PITTSBURGH THEOLOGICAL MONOGRAPHS

New Series

Dikran Y. Hadidian

General Editor

16

FREDERIC HENRY HEDGE

Nineteenth Century American Transcendentalist

Frederic Henry Hedge

Frederic Henry Hedge

Nineteenth Century American Transcendentalist

Intellectually Radical Ecclesiastically Conservative

By

Bryan F. LeBeau

PICKWICK PUBLICATIONS
Allison Park, Pennsylvania

4137 Timberlane Drive, Allison Park, PA 15101

Printed in the United States of America

Library of Congress Cataloging in Publication Data
Le Beau, Bryan F.
Frederic Henry Hedge, nineteenth century American transcendentalist.

(Pittsburgh theological monographs; new ser. 16)
Bibliography: p.
Includes index.
1. Hedge, Frederic Henry, 1805–1890. 2. Transcendentalism (New England)
I. Title. II. Series.
BX9869.H39L43 1985 288'.092'4 [B] 85-570
ISBN 0-915138-71-9

Printed and Bound by Publishers Choice Book Mfg. Co.
Mars, Pennsylvania 16046

To My Mother And Father

CONTENTS

ACKNOWLEDGEMENTS

Publication of this book was made possible by the assistance of several individuals and through the use of numerous research institutions. First among those individuals to be credited is Paul Baker, whose perceptive suggestions led to many substantive improvements. Significant contributions were also made by Kenneth Silverman and James Carse who read and commented on successive drafts of this study.

Most of the research on this book was conducted at the Harvard University Archives and Libraries, Andover-Harvard Theological Library, Massachusetts Historical Society, Boston Public Library, New York Public Library, Union Theological Seminary Library, Elmer Holmes Bobst Library, Bangor Public Library, and Concordia College Library. A debt of gratitude is owed all those institutions as well as the staff of the Greenburgh Public Library for their assistance in locating and securing materials for research purposes.

Finally, I would like to thank Dikran Y. Hadidian, General Editor of Pickwick Publications, for his encouragement and for the many hours spent preparing this manuscript for publication; and my wife, Chris, for her continued support and understanding.

Acknowledgments

INTRODUCTION

Frederic Henry Hedge possessed one of the most remarkable minds of the nineteenth century. He was a wealth of intellectual resources, through whom passed the main currents of American thought of his time. He touched the minds of many of the leading thinkers of his age and earned the title "teacher of teachers." [1] His commitment to progressive thought was reflected in Thomas Carlyle's comment: "Wherever new thought is marching onto the field, there we find Mr. Hedge in the front rank." [2]

Frederic Hedge was one of the two prime movers of nineteenth century American Unitarianism. William Ellery Channing provided the impetous for Unitarians, but Hedge gave them a consistent theology and defended them against outside attack and internal divisiveness. At the same time his ideas on the "Broad Church" placed him near the limits commonly set by that denomination. The "Humanitarian Church" or the "Liberal Pulpit," with its unorganized ecumenical, spiritual fellowship, claimed him. In that fellowship he sought the realization of the universal church of Christianity. [3]

Hedge is most widely known for his involvement with American Transcendentalists. His articles in the Christian Examiner in 1833 and 1834 provided the first positive American recognition of the claims of Transcendentalism as a constructive force. His first-hand and extensive knowledge of the German language, German literature, and German philosophy earned him the title "Germanicus" Hedge, or the "fountain . . . of the very atmosphere of German thought," among the American Transcendentalists. [4] He was instrumental in the organization of the Transcendental Club, which became known to its members as the Hedge Club. It met whenever he came to Boston or Cambridge from his congregation in Bangor, Maine. Finally, his initiative led to publication of The Dial, American Transcendentalism's literary organ.

Estimates of Hedge's fidelity to American Transcendentalism have varied. Some scholars have stressed his disagreements with more popular figures such as Ralph Waldo Emerson and the notes of disappointment he and Emerson exchanged concerning

Hedge's conclusions. Other scholars have commented on his languishing support of The Dial after he had been a major force in its creation, or his less than enthusiastic review of Transcendentalism after its main currents had run their course. Evaluations of Hedge's Transcendental vision come to three conclusions:

1. His intellect and wide knowledge of literature, philosophy, and theology--especially German--influenced American Transcendentalists, but he never joined them.

2. He was a Transcendentalist in the early years of the movement, but he later "regressed" to a more conservative stand.

3. He was a Transcendentalist, but he disagreed with more popular figures in that group on certain basic points.

Undoubtedly some of the difficulty in establishing Hedge's position within the Transcendental movement stems from a problem of definition. Even those who were involved in the Transcendental Club meetings of the 1830s reported that the membership agreed on little. More likely, however, difficulties arise because no one has yet dealt with Hedge's Transcendental views in the context of his complete intellectual scheme.

Frederic Henry Hedge was indeed a Transcendentalist as defined in its most basic terms. If he disagreed with others in the movement, he did so over radical tendencies. Transcendentalism was first and foremost a religious movement, which evolved to counter the effects of Lockean sensualism, Humean skepticism, and arid Unitarianism. Just as importantly, Transcendentalism was a method or critique, rather than a system of fixed beliefs. It provided a mode of knowing rather than a philosophy of what was known. Finally, it sought to restore the divine in man. To these points Hedge remained faithful.

Beyond Hedge's basic Transcendental beliefs, he belonged to no one school of thought. He was a progressive thinker, an idealist, and a liberal Christian. Yet he remained within the mainstream of Unitarianism. He accepted from Transcendentalism, or from any other philosophy, what best suited his own clear and definite objectives, on which he was unwilling to compromise. These objectives included the negation of extremes of left or right in order to effect the resurrection of the Christian Church as a providential instrument. As a providential instrument the Christian Church would serve to develop man's highest powers toward the consummate spirit best represented in the life and death of Jesus Christ. This consummate spirit, he believed, was the birthright of all men.

To know the mind of Frederic Hedge is to understand the mainstream of American Transcendentalism. To follow the evolution of his intellectual scheme is to encounter major elements of nineteenth century intellectual history. This study is intended to provide that knowledge. It shows that Frederic Henry Hedge remained faithful to the generally agreed upon objectives of American Transcendentalism formulated at its inception. He refused to follow figures such as Ralph Waldo Emerson, Margaret Fuller, Bronson Alcott, and George Ripley in their increasingly individualistic or secular straying from the center of the movement. As a result he forfeited the popularity that these figures gained in the course of time as their views became indelibly associated with American Transcendentalism. He became instead a leading spokesman for the moderate mainstream of American Transcendentalism, an area yet to be fully explored.

NOTES

1. William H. Lyon, **Frederic Henry Hedge: Seventh Minister of the First Parish in Brookline** (Brookline, MA.: First Parish in Brookline, 1906), 13.

2. "To Ralph Waldo Emerson," 31 August 1847, **Correspondence of Thomas Carlyle and Ralph Waldo Emerson, 1834-1872,** ed. C. E. Norton (Boston: Houghton, Mifflin Company, 1883), II, 140.

3. George Willis Cooke, **Unitarianism in America: A History of Its Origin and Development** (Boston: American Unitarian Association, 1902), 417.

4. Henry A. Pochmann, **German Culture in America: Philosophical and Literary Influences: 1600-1900** (Madison: The University of Wisconsin Press, 1957), 144.

Chapter One

THE FORMATIVE YEARS

The life of Frederic Henry Hedge stands at the confluence of four prominent New England families. Hedge's mother, Mary Kneeland Hedge, was descended from the Holyoke and Kneeland families. The Holyoke lineage included a president of Harvard College (Edward Holyoke) and the first person to receive a doctor of medicine degree from Harvard (Edward Augustus Holyoke). The latter served as the first president of the Massachusetts Medical Society and president of the American Academy of Arts and Sciences. Mary Kneeland's father, Dr. William Kneeland, also a medical doctor, was elected steward of Harvard and also served as president of the Massachusetts Medical Society. [1]

Hedge's paternal grandfather, Reverend Lemuel Hedge, was a noted scholar and minister, whose congregation resided in Warwick, Massachusetts. He held a B.A. and an M.A. from Harvard. [2] Frederic's paternal grandmother, Sara White Hedge, was also descended from a prominent New England family. [3]

Levi Hedge, Frederic's father, received his B.A. and M.A. from Harvard and LL.D. from Yale. He served as professor of logic and metaphysics at Harvard from 1810 to 1827. In 1827 he was appointed Alford Professor of Natural Religion, Moral Philosophy, and Civil Polity, a post he held for five years. College faculty and students granted him a less formal title, "old brains." Levi's text, **Elements of Logick, or a Summary of the General Principles and Different Modes of Reason** (1816), was a standard text at Harvard for a number of years. It stressed post-Lockean thought, especially that of the Scots, and undoubtedly influenced young Frederic, Ralph Waldo Emerson, and other New England Transcendentalists who attended Harvard at that time. [4]

Frederic Hedge was born in Cambridge, Massachusetts, on December 12, 1805. From his own recollections, he was a "timid and somewhat puny child," who was fond of reading poetry and prose such as Pope's **Essay on Man** and Cervantes' **Don Quixote.**

He noted that he read the latter work "over and over again." [5] He early developed a talent for languages, memorizing the **Eclogues** of Virgil in the original before the age of seven and ten long passages of Homer by ten. [6]

Except for five or six months spent at a small classical school in Cambridge, Hedge received his education at home under the direction of his father and tutors. One tutor, George Bancroft, later to become one of America's most popular historians, lived with the Hedges while he pursued graduate study at Harvard. Understandably, Hedge wrote that as a child, "he had no companions in study," nor any "class rivalry to cramp or cheer." [7] By the age of twelve Hedge passed the entrance examination for Harvard College. [8] His father, however, felt he was too young to enter the school, and that he should first receive a more complete education abroad. This decision had a lasting influence on his life. [9]

On June 27, 1818, at the age of twelve, Hedge left for Germany with his tutor George Bancroft. Bancroft, who went to study at the Universities of Berlin and Heidelberg, anticipated the problems language and cost would cause for the proper care of his young charge. He did not foresee the difficulties that arose from the "conflicting currents of his [Hedge's] natural aptitude and unformed youth," [10] possibly because Bancroft was himself only eighteen years old.

Edward Everett, a colleague of Levi Hedge, guided Bancroft in his care of Frederic. Everett toured Europe at the same time and offered advice on the youngster's education and housing. Upon Everett's advice Bancroft settled Hedge in Göttingen near the gymnasium, Gotha. He housed him with a Reverend Oppermann, pastor of a village adjacent to Göttingen, and placed him under a tutor to improve his language proficiency prior to entrance into Gotha. [11] Bancroft then left Frederic and pursued his own studies, but he kept in close contact both by mail and occasional visits.

In November 1818, Bancroft reported to Everett that Frederic was doing well in his preparation, but he noted, without elaboration, that Hedge was "more of a boy" than he had imagined. Bancroft was not altogether pleased with the arrangement at Göttingen. What concerned him most was the cost of Hedge's residence and his education at Gotha. It would cost him nearly $300 per year, or $100 in excess of what Levi Hedge had allowed. [12]

Bancroft subsequently removed Hedge from Göttingen and, upon the advice of Edward Everett, sent him to the gymnasium at Ilfeld in Hanover. Ilfeld was generally considered one of the best gymnasia in Germany. [13] At Ilfeld, Hedge was placed under the care of one of Everett's local contacts. He was to "enjoy all the good things of the institution, and to have private lessons," at an annual cost not to exceed $250, a figure agreed upon by Hedge's father. [14]

Problems began to develop at Ilfeld, however, as Frederic became "more of a boy." In August 1819, Bancroft wrote that Hedge continued to do well academically, but that he was "guilty now and then of indiscretion." He explained that Frederic's temper had not been "properly disciplined in his childhood," and that his "passionate temperament" might get him into difficulty, as it had already "occasioned something unpleasant." [15] Bancroft did not explain the "unpleasant" occasion.

During the months of September and October, Hedge continued to be "admonished" by his instructors, and he began to have "bouts with depression." [16] By December his behavior brought Bancroft "to the point of despair." He had received a letter from Ilfeld "filled with bitter and passionate complaints" against Frederic, "using words like rudeness, impertinence, and unverbesserliche Faulheit" (incorrigible laziness). The letter ended by insisting on his removal from Ilfeld "mit möglichster Eile" (with all possible haste). The immediate cause for Hedge's dismissal was "disrespect to one of his teachers." [17]

Bancroft made no attempt to excuse Hedge's behavior, but he later commented on what might have caused it. In a letter to Frederic's father, Bancroft explained that in reflecting on Frederic's own account of the affair leading to his removal from Ilfeld, "the teacher must have been nearly as much to blame as he [Frederic] was." He went on to speak of Frederic's "isolated situation," especially at age thirteen:

> It is not be wondered at, that he felt little impulse to books, little ardour in his studies. He was, as it were a young plant, moved from its natural soil and climate, drooping and fainting, [until he became] . . . fairly accustomed to the foreign earth. [18]

Bancroft explained that motives were different in Germany than those Hedge was accustomed to in America. Frederic had heard of "prizes and good scholarship, of college clubs and parts at commencement," but at Ilfeld nothing was done but "to offer him the means of becoming wise, it being presumed that every youth felt the benefits of learning." [19]

Bancroft believed that Frederic's difficulties may have been further complicated by a lack of direction from his father. In a letter to Edward Everett, Bancroft mentioned that "the root of the evil" lay with Professor Hedge. The professor did not know what he would have his son become; he had only "indistinct notions of excellence." Hedge's attitude reflected his father's indecision. Bancroft concluded, however, that regardless of extenuating circumstances, if Hedge had not had a "change of heart" at Schulpforta, the school to which he was transferred, he would have been returned to America. [20]

In the closing years of Hedge's life, Joseph Henry Allen, a close friend of Hedge and his successor at Bangor and the Harvard Divinity School, suggested that Frederic write his memoirs. Hedge agreed but completed only a few brief pages before ill health prevented his continuing. The completed section, which he titled, "Recollections of Student Life in Germany," gave a far more personal view of Ilfeld than that found in the letters of Bancroft.

At the opening of Hedge's narrative, he discussed the curiosity of the students at Ilfeld upon his arrival. Although they had studied the people, history, and climate of the United States, they first expected to see "a copper coloured savage." Further, they questioned him about "the tropical plants and tropical animals, as if all America lay in the tropical zone." Hedge attributed this line of questioning to the failure of the students' book knowledge to overcome popular misconceptions born of "the glamour attending the word 'America' " in the early years of the nineteenth century. Hedge was pleased with their interest, however, because of their attempts to learn all they could of this stranger, they overlooked the hazing usually practiced on newcomers. [21]

Hedge recalled that Ilfeld had been a monastery before becoming a school, and that its living accommodations had changed little. They consisted of small rooms with stone floors, in a line, opening onto a common corridor. All rooms were heated by stoves placed in the corridor between room openings, one for every two rooms. Below one part of the building was a crypt with tomb stones faced with effigies in relief of deceased monastic brothers. Students returning to their dormitory after hours, found the doors locked and had to pass through the crypt, an experience they did not relish. [22]

The students' daily lives were closely scheduled and provided little opportunity for pursuits of a frivolous nature. In the evening, study was expected and enforced by room checks. Instructors visited each room at 9:00 p.m. to insure that all were studying, and again at 11:00 p.m. to be certain that all had gone to bed. If a student had to miss class due to illness, the school required him to submit a note written in Latin (the school's official language of instruction) requesting permission to remain in his room. If permission was granted, he stayed in his room for the day. He was expected to study, if his health permitted, and he received only "a piece of dry bread for his sustenance." [23]

Ilfeld required students to attend church on Sundays at 11:00 a.m. Hedge felt that although services were long, discipline was lax. Students often read novels during the service, unless they were too cold. Hedge complained of times when the students were so cold as to be almost in a state of "suspended animation." He recorded that he had never before nor afterwards experienced such cold. [24]

In general Hedge believed that discipline was excessive but "not searching and not quickening." Punishment was graded to reflect the severity of the error and its frequency. Minor faults were met by loss of dinner. More serious infractions led to confinement within one's room. Errors in excess of those, yet short of meriting expulsion, as did Hedge's act of "disrespect," resulted in "incarceration" in an attic room "with tasks sufficient to occupy the solitary hours and prevent the morbid action of the mind." [25]

On a more positive note, Hedge praise Ilfeld's food and occasional social affairs. Students supplied their own breakfasts, for which they kept charcoal and tableware. The school supplied two meals per day, one at noon and the other at 6:00 p.m. Hedge rated these meals "well served." Students sat at long tables with a teacher and were read to from the "upper table" by the Primaner in monastic tradition. The readings usually included fiction, however, and were for entertainment as much as for enlightenment. [26]

As to the social gatherings at Ilfeld, Hedge spoke of group walks to town, where they occasionally attended plays, and of the two balls held each year with ladies invited from within a ten-mile radius of the school. Dancing lasted until late in the evening, and the revelers drank "concoctions" of spiritous liquors "of a mild nature," called "bishops." Bishops were composed chiefly of port and wine. Physical distress usually resulted on the following day, relieved only by the traditional declaration of a school holiday. [27]

In his recollections Hedge spoke of the organization and function of student life. As in most schools of the day, age had its rank. In this case it was enforced by both tradition and the student senate. Boys sixteen years of age and older, who had been at school for a minimum of a year and a half, "exercised an absolute and undisputed sway over the younger portion." For example, all students signed allegiance to a written code of laws and were conferred with a name by veterans, based on "some personal peculiarity." Hedge did not disclose his "cloister name." Cloister names could not be used by younger students, however, when addressing elder ones. These same codes ruled out bullying and cheating. Violaters were boycotted by others. Finally, discrimination was not tolerated, despite the fact that many students were the children of noblemen. [28]

Hedge did not find instruction at Ilfeld "fructifying." He criticized its overemphasis on the university method of teaching by lectures, which left pupils little prepared. Students took notes, but they were not examined on them. Promotion was determined by "no very rigorous test." Evaluating his own success at Ilfeld, Hedge admitted he "made little progress except in writing Latin, the one exercise Ilfeld rigorously enforced. [29]

By January 1821, Hedge was transferred to the gymnasium at Schulpforte in Saxony. Schulpforta was a Prussian state school and like Ilfeld was rated among the best of the day. [30] He lodged with Karl Koberstein, a literary historian, who became quite fond of Hedge. Schulpforta proved to be a more pleasant experience for Hedge than Ilfeld. By March Bancroft wrote to Levi Hedge with a pleasure he had not felt for months. Frederic, he reported, had become "more contented, more industrious, and more gentle in his deportment" than he had ever been in his life abroad. [31] He had been "weaned to the ways of foreigners," and had grown to appreciate his opportunities for learning at Schulpforta. Further, Hedge had become very well liked. Bancroft concluded:

> Hedge has an earnest and reflective turn of mind, is well disposed, and capable of effecting much. . . . He converses with sobriety, has asked me a great many questions which indicates his reflecting a good deal about morals and religion, and seems actually bent on making honorable progress in good learning. [32]

Hedge's own recollections included little about Schulpforta. What was written, in union with comments made elsewhere, however, indicates his clear preference for this gymnasium over Ilfeld. In his "Recollections" he referred to Schulpforta as a Prussian institution, "manifest in its discipline, its vitality, its thoroughness." In was under "the care of the best government of modern times," and was often visited by the minister of instruction. Its curriculum was similar to other gymnasia in Germany, and its faculty was larger than that of Harvard at the same time. [33]

Hedge had fond memories of two friendships made at Schulpforta. The first was of Karl Koberstein, with whom Frederic boarded. [34] (Students from outside Saxony were not offered school dormitory space.) In Hedge's estimation Koberstein had written "the most complete history of German literature of the time." The second bond was with Carl, the future Baron von Münchhausen, nephew of the "veritable, unveracious storyteller of that verse." Frederic remembered helping Carl with his Latin in return for assistance in mathematics. Frederic wrote Carl's "confession" in Latin for his Lutheran Confirmation. Carl once saved Frederic's life, pulling him from a river, unconscious, after the two had attempted to swim across it. [35]

Years later Hedge admitted that he was too young to appreciate the advantages of his opportunity to study in Germany and that he would have made better progress if he had stayed in Cambridge. As a foreigner, he "had been left too much to his own devices," when his youth needed discipline. He quickly credited his German education, however, with giving him a thorough knowledge of the German language; an acquaintance with the literature of Goethe and other German writers; an early initiation in the realm of German idealism, "then, to our people an unknown world"; and the opening of his mind "to a knowledge of what is meant by a life of thought and letters." The conveying of this knowledge, he confided to a friend, may have been his "characteristic" service to "the somewhat provincial dialect of letters and scholarship then prevailing in New England," and to "our so-called Transcendental movement." Others have agreed with Hedge's assessment of his service. [36]

In July 1871, Hedge addressed an audience of German-Americans at Faneuil Hall in Boston. He reflected on his youthful days in Germany and the impact they had had on his life. "I am a German by intellectual descent. . . . Germany is the fatherland of my mind. It was there I first drew the breath of intellectual life and imbibed my first ideas of poetry and philosophy." [37]

Late in the year 1822 at the age of seventeen, Frederic Hedge returned to the United States. Bancroft had already preceded him in June of that year. In 1823 Hedge entered Harvard as a junior. Joseph Allen observed that Hedge, by this time, had already developed "the temper of the teacher, the preacher, and the interpreter of thought or beauty to the higher life of man." [38] His first inclination, however, was to study science, probably for a career in medicine. Allen recalled that Hedge regretted he was "born too early (as he thought) to be baptized into the newer life of science." [39] Under his father's influence Frederic studied theology. [40]

Regardless of his vocation, Hedge's avocation was poetry. During his years at Harvard, he became vice-president and poet of the Hasty Pudding Club. At the Spring Exhibition in his senior year, he delivered "The Sceptics Soliloquy," a "free rendering of the first part of Tiedge's 'Urania.' " He became poet of his graduating class and delivered a valedictory poem entitled "The Student" on July 19, 1825. [41] At his commencement in August 1825, he presented his poem, "Ruins of the East," which received "reiterated applause." [42]

Hedge continued to write poetry after graduating from Harvard College, although it did not earn him his reputation. Some of his verse was well received, but more for its mastery of meter than its poetic imagination. His more notable accomplishments as a versifier include election to poet of the Phi Beta Kappa Society in 1828; delivery of class poems at his 40th and 50th reunions; and publication of poems with Annis Lee Wister, in **Metrical Translations and Poems** (1888). Hedge's poetic temperament influenced his prose and, at times, his critical exercises and interpretive approach. Critics have commented that his occasional lapses in logical ardor were due to his flare for the poetic. [43]

Hedge earned what has been referred to as a "respectable college record" at Harvard. [44] Much to his father's chagrin, continued difficulties with mathematics prevented his taking highest honors. [45] Within the two years, however, Frederic rapidly established himself as a "fountain of knowledge in the ways of German." This resulted in close ties with Edward Everett, his early advisor, the only man at Harvard who shared his experience, ability, and interest in German. [46]

In the same two years at Harvard, Hedge's growing reputation in "the ways of German" brought him into contact with several Transcendentalists to be, including, most notably at this point, Margaret Fuller. Hedge met Fuller, then age thirteen, during his first year at Harvard, when Timothy Fuller, Margaret's socially conscious father, pushed her into giving her first party. She invited the "Boston misses" from Park School and several other Cambridge acquaintances and their guests. Hedge was among the guests. Fuller spent the evening talking to the Cambridge group, causing the ladies to leave "in a huff." Fuller impressed Hedge with her conversation, and he grew determined to know her better. [47]

Margaret's developing interest in German literature drew her and Frederic closer. She frequently borrowed from his German library, considered one of the best in the Boston area, and she soon became his "intimate intellectual companion," spending hours in conversation with him over points raised in her studies. He became a source of inspiration, confidence, and criticism for her work, especially her German translations and unpublished biography of Goethe. Finally, he brought Fuller to Ralph Waldo Emerson's attention, initiating that lasting friendship. [48]

When Hedge graduated in 1825, Harvard considered him for a position as instructor of German. Carl Follen had become Harvard's first professor of German that year, and he needed assistance. [49] Hedge chose, instead, to attend the Harvard Divinity School.

Frederic's years at the Divinity School were important not only for the direction they gave his life, but also for the contacts he made. To begin with Hedge immersed himself in the studies which served as a major informational source for his writings: natural religion, Hebrew, biblical criticism, ecclesiastic history, and pastoral theology. His most influential instructors included Henry Ware, Sr., Hollis Professor of Natural Religion, and George Ticknor and Andrews Norton, both of whom specialized in biblical criticism. Ticknor taught the basics of the new German Higher Criticism. Norton, Dexter Professor of Sacred Literature, would become a major spokesman for anti-Transcendentalists, and he exhibited some of those tendencies when Hedge was at the Divinity School. Hedge became "conscious of his limitations and sometimes galled by his intolerance," but he nevertheless grew to respect him. [50]

At the Divinity School, Hedge also met Emerson with whom he formed an "intimate and cross-influencing relationship." Emerson was preparing for the ministry, but he was not then an enrolled member of the school nor did he take part in its exercises. [51] Both he and Hedge showed a fondness for progressive thought. Hedge's earliest memories of his friendship with Emerson at the Divinity School recalled Emerson's "very positive opinion" in the field of ethics. He quoted one statement of Emerson's in particular:

> Owe no conformity to custom, against your private judgment. Have no regard to the influence of your example, but act always from the simplest motive. [52]

One of Hedge's associates, John Chadwick, recalled that Hedge's "admiration, reverence, and love" as well as his encouragement, led Emerson to publish many of his early poems and to further cultivate his intellectual gifts. [53] Hedge later reminisced how his influence was limited in one area close to his heart:

> I tried to interest him [Emerson] in German literature, but he laughingly said that he was entirely ignorant of the subject, and he should assume that it was not worth knowing. [54]

Within a few years Emerson changed his mind and became a serious student of German literature. Hedge became his closest adviser on the subject. [55]

Frederic Hedge graduated from Harvard Divinity School in 1829, one of a class of nine. The Divinity School at this time granted no degrees but simply pronounced its students "worthy of ministerial rank" and issued them licenses. Hedge was prepared for his life to follow. [**56**]

NOTES

1. College overseers disallowed William Kneeland's election as steward by the Harvard corporation in 1778 because of his "sympathy" for the loyalist cause during the American Revolution. William H. Lyon, **Frederic Henry Hedge: Seventh Minister of the First Parish in Brookline, 1856–1872** (Brookline, Ma.: First Parish in Brookline, 1906), 4; Stillman Foster Kneeland, **Seven Centuries in the Kneeland Family** (New York: Stillman Foster Kneeland, 1897), 69; Joseph Henry Allen, **Sequel to "Our Liberal Movement"** (Boston: Roberts Brothers, 1897), 63; Martha Ilona Tuomi, "Dr. Frederic Henry Hedge: His Life and Works to the End of His Bangor Pastorate, 1805-1850," M.A. Thesis, University of Maine, 1934, 7.

2. Lemuel Hedge committed the indiscretion of expressing his doubts as to the ability of the colonists to maintain their liberty by force of arms in a letter to his Harvard classmate, Joseph Warren. The letter was found on Warren's body when he was killed at the Battle of Bunker Hill. Hedge's fellow townspeople promptly labeled him a Tory and voted to "disarm and confine him, and also to dismiss him." A mob hustled him to Northampton, Massachusetts, "hastening, if not causing, his early death by their indignity." John W. Chadwick, **Frederic Henry Hedge: A Sermon** (Boston: George H. Ellis, 1890-1891), 20.

3. Tuomi, 1.

4. Ernest Sutherland Bates, "Levi Hedge," **Dictionary of American Biography** (1932), IV, 499; Allen, **Sequel to "Our Liberal Movement,"** 63; Tuomi, 1; Levi Hedge, **Elements of Logick; or A Summary of the General Principles and Different Modes of Reasoning** (1816: rpt. Cooperstown, N.Y.: H. & E. Phinney, 1849).

5. Chadwick, 21.

6. Raymond William Adams, "Frederic Henry Hedge," **Dictionary of American Biography** (1932), IV, 498; Lyon, 4.

7. Allen, **Sequel to "Our Liberal Movement,"** 64.

8. Tuomi, 19.

9. Ronald Vale Wells, **Three Christian Transcendentalists: James Marsh, Caleb Sprague Henry, Frederic Henry Hedge** (1943; rpt. New York: Octagon Books, 1972), 96; Orie W. Long, **Frederic Henry Hedge: A Cosmopolitan Scholar** (Portland, Me.: The Southworth-Anthoensen Press, 1940), 2; Howard N. Brown, "Frederic Henry Hedge," in **Heralds of a Liberal Faith**, ed. Samuel A. Eliot (Boston: American Unitarian Association, 1910), IV, 161.

10. Long, **Frederic Henry Hedge**, 2-3; Tuomi, 18; Orie W. Long, **Literary Pioneers: Early American Explorers of European Culture** (New York: Russell and Russell, Inc., 1963), 108.

11. Long, **Frederic Henry Hedge**, 63.

12. George Bancroft, Letter to Edward Everett, 14 November 1818, Bancroft Collection, Massachusetts Historical Society, Boston, Massachusetts; George Bancroft, Letter to Edward Everett, 25 September 1819, Bancroft Collection, Massachusetts Historical Society, Boston, Massachusetts.

13. Carl Diehl, **American and German Scholarship, 1770-1870** (New Haven: Yale University Press, 1978), 95.

14. George Bancroft, Letter to Edward Everett, 20 February 1819, Bancroft Collection, Massachusetts Historical Society, Boston, Massachusetts.

15. George Bancroft, Letter to Edward Everett, 1 August 1819.

16. Bancroft, Letter to Everett, 25 September 1819; George Bancroft, Letter to Edward Everett, 4 November 1819.

17. George Bancroft, Letter to Edward Everett, 28 December 1820; George Bancroft, Letter to Levi Hedge, 6 March 1821; George Bancroft, Letter to Edward Everett, 2 April 1821.

18. Bancroft, Letter to Levi Hedge, 6 March 1821.

19. Ibid.

20. Bancroft, Letter to Everett, 2 April 1821.

21. Frederic Henry Hedge, "Recollections of Student Life in Germany," in Allen **Sequel to "Our Liberal Movement,"** 65.

22. Ibid.

23. Ibid.

24. Ibid., 68.

25. Ibid., 67-68.

26. Ibid., 68.

27. Ibid., 69.

28. Ibid., 69-71.

29. Ibid., 67-68, 71.

30. Diehl, **American and German Scholarship**, 95.

31. Bancroft, Letter to Levi Hedge, 6 March 1821.

32. Ibid.

33. Hedge, "Recollections," 73.

34. Ibid., 71.

35. Ibid., 73-74.

36. Hedge, "Recollections," 73; Long, **Frederic Henry Hedge**, 14; Chadwick, 21; Joseph Henry Allen, "A Memory of Dr. Hedge," The Unitarian Review and Religious Magazine, Sept. 1890, 269.

37. Frederic Henry Hedge, "Address to Germans of Boston, Faneuil Hall, July, 1876," The Index, 27 August 1870, 2-3.

38. Allen, "A Memory of Dr. Hedge," 267.

39. Chadwick, 23; Allen, "A Memory of Dr. Hedge," 267.

40. Ibid.

41. Preserved at the Harvard University Archives, Cambridge, Massachusetts.

42. Long, **Frederic Henry Hedge**, 15-16.

43. Chadwick, 22; Allen, **Sequel to "Our Liberal Movement,"** 76; Long, **Frederic Henry Hedge**, 16; Lawrence Buell, **Literary Transcendentalism: Style and Vision in the American Renaissance** (Ithaca, N.Y.: Cornell University Press, 1973), 52. Frederic Henry Hedge and Annis Lee Wister, **Metrical Translations and Poems** (Boston: Houghton, Mifflin and Company, 1888).

44. Long, **Frederic Henry Hedge**, 15.

45. Tuomi, 181.

46. Long, **Frederic Henry Hedge**, 17, 21.

47. Arthur W. Brown, **Margaret Fuller** (New York: Twayne Publishers, Inc., 1964), 23; Julia Ward Howe, **Reminiscences: 1819-1899** (1899; rpt. New York: Negro University Press, 1969), 300-301; Tuomi, 35.

48. Long, **Frederic Henry Hedge,** 21; Margaret Fuller, **Memoirs of Margaret Fuller Ossoli,** eds. William Henry Channing, James Freeman Clarke, and Ralph Waldo Emerson (London: Richard Bentley, 1852), I, 90; Thomas Wentworth Higginson, **Margaret Fuller Ossoli** (1884; rpt. New York: Haskel House Publishers, Ltd., 1968), 22, 44; Frederick Augustus Brown, **Margaret Fuller and Goethe. The Development of a Remarkable Personality, Her Religion and Philosophy, and Her Relation to Emerson, James Freeman Clarke and Transcendentalism** (1910; rpt. New York: Henry Holt and Company, 1910), 45; Arthur Brown, **Margaret Fuller,** 34-35.

49. Long, **Frederic Henry Hedge,** 17.

50. Octavius Brooks Frothingham, **Recollections and Impressions** (New York: G. P. Putnam's Sons, 1891), 29-31; Chadwick, 23; Peter King Carley, "The Early Life and Thought of Frederic Henry Hedge: 1805-1850," Ph.D. Dissertation, Syracuse University 1972, 70-72, 76-77.

51. James Elliot Cabot, **A Memoir of Ralph Waldo Emerson** (Boston: Houghton, Mifflin and Company, 1895), I, 138; Tuomi, 40-41.

52. Frederic Henry Hedge, "A Memoir of Ralph Waldo Emerson," Cabot, I, 139; Tuomi, 40-41.

53. Cabot, I, 138; Chadwick, 23.

54. Hedge, "A Memoir of Ralph Waldo Emerson," I, 139.

55. See for example: Hedge, "A Memoir of Ralph Waldo Emerson," I, 23; "To Thomas Carlyle," 17 September 1836, **Correspondence of Thomas Carlyle and Ralph Waldo Emerson, 1834-1872,** ed. E. E. Norton (Boston: Houghton, Mifflin Company, 1883), I, 39-40; "To Thomas Carlyle," 22 April 1840, **Correspondence,** I, 285; Ralph Waldo Emerson, **The Journals of Ralph Waldo Emerson,** eds. Edward W. Emerson and William E. Forbes (Cambridge, Ma.: The Riverside Press, 1909-14), IV, 94.

56. Carley, "The Early Life," 84.

Chapter Two

A LIFE FULFILLED

On May 20, 1829, Frederic Hedge was ordained at the Congregational Church and Society in West Cambridge (now Arlington), Massachusetts. On September 7, 1829, he married Lucy L. Pierce, daughter of the Reverend John Pierce of Brookline, Massachusetts, and a friend of Margaret Fuller. Frederic was highly successful in his first position, and Lucy complemented his efforts well. While he cultivated the spiritual lives of the parish, she catered to its ill and needy. [1]

While Hedge was at West Cambridge, he began to "unfold," as Emerson put it. He grew closer to influential figures in the area, including not only Fuller and Emerson (established at the Second Church in Boston), but also George Ripley (at the Purchase Street Church, Boston) and Convers Francis (living in Watertown). These friends often met in Boston at Peabody's bookstore, where they looked at foreign periodicals and discussed current issues. [2]

Hedge took a dramatic step forward in 1833, with his publication of "Coleridge's **Literary Character**" in the Christian Examiner, one of the most influential journals of the time. [3] The article reviewed not only Coleridge's ideas but their background in German philosophy. It gave an explanation of the basic tenets of Kant, Fichte, and Schelling, and the general import of their system and provided the first American recognition of the claims of Transcendentalism, especially as a positive, constructive force. [4] Emerson called the article "a living, leaping logos," wrote of the influence it and Hedge were having in the development of his intellectual life, and recommended the article to Thomas Carlyle. [5] Within two years Hedge also published highly regarded articles on Emmanuel Swedenborg and on phrenology. [6] He felt that all three articles "looked in the Transcendental direction" and were reactions "against the orthodoxy expounded at the Harvard Divinity School." Emerson considered them "the best that have appeared in the Examiner." [7]

In 1833 Hedge received an offer to become minister of the Independent Congregational Church in Bangor, Maine. He rejected the offer, since he knew little of the congregation. [8] In 1834, however, Emerson preached there and wrote to Hedge of the "shrewd liberal men" of the congregation and of their desire to get a minister of ability, for whom they would pay well. He continued, "I am almost persuaded to sit down on the banks of this pleasant stream, and, if I could only persuade a small number of persons to join my colony, we would have a settlement thirty miles up the river at once." [9]

Bangor was a lumber "boom town" and shipping center. Many of its wealthiest and most educated townspeople, including a mix of Unitarians, Congregationalists, and Methodists, belonged to the Independent Church. Hedge followed Emerson there, preached to the congregation, and was again offered a position. He accepted the job at $1500 per year, nearly twice his West Cambridge salary, and left to settle in Maine in May 1835. [10]

Hedge's transfer to Bangor was not well accepted by all, nor did it begin auspiciously. Margaret Fuller was typical of Hedge's contemporaries who viewed his move with concern. She wrote to him soon after he left, voicing her fears of his "going into mental solitude." [11] A later critic noted although Hedge was one of the earliest and most influential Transcendentalists, if he had not left the Boston area he would have been even more prominent. [12]

Added to the voices of concern were the hardships Hedge faced during his first winter in Bangor. Just as Frederic was about to move to Bangor, Lucy grew ill, so he went without her. Her illness lingered on until heavy snows prevented her joining him with their two young children. Frederic therefore spent most of the winter alone, often ill and exhausted. A protracted salary dispute only exacerbated the situation. By spring, however, he had regained his health, settled his salary dispute, and brought Lucy to him. [13]

To some of his contemporaries, Hedge's move to Bangor was a fortunate one. If a few contended that it removed him from possible leadership in the Transcendental movement, others asserted that he was too young to be a leader in 1835 anyway. They reasoned that he was "a little overawed among so many prominent and popular brothers and needed a removal to the frontier, where he would have to depend on the responsibility and the stimulus of being the sole representative of his faith in a large region." [14] An acquaintance recorded Hedge's personal view:

> It was a kind of exile, but, on the whole, it was an advantage to me, favoring independence and allowing a freer intellectual development than I could, perhaps, have attained in a parish nearer home, under the pressure of ecclesiastical influences. [15]

A broader and more independent vision resulted. [16]

For the most part Frederic Hedge's ministry was well received in Bangor. Contemporaries reported that his pulpit voice was "sonorous" and that his rhetoric was not "flowing." Others recalled he was "a man of the study rather than of the world," and that he was "more at ease with thoughts rather than with persons," preferring to reach people through the head rather than the heart. These same sources, however, admitted that he succeeded in creating a fit "dwelling place for the Holy Ghost," and in cultivating warmth within the congregation through his "modest, simple, affectionate nature." [17]

Although a frontier town, Bangor was a commercial center and the Independent Church earned a reputation for its percentage of men of learning and accomplishment. In 1842, Reverend John Pierce, Hedge's father-in-law, visited Bangor and reported that the congregation included thirty lawyers, five judges, and one ex-governor. [18] Hedge was proud of the unusual number of college graduates in his congregation, greater, he thought, than could be found in almost any other. He used this talent to establish the Bangor Lyceum, to which he gave the inaugural lecture. [19]

Soon after Emerson had visited Hedge in Bangor, he made the following report to Thomas Carlyle:

> Henry Hedge is a recluse, but Catholic scholar, in our remote Bangor, who reads German and smokes in his solitary study through eight months of snow in the year, and deals out every Sunday his witty apothegms to the lumber merchants and township owners of the Penobscott River, who have actually grown intelligent interpreters of his riddles by long hearkening after them. [20]

Hedge's years in Bangor were not so inactive nor were they spent in the degree of isolation Emerson implied. His pastoral duties were extensive, but he still found time to increase the volume of his writing and organizational involvement. His numerous visits to Boston assured his continuing role in its intellectual circles. One of his earliest achievements in this period was the establishment of the Transcendental Club.

The first suggestion for the organization of what was to be called the Transcendental Club came from Hedge to Margaret Fuller in the summer of 1833. Following their conversation, Fuller wrote to Hedge that she was willing to join such a society "as he spoke of." She did not discuss the exact nature of the group, but it would appear that more than socializing was intended. Fuller included an offer to write for that club, if it were formed. [21] The idea surfaced once again in the spring of 1835. In another letter from Fuller to Hedge, she again voiced her support for such an organization as well as for his idea for a journal. [22]

In the summer of 1835, Hedge proposed his idea to Emerson. At this point, however, he flirted with the possibility of limiting membership in his proposed group to the ministry. Emerson objected to the limitation, citing Bronson Alcott as an example of someone who would be excluded under such a rule, but he favored the basic proposal. Nothing was done until the following summer, probably the result of Hedge's move to Bangor. [23]

In May 1836, Hedge attended the Berry Street Conference in Boston, the meeting of an informal advisory body of Unitarian ministers in Massachusetts. In his own words, he was "stunned by the lamentable want of courage shown by the members in their discussion of subjects [theological and moral], and the utter neglect of truth for expedients." He spoke to George Ripley and George Putnam of his concern and suggested that a group was needed to supply the forum in which "to speak without fear of elders and betters." [24]

In contrast to his stand in 1835, Hedge suggested that membership in his proposed organization be open to all "like minded persons," in spirit, if not in opinion. It would include "men who earnestly seek the truth and who, with perfect freedom in the avowal of their own opinions, however abhorent in the general facts, unite perfect toleration of other men's freedom and opinions." In other words, he would exclude only those whose presence would preclude discussion on any topic. [25]

Hedge later reflected on objectives of the Transcendental Club:

> What precisely we wanted it would have been difficult for either of us [Hedge or Emerson] to state. What we strongly felt was dissatisfaction with the reigning sensual philosophy dating from Locke, on which Unitarian theology was based. [26]

Elsewhere he noted:

> There was a promise in the air of a new era of intellectual life. We four [Ripley, Putnam, Emerson, and Hedge] concluded to call a few like-minded seekers together on the following week. [Reflections on the Willard Hotel meeting.] [27]

Beyond this, little agreement existed. James Freeman Clarke, himself a participant, recalled that members called themselves "the club of the like minded," because, "no two of us thought alike." [28] Hedge added that in his mind there was actually no club at all, "properly speaking." There was no organization, no presiding officer, and no votes taken. He could not even recall how the name "Transcendental Club" came into being. "It certainly was never assumed by the persons so called," he added. [29]

Actually, critics applied the name "Transcendental Club" to the "like-minded." The name described the group's basic philosophical principles, but it also reflected the attitude of the critics toward Transcendental beliefs. To underscore their attitude critics often quoted Charles Dickens: "I was given to understand that whatever was unintelligible would be certainly Transcendental." Dickens wrote that he was led to believe this upon his arrival in Boston in 1842. Upon his own investigation, however, he found Transcendentalism had "its good and healthful qualities," as well as its few "vagaries." "What school has not?" Dickens noted in reference to its vagaries. He concluded, "If I were a Bostonian, I think I would be a Transcendentalist." Understandably, Dickens' later comments were ignored by those who chose to use his formal statements as a criticism of Transcendentalism. [30]

Transcendental Club members found it difficult to accept the name, not because it failed to represent their spirit and aims, but because it was "too ambiguous and involved several popular and technical definitions no one of which was suitable for what the group had in common." They considered, but failed to adopt, titles such as "Disciples of Newness," "New School," "Eclectics," and "Symposium." They finally answered to the name "Transcendental Club," because the public would accept no other. [31]

To its members, the Transcendental Club became Hedge's Club or the Hedge Club. He was its founder, and his arrival from Bangor signaled club meetings. [32] Hedge played an even more important role, however. Club members recognized him as a leader in both philosophical thought and German literature. George Ripley, for example, attributed his progress in metaphysics to the "guidance of our learned Professor Hedge." [33] Ralph Waldo Emerson listed him as his choice for instructor of metaphysics and philosophy of history for his never-to-be model university, that which would revolutionize New England education. [34]

By most estimates, then and now, Hedge was the best trained and most methodical thinker of New England Transcendentalists. [35]

New England Transcendentalists dubbed Frederic "Germanicus Hedge," the "fountain of knowledge in the way of German." They deferred to him as the "authority in matters of German philosophy," [36] and German philosophy was the most important foreign influence on American Transcendentalism. George Ripley noted that his "thirst for German philosophy" was quenched by Hedge, [37] while Theodore Parker recalled that Hedge knew more about German philosophy than any other man of his acquaintance. In the early years of the club meetings Parker sought Hedge for a course of readings in the field. [38]

Hedge was the only one of the original New England Transcendentalists who had experienced both the German language and German literature at first hand. The rest either learned the language in America or read translations and critiques. Harvard did not have its first German language instructor until Charles Follen in 1825. Early translations were uniformly poor, and critiques, including those of Coleridge and Carlyle, reflected the attitude of their composers. [39]

Hedge had not been the first New Englander to study in Germany. George Ticknor, Edward Everett, and Joseph Cogswell, who had preceded Hedge by a few years, had sought progressive methods or instruction utilized at the Universities of Berlin, Halle, and Heidelberg. [40] The second wave of American students who traveled to Germany in the late 1810s, included John Motley, Henry Dwight, William Emerson, George Calvert, Henry Wadsworth Longfellow, and George Bancroft, accompanied by Frederic Hedge. The second wave tended to study philosophy, and when they returned most of them introduced the study of German literature. Longfellow became the first American college instructor to interpret and teach Johann Wolfgang von Goethe. Many Americans considered German literature "indecent" or "immoral," and the stigma remained, no doubt aggravated by Bancroft's well publicized disdain for the German "national character," and for Goethe's "dirty" and "bestial" literature. Critics attacked Goethe's literature for emphasizing "uncontrollable passions," for "dangerously libeling human nature" by representing vice rather than virtue "as lovely and exciting sympathy," and for making heroes of the "profligate" rather than "esteeming sources of purity of thought and loftiness of soul."[41]

Scholars generally agree that Hedge was the first American whose "understanding of German thought and art was unequivocal." They feel he rose above the intercultural clash of moral or religious values, as well as the "self-doubt" of the society that sent him. Both factors, critics agree, hampered the accumulation of knowledge by earlier students. Further, scholars suggest that Hedge was the first exponent of German thought to gain a measure of American acceptance of German literature. He became "patriarch of the movement for the study of German letters in America," as well as the indisputable source of German philosophy for American Transcendentalists. [42]

In time the Hedge Club included twenty-six members, including seventeen Unitarian ministers and five women. [43] It was devoted to new ideas in ethics, philosophy, theology, literature, and religious reform. Each member contributed certain intellectual qualities. For example, if Hedge supplied the philosophic mind, Emerson gave penetrating insight, Alcott, pure idealism, and Ripley, practical understanding. If Emerson and Ripley were the first to argue for a program of reform, Parker was their main supporter, and Hedge sought to work reformism into the context of universal Christianity. [44] The Transcendental Club met nearly thirty times over the next four years, and Hedge attended three-quarters of those sessions despite the travel distance involved. [45] After 1840 the club met less regularly as the growing individualism of the group took its toll. [46]

In 1835, Frederic Hedge proposed publishing a journal with contributions from the "like-minded." He suggested it be devoted to "spiritual philosophy" and include articles and translations by "leaders in that school of thought." [47] He would edit the journal, with the help of Emerson and Ripley, and its title would be the Transcendentalist or the Spiritual Inquirer. This project was postponed, however, when he moved to Bangor, and could not take the position. Emerson, with Hedge's encouragement, tried to interest Thomas Carlyle in editing a transatlantic version of the journal, but he declined. [48]

Hedge brought up the idea of a Transcendental journal once again at a club meeting on September 18, 1839, at the home of Cyrus Bartol. The group asked him to be editor, but he declined. Margaret Fuller assumed the position, however, and The Dial began publication in 1840. [49] According to Fuller, the purpose of the journal was not to establish the "Gospel of Transcendentalism" but rather to create

> a perfectly free organization for the expression of individual thought and character . . . no party measures to be carried, no particular standard to be set up . . . not to accomplish any outward object, but merely to afford an avenue for what of liberal and calm thought might be originated among us, by the wants of individual minds. [50]

During the four years of The Dial's existence, Hedge made four contributions: an article, two translations, and one poem. [51] "The Art of Life, the Scholar's Calling" is considered to be one of the three items serving as the literary keynote of the new publication, the other two being Emerson's "The Editors to the Readers" and Fuller's "Essay on Critics." [52] Yet, it is generally held that despite his involvement in its founding, Hedge's interest in The Dial soon languished. Many believe that this signaled the first stage of his disenchantment with other Transcendental leaders. (This will be discussed later.)

Hedge's active involvement with other Transcendentalists upon occasion strained the relationship he had with his own congregation. He explained two such incidents in a letter to Convers Francis in 1842, setting the tone by wishing Francis a Happy New Year, "if it is allowable in these conservative days to wish or speak of anything new." He then related that in the preceding summer three or four members of his congregation, including two Methodist deacons, "got frightened about Transcendentalism ... and suspected that I am no better than I should be in point of orthodoxy." He suspected that there was "an organized attempt to brand and call out of the ministry" certain individuals who were thought not to be "sufficiently active in forwarding party views and objects." This he saw as a tendency in the ministry at large, being met by an equally distasteful and intolerant "headlong radicalism." Since both these positions were mutually exclusive and unpalatable, he could find only two or three ministers with whom he could feel any sympathy, including Francis. [53] Clearly, Hedge was finding his position a lonely one, both in Boston and Bangor.

Hedge continued, in his letter to Francis, that later in the fall of 1841 he had used the word "Tory," as opposed to "Whig," in a sermon to represent a "worldly type." He was developing the idea of good versus bad, and he felt the analogy was agreed upon. Instead, "several of the democracy" of his congregation understood the term as an intended reproach upon their party. At the height of the controversy that ensued, he offered to resign but, as he put it, he was "foolish enough to withdraw his decision," when asked to do so by the majority of the congregation. [54]

Hedge concluded his remarks with the following paragraph:

> So here I am still grinding in the old mill, without any prospect of relief. I should be content to stay if I could believe that I was doing good enough to compensate for the sacrifice. And yet perhaps I do as much good here as I should anywhere else, or anyone else would do in my place with such a peculiar heterogeneous people

> [elsewhere explained as a mix of ultraliberals and ultraconservatives]. I believe that if I were to leave them, they would find it very difficult to unite in another minister and that makes me less resolute about going than I should be if I consulted my own inclination alone. [55]

Several months later Hedge wrote once again to Francis expressing his concern over developments in Boston. Polarization continued:

> There is a rigid, cautious, circumspect, conservative ring in the air of Cambridge which no one, especially those incurred with the stigma of Transcendental and heretical tendencies, who has resided there for any considerable time can escape.

At the same time, radicals could not be placated, and Hedge feared for the ministerial profession. He noted, for example, that "open and avowed dissent" of Emerson and Parker, especially as to "the inspiration of the Bible, had given a sort of respectability to doctrines and tendencies which were considered infamous a few years ago," leading to "a vast amount of skepticism in the world." [56]

What Hedge feared most, however, were other radicals "with large ideas and small faculty, who have not obtained what they covet from existing institutions and who think they shall find this amount in general overturn." On this point he referred to "all sorts of radicalism abroad," and particularly to socialism which "grassates like the cholera." [57] Hedge continued:

> If the principle of dissent from existing institutions and beliefs continues to spread at the rate it has done for the last two years . . . the entire clerus, professional and parochial, will be ousted in ten years from this. [58]

Hedge concluded his letter to Francis with what must have reflected the low point of his ministry in Bangor, "I consider myself a loser in this business, and I begin to wonder how I come to be so disinterested." [59]

In 1847, Frederic Hedge reached two milestones in his life. In the spring he published his first major volume, **Prose Writers of Germany.** He made no pretense of including translations of all major works of German writers, but instead, included what he considered to be the "classics," or the best of the "first class." The book included twenty-eight selections and involved eight translators besides Hedge. [60] **Prose Writers** was the first effort of such scale in the United States; its five editions served as a major resource for students of German literature. One contemporary felt it "rendered to the American public a service comparable to that performed by Carlyle's translations from the German for the English public" a quarter of a century before. [**61**] In the spring of 1847 Hedge decided to visit Europe once again. His years in Bangor had been difficult ones. He had not taken any of the vacation time to which he was entitled, and he was ill and worn out. The congregation agreed to defray his expenses, as well as to pay for his replacement. [**62**]

On June 5, 1847, Hedge left for Europe where he toured, in part, with his friend George William Curtis. He landed in Liverpool and traveled to London, where, with a letter of introduction from Ralph Waldo Emerson, he met Thomas Carlyle. In that letter Emerson referred to Hedge as "an old friend," and as "a chief supporter of the cause of good letters" in America. Emerson noted that although he had sent a good many friends to Carlyle, few were "on as many grounds entitled to know" Carlyle as Hedge. [**63**] Carlyle gave his impression of Hedge in a letter to Emerson:

> Hedge is one of the sturdiest little fellows I have come across for many a day. A face like a rock, a voice like a howitzer, only his honest gray eyes reassure you a little. . . . We may have met only once, but hope (mutually, I flatter myself) it may be often by and by.

And on Hedge's other qualities:

> Wherever new thought is marching on the field, there we find Mr. Hedge in the front rank. [**64**]

From England Hedge traveled to Belgium, Germany, and Italy. If his visit to Germany renewed his love of that country, Italy was his greatest delight. He spent the winter of 1847/48 in Rome, where he visited Margaret Fuller, playing her role in the Italian Revolution of 1848 as the wife of Marchese Ossoli. Hedge found Italy to be the only country superior to Germany in historic and artistic interest. Of special interest were incidents from the Revolution of 1848 in Rome and the counter-offenses by figures such as Pope Pius IX. [**65**]

In December 1849, on his return from Europe, Hedge submitted his letter of resignation to the congregation at Bangor. Some embarrassment arose because notice of his acceptance of the Providence position appeared in the Christian Examiner before he had notified his Bangor congregation. [**66**] In his farewell sermon on March 3, 1850, Hedge noted that he had spent the best years of his life in Bangor, but that these years had been difficult ones, "tasking" all his powers. He felt the chief burden of his years at Bangor had been his devotion to the pulpit. He added that he did not regret this devotion, but that he had found it difficult to speak to the same audience every Sunday. Further, he felt he had been so tied to his pulpit that he had failed to go out among his people "in the pastoral sense." He regretted that he had not done more "to arouse the interest" of his people "in missionary work of the church." [**67**]

Finally, Hedge concluded:

> Without discussing the reasons which have moved me to lay down my ministry here, I will only say that the need of relief from the constant pressure of intellectual labor, in the absence of professional exchanges, the fear of degenerating for want of that relief, of failing to satisfy the demands of this position, has been my chief enducement. [**68**]

Hedge had hoped to find a position in the Boston area, possibly an "historical professorship at Cambridge." When that was not forthcoming, he settled for Providence, Rhode Island, closer by far to Boston than Bangor. [**69**] Although he spent less than seven years with the Westminster Congregational Society in Providence, his family formed close ties with its members which lasted beyond Frederic's death. Sixty years after Hedge had left Providence, and twenty-seven years after his death, members of the congregation attended the funeral of his daughter, Charlotte. [**70**] Moreover, his years in Providence were productive. In 1853 he published **Christian Liturgy, for the Use of the Church** and, with Frederick D. Huntington, **Hymns for the Church of Christ.** [**71**] In 1852, Hedge received an honorary Doctor of Divinity from Harvard.

In 1857 the First Parish of Brookline, Massachusetts, "unanimously" called Hedge from Providence to succeed the Reverend Frederick Knapp. Knapp had resigned because of illness, following a brief stay as successor to the Reverend John Pierce, Hedge's father-in-law. Although overjoyed by this long awaited opportunity, Hedge was reluctant to leave his Providence congregation without pastoral care. He did so only on condition that within seven months they find a successor with whom they could unite. They did. [**72**] He became the first minister of the Brookline congregation not taken directly from the Harvard Divinity School and also the first to leave before retirement, unless forced to do so on account of ill health. [**73**]

Hedge's move to Brookline signaled his rise to leadership in New England's intellectual circles. Within a year he became professor of ecclesiastical history at Harvard Divinity School and editor of the Christian Examiner. In 1859, as newly elected president of the American Unitarian Association, he delivered a major address at the Schiller Centennial in Boston, praising the poetic genius of Schiller and calling him the German national consciousness and heart of the people. [74]

In 1860 Hedge published **Recent Inquiries in Theology**, a collection of essays and reviews by "eminent" English churchmen on contemporary theological issues. The clerical authors included shared a "fellowship of a liberal faith" and opposition to the "fructification" resulting from Locke. [75] **Recent Inquiries** was highly regarded for representing the "most significant fruits of modern scholarship" and for the courage of dealing with issues between the old traditional faith and new knowledge. This, after all, was a topic Hedge not only personally pursued but that he sought to bring to the attention of those around him. [76]

Under Hedge's editorship the Christian Examiner became one of the leading journals of the day. In his own words he espoused no cause as editor, but he tried to make the Christian Examiner "a condign organ for the best thought of the country and to attract the best thinkers to it by giving them the assurance of good company." He felt he was successful in this, as did most others, and that in the "resumé of current literature" the journal excelled all other American periodicals. As to his own part in this, he claimed his work "had been merely to organize the journal, to lay down the paradigm, and to exercise a negative control, keeping out and staving off . . . the crude stuff and multitudinous inanity that seeks admission into every periodical, appealing to editorial good nature." The rejection of "foul manuscripts from people he wished to please, he considered his hardest labor. [77]

Hedge is generally remembered as one of the most effective presidents of the American Unitarian Association. At a time of serious internal discord and factionalization, he rose above party and was welcomed by all. He was bold and daring in his own speculations, but he was cautious in his acceptance of new theories into the church. Thus, regardless of his intellectual association, his devotion to Unitarianism was never seriously questioned. [78]

In 1861 Hedge resigned as editor of the Christian Examiner, and in 1863 he finished his fourth and final term as A.U.A. president. Although maintaining his pastoral duties and remaining on the A.U.A. Executive Board until 1866, he was preparing his most important and widely read intellectual exposition, **Reason in Religion**, which appeared in 1865. It was an explication of his major faith in life, liberal religion. [79] One contemporary saw the book as "by far the ablest and most influential expression" of liberal theology of its time. Another felt it established Hedge as "an acknowledged leader among Unitarian divines" and "a man eminent in the walks of theology and letters." Henry Wadsworth Longfellow called the work Hedge's "Holy Grail." One modern scholar considers it "perhaps the classic statement of Transcendental Christianity." [80]

The rest of the decade was punctuated by a third trip to Europe in 1866; a widely hailed appearance at Faneuil Hall in 1870, speaking on behalf of the German effort in the Franco-Prussian War; [81] the publication of numerous journal articles; and the appearance of **The Primeval World of Hebrew Tradition**, also in 1870. **The Primeval World** was a textual exegesis of Old Testament passages from Genesis dealing with topics such as creation, man and the image of God, and man's fall from grace. [82] Hedge also frequented meetings of the Boston Radical Club, organized in 1867 to discuss radical ideas and reform movements. Among those appearing at club meetings were Ralph Waldo Emerson, Octavius B. Frothingham, and James Freeman Clarke. [83]

In 1872, Hedge resigned from his position in Brookline to become professor of German at Harvard. [84] By 1876 his responsibilities in that department increased to the point where he was forced to resign from his post in the Divinity School. He remained in the Divinity School for the next two years as instructor on special topics. Although Hedge's scholarship was unquestioned, and students reported being deeply influenced by his intellect, his demeanor and classroom methodology received only fair ratings at best. The more gracious reports held him as "not especially successful as a teacher." Others more bluntly called him "the worst teacher of German that ever lived." [85] His students found his exposition "arid" and saw him as a "testy and fussy old gentleman," who was "difficult of approach and slow of sympathy." [86] Hedge's colleagues agreed that he did not "suffer fools gladly," but they found him "generous, considerate, tender, even humble minded," especially once they passed through "the magic circle of friendship." [87]

Throughout the 1870s Hedge maintained a busy schedule of teaching, writing, and speaking activities. In 1877 he spoke before the Goethe Club of New York City, of which he was an honorary member, [88] and published **Ways of the Spirit and Other Essays**, a collection of writings on topics such as historic Christianity, atonement, theism, and the proof of God's existence. [89] In 1879, he began an irregularly scheduled lecture series at the Concord School of Philosophy which lasted until 1887. [90] By 1880 Hedge found it difficult to keep his continuously growing, hectic schedule. In that year he wrote to Henry Bellows complaining that he was beginning to find it necessary to decline several special speaking engagements. [91] In February 1881, he submitted his resignation from Harvard, effective the following August. It was accepted with expressions of praise as to his service and the value of his influence on the university, but he did not completely stop teaching until 1884. [92] In a letter to Caroline Dall on March 23, 1881, Hedge explained his resignation:

> I have resigned my office not from consciousness of any want of strength to do at least as much as I have been doing the last year, but on general principles, and because I think old men should retire before they become actually superannuated and make way for younger talent and fresh powers. [93]

Hedge's active life was far from over. In 1882 he delivered notable eulogies on the deaths of Henry Bellows and of Ralph Waldo Emerson. [94] In September 1882, he spoke of Luther at the Ministers' Institute in Lowell, Massachusetts. [95] On November 10, 1883, Hedge appeared at the 400th anniversary celebration of the birth of Martin Luther at the Arlington Street Church in Boston and spoke from memory for more than an hour and a half, closely holding the attention of his audience. [96]

The following year Frederic Hedge published **Atheism in Philosophy.** Its theme can be seen in the quotation from Plato which Hedge cited at the opening of the text:

> Philosophy, Socrates, if pursued in moderation and at the proper age, is an elegant accomplishment; but too much philosophy is the ruin of human life. [97]

The philosophy that Hedge disparaged denied the "supermundane, conscious intelligence of the universe," preferring to see it as "the product of blind force, as a self-subsisting, self-governing, independent being." [98]

Hedge received an honorary LL.D. in 1886 at the 250th anniversary of Harvard University in recognition of his faithful service to scholarship. [99] In the same year he published **Hours with German Classics: Masterpieces of German Literature Translated into English.** His contemporaries considered **Hours with German Classics** "the most complete treatment of German literature" in English at that time. Hedge noted, however, that he did not intend to be totally inclusive but to "exhibit some of its characteristic phases as exemplified by writers representing the national genius." [100]

Hedge made his last public appearance at the Unitarian Festival of Anniversary Week in Boston in May 1888. He was received with a "hearty greeting." [101] In the same year he published **Martin Luther and Other Essays** and **Metrical Translations and Poems. Martin Luther** contained essays on such people and topics as Martin Luther, Count Zinzendorf, Christianity in Conflict with Hellenism, and Feudal Society. [102] **Metrical Translations**, edited with Annis Lee Wister, included Hedge's translations of works by Goethe, Friedrich von Schiller, and others as well as original poems of his own, such as "Class of Twenty-Five on Their Fortieth Anniversary" and "The Idealist." [103] Clearly, Hedge's mind remained active. James Freeman Clarke made the following comment in a letter to him in 1888: "Your thoughts are a great stimulus to my intellect. They set my thoughts in motion." [104]

Frederic Hedge spent the last two years of his life suffering from eczema, "tortured with disease," and periodically, "imprisoned in paralysis." [105] During his moments of paralysis, he alternated between cravings for forgetfulness and rest and the fear of aphasia, which had plagued the last years of his friend, Emerson. His memory never suffered substantial loss, however, though he could no longer sustain literary efforts. [106] He died on August 21, 1890, at his home in Cambridge.

In 1891 Hedge's **Sermons** was published posthumously. It included selected orations given by him during his lifetime. The collection was a fitting tribute to him, and it is appropriate to end this chapter with its recognition, for although the preceding information establishes Hedge's impact on the intellectual life of nineteenth century New England, the nature of his speculation remains to be considered. Chief among the subjects to be covered are his view of the nature of life, the existence and role of the soul, and the sources of human and divine authority. These were the focus of **Sermons** as they were of Hedge's intellectual life. [107]

NOTES

1. Ronald Vale Wells, **Three Christian Transcendentalists: James Marsh, Caleb Sprague Henry, Frederic Henry Hedge** (1943; rpt. New York: Octagon Books, 1972), 97; William H. Lyon, **Frederic Henry Hedge: Seventh Minister of the First Parish in Brookline** (Brookline, Ma.: First Parish in Brookline, 1906), 9.

2. Martha Ilona Tuomi, "Dr. Frederic Henry Hedge: His Life and Works to the End of His Bangor Pastorate, 1805-1850," M.A. Thesis, University of Maine 1934, 43.

3. Frederic Henry Hedge, "Coleridge's **Literary Character**," Christian Examiner, 14 (1833), 108-129.

4. Donald N. Koster, **Transcendentalism in America** (Boston: Twayne Publishers, 1975), 1. William T. Harris, "Frederic Henry Hedge," Journal of Speculative Philosophy, 11 (1877), 107.

5. "To Thomas Carlyle," 20 November 1834, **The Correspondence of Emerson and Carlyle**, ed. Joseph Slater (New York: Columbia University Press, 1964), 110. See also James Elliot Cabot, **A Memoir of Ralph Waldo Emerson** (Boston: Houghton Mifflin Company, 1895), I, 216; Henry David Gray, **Emerson: A Statement of New England Transcendentalism as Expressed in the Philosophy of Its Chief Exponent** (1917; rpt. New York: Frederick Ungar Publishing Co., 1958), 23.

6. Frederic Henry Hedge, "Emmanuel Swedenborg," Christian Examiner, 15 (1833), 193-218; Frederic Henry Hedge, "Pretensions of Phrenology Examined," Christian Examiner, 17 (1834), 249-269.

7. Frederic Henry Hedge, Letter to Caroline H. Dall, 1 February 1877, as recorded in Caroline H. Dall, **Transcendentalism in New England: A Lecture Before the Society for Philosophical Enquiry, Washington, D.C., May 7, 1895** (Boston: Roberts Brothers, 1897),16.

8. Frederic Henry Hedge, Letter to John Graham Palfrey, 16 June 1833, Frederic Henry Hedge Papers, Harvard University Archives, Cambridge, Massachusetts.

9. Ralph Waldo Emerson, Letter to Frederic Henry Hedge, 12 July 1834, Frederic Henry Hedge Papers, Bangor Historical Society, Bangor, Maine.

10. Joel Myerson, "Frederic Henry Hedge and the Failure of Transcendentalism," Harvard Library Bulletin, 23 (1975), 399; Tuomi, 51, 56.

11. Frederic Henry Hedge, Letter to Margaret Fuller, 1 February 1835, Frederic Henry Hedge Papers, Harvard University Archives, Cambridge, Massachusetts.

12. Harold Clarke Goddard, **Studies in New England Transcendentalism** (1908; rpt. New York: Hillary House Publishers, Ltd., 1960), 5.

13. Letter, Lucy Hedge to Frederic Henry Hedge, 17 December 1835, Poor-Hedge Letters, Schlesinger Library, Radcliffe College, Cambridge, Massachusetts; Letter, Frederic Henry Hedge to Lucy Hedge, 1 April 1836, Poor-Hedge Letters, Schlesinger Library, Radcliffe College, Cambridge, Massachusetts.

14. Bliss Perry, "Frederic Henry Hedge," in **The Early Years of the Saturday Club, 1855-1876**, ed. Edward Waldo Emerson (Boston: Houghton Mifflin Company, 1918), 278; Lyon, 6; Joseph Henry Allen, **Sequel to "Our Liberal Movement"** (Boston: Roberts Brothers, 1897), 78.

15. As quoted in John W. Chadwick, **Frederic Henry Hedge: A Sermon** (Boston: George H. Ellis, Publisher, 1890-91), 25.

16. Howard N. Brown, "Frederic Henry Hedge," in **Heralds of A Liberal Faith** (Boston: American Unitarian Association, 1910), IV, 162; Joseph Henry Allen,

"Frederic Henry Hedge," Unitarian Review and Religious Magazine, Oct. 1890, 292.

17. Perry, 28; Lyon, 3, 11; Brown, 162; Julia Ward Howe, **Reminiscences: 1819–1899** (1899; rpt. New York: Negro University Press, 1969), 295.

18. Lyon, 6.

19. Wells, 97; Lyon, 7; Tuomi, 59.

20. "To Thomas Carlyle," 4 June 1847, **Correspondence of Thomas Carlyle and Ralph Waldo Emerson, 1834–1872**, ed. C. E. Norton (Boston: Houghton Mifflin Company, 1883), II, 135.

21. Letter, Margaret Fuller to Frederic Henry Hedge, 4 July 1833, as quoted in Thomas Wentworth Higginson, **Margaret Fuller Ossoli** (1844; rpt. New York: Haskel House Publishers, Ltd., 1968), 4.

22. Ibid., 5 March 1835, 142.

23. William R. Hutchison, **The Transcendentalist Ministers: Church Reform in the New England Renaissance** (New Haven: Yale University Press, 1959), 30–31.

24. Letter, Frederic Henry Hedge to Ralph Waldo Emerson, 14 June 1836, Poor-Hedge Letters, Schlesinger Library, Radcliffe College, Cambridge, Massachusetts.

25. Ibid.

26. Letter, Frederic Henry Hedge to James Elliot Cabot, 3 December 1836, Frederic Henry Hedge Papers, Harvard University Archives, Cambridge, Massachusetts.

27. As quoted in Hutchison, 31.

28. As quoted in Paul Boller, Jr., **American Transcendentalism, 1836–1860: An Intellectual Inquiry** (New York: G. P. Putnam's Sons, 1974), xvii.

29. Letter, Frederic Henry Hedge to Caroline H. Dall, 1 February 1877, as quoted in Dall, 16.

30. Charles Dickens, **American Notes** (1842; rpt. New York: Oxford University Press, 1957), 24. See also Dall, 16; Boller, 35; Walter Harding, **The Days of Henry Thoreau** (New York: Alfred A. Knopf, 1966), 63; Gray, 7.

31. Hutchison, 23; Harding, 63.

32. Boller, xiv; Henry A. Pochmann, **German Culture in America: Philosophical and Literary Influences: 1600–1900** (Madison: University of Wisconsin Press, 1957), 144.

33. As quoted in Pochmann, 121.

34. Crowe, 122.

35. Pochmann, 143-144; Crowe, 80.

36. Pochmann, 144; Gray, 23.

37. As quoted in Myerson, "Frederic Henry Hedge," 159.

38. Ibid.

39. Stanley M. Vogel, **German Literary Influences on the American Transcendentalists** (New York: Archon Books, 1970), 50; Harvey Gates Townsend, **Philosophical Ideas in the United States** (New York: American Book Company, 1934), 83; Nelson R. Burr, **A Critical Bibliography of Religion in America** (Princeton: Princeton University Press, 1961), 60.

40. Vogel, 27; Carl Diehl, **Americans and German Scholarship, 1770-1870** (New Haven: Yale University Press, 1978), 2, 50; Orie W. Long, **Literary Pioneers: Early American Explorers of European Culture** (New York: Russell and Russell, Inc., 1963), 77; Pochmann, 63.

41. Long, **Literary Pioneers**, 16, 68, 108, 117, 204; Vogel, **German Literary Influences**, 36, 42; Pochmann, **German Culture**, 336-337.

42. The role of Frederic Hedge in German scholarship in America is considered herein only as it relates to this study. The topic is more extensively covered in Orie W. Long, **Frederic Henry Hedge: A Cosmopolitan Scholar** (Portland, Me.: The Southworth-Anthoensen Press, 1940); Vogel, 65; Pochmann, 85, 143, 259, 336; Diehl, 149.

43. Hutchison, **The Transcendentalist Ministers**, 31-32.

44. Hutchison, 3; Higginson, 144; Boller, xiv; Harding, 121; Crowe, 84.

45. Myerson, "Frederic Henry Hedge," 402.

46. Harding, 121.

47. As quoted in Long, **Frederic Henry Hedge**, 23; Brown, 162; Octavius B. Frothingham, **A Memoir of William Henry Channing** (Boston: Houghton Mifflin Company, 1886), 109; Letter, Ralph Waldo Emerson to Thomas Carlyle, 30 April 1835, **Correspondence of Emerson and Carlyle**, 125.

48. "To Thomas Carlyle," 13 May 1835, **Correspondence of Emerson and Carlyle**, 125; "To Thomas Carlyle," 30 August 1835, **Correspondence of Emerson and Carlyle**, 129-130.

49. Joel Myerson, **The New England Transcendentalists and the Dial: A History of the Magazine and Its Contributors** (Rutherford, N.J.: Farleigh Dickinson University Press, 1980), 188.

50. Margaret Fuller, **Memoirs of Margaret Fuller Ossoli,** eds. William Henry Channing, James Freeman Clarke, and Ralph Waldo Emerson. (London: Richard Bentley, 1852), II, 20, 199-200.

51. Frederic Henry Hedge, "The Art of Life, the Scholar's Calling," The Dial, 1 (1840), 175-182; Frederic Henry Hedge, "Questionings," The Dial, 1 (1841), 290-291; Frederic Henry Hedge, "Uhlands's 'The Castle by the Sea,'" The Dial, 3 (1842), 74-75; Frederic Henry Hedge, "Schelling's Introductory Lecture in Berlin, 15 November, 1841," The Dial, 3 (1843), 398-404.

52. Hedge, "The Art of Life"; Long, **Frederic Henry Hedge,** 23.

53. Letter, Frederic Henry Hedge to Convers Francis, 26 January 1842, Washburn Collection, Massachusetts Historical Society, Boston, Massachusetts.

54. Ibid.

55. Ibid.

56. Letter, Frederic Henry Hedge to Convers Francis, 14 February 1843, Washburn Collection, Massachusetts Historical Society, Boston, Massachusetts.

57. Ibid.

58. Ibid.

59. Ibid.

60. Edition used: Frederic Henry Hedge, **Prose Writers of Germany** (New York: C. S. Francis and Company, 1856).

61. Edward Waldo Emerson, **The Early Years of the Saturday Club,** 279. See also Lyon, 12; Brown, 163; Vogel, 117; Chadwick, 24; Harris, 107; Pochmann, 583; H. H. Furness, "Prose Writers of Germany," Christian Examiner, 44 (1848), 268.

62. Tuomi, 73.

63. "To Thomas Carlyle," 4 June 1847, **Correspondence of Emerson and Carlyle,** 425.

64. "To Ralph Waldo Emerson," 31 August 1847, **Correspondence of Emerson and Carlyle,** 428.

65. Long, **Frederic Henry Hedge,** 28; Allen, **Sequel to "Our Liberal Movement,"** 79. Hedge later commented on his concern for Margaret Fuller. During

his visit to Rome, he found her suffering from "severe fits of depression." Howe, 301.

66. Letter, "Frederic Henry Hedge to a Friend in Bangor, Me.," 21 November 1849, included in Wells, 209.

67. Frederic Henry Hedge, **A Sermon Preached to the Independent Congregational Society, March 3, 1850 on Closing His Pastoral Connection With That Society** (Bangor, Me.: Samuel S. Smith, 1850), 7, 13.

68. Ibid., 14.

69. Letter, "Hedge to a Friend," 21 November 1849.

70. Wells, 97.

71. Frederic Henry Hedge, **Christian Liturgy for the Use of the Church** (Boston: Crosby, Nichols, and Company, 1853).

72. Lyon, 9.

73. Ibid., 8.

74. Lyon, 12; Long, **Frederic Henry Hedge**, 46-47.

75. Edition used: Frederic Henry Hedge, **Recent Inquiries in Theology, By Eminent English Churchmen; Being "Essays and Reviews"** (Boston: Walker, Wise, and Company, 1861). **Recent Inquiries in Theology** was also published in London, England.

76. George E. Ellis, "Old Faith and New Knowledge, A Review of Frederic Hedge's **Recent Inquiries in Theology**," Christian Examiner, 69 (1860), 362, 378.

77. Letter, Frederic Henry Hedge to Henry W. Bellows, 16 May 1850, Bellows Collection, Massachusetts Historical Society, Boston, Massachusetts; Letter, Frederic Henry Hedge to Nathan Appleton, 23 September 1859, Appleton Collection, Massachusetts Historical Society, Boston, Massachusetts. See also Wells, 197; Pochmann, 583.

78. Raymond William Adams, "Frederic Henry Hedge," **Dictionary of American Biography** (1932), IV, 498; Letter, Frederic Henry Hedge to Reverend Charles Lowe, 7 June 1866, Frederic Henry Hedge Collection, Andover-Harvard Theological Library, Cambridge, Massachusetts.

79. Letter, Hedge to Lowe, 7 June 1866; Frederic Henry Hedge, **Reason in Religion** (Boston: Walker, Fuller, and Company, 1865).

80. Edward Waldo Emerson, **The Early Years of the Saturday Club**, 464; Lyon, 12; Joseph Henry Allen, "A Memory of Dr. Hedge," The Unitarian Review

and Religious Magazine, Sept. 1890, 269; Joseph Henry Allen and Richard Eddy, **A History of the Unitarians and Universalists in the United States** (New York: The Christian Literature Co., 1894), 229; "Reason in Relgion," The New Jerusalem Magazine, Nov. 1865, 290; Burr, 69.

81. Frederic Henry Hedge, "Address to Germans of Boston, Faneuil Hall, July, 1870," The Index, 27 August 1870, 2-3. See also Long, **Frederic Henry Hedge**, 48.

82. Frederic Henry Hedge, The Primeval World of Hebrew Tradition (Boston: Roberts Brothers, 1870).

83. Howe, 281-282.

84. Letter, John Thornston Kirkland (President of Harvard College) to Frederic Henry Hedge, 16 September 1872, Frederic Henry Hedge Papers, Harvard University Archives, Cambridge, Massachusetts.

85. Eliot, IV, 63; Edward Waldo Emerson, **The Early Years of the Saturday Club**, 272; Long, **Frederic Henry Hedge**, 42.

86. Perry, 280; Chadwick, 25.

87. Brown, 164. Ralph Waldo Emerson, **The Journals of Ralph Waldo Emerson**, eds. Edward W. Emerson and W. E. Forbes. (Cambridge, Ma.: The Riverside Press, 1909-14), V, 248; Allen, "A Memory of Dr. Hedge," 269.

88. Long, **Frederic Henry Hedge**, 48.

89. Frederic Henry Hedge, **Ways of the Spirit and Other Essays** (Boston: Roberts Brothers, 1877).

90. Pochmann, 233.

91. Letter, Frederic Henry Hedge to Henry W. Bellows, 12 April 1880, Bellows Collection, Massachusetts Historical Society, Boston, Massachusetts.

92. **Harvard College Records**, Harvard University Archives, XIII, 48. Long, **Frederic Henry Hedge**, 43; Allen, "Frederic Henry Hedge," 294.

93. Letter, Frederic Henry Hedge to Caroline H. Dall, 23 March 1881, Dall Collection, Massachusetts Historical Society, Boston, Massachusetts.

94. Frederic Henry Hedge, "Memorial Address," in Joseph Henry Allen, **Our Liberal Movement in Theology: Chiefly as shown in Recollections of the History of Unitarianism in New England** (Boston: Roberts Brothers, 1892), 203-218.

95. The Ministers' Institute instructed ministers who did not have the time or opportunity for original research. Hedge at first preferred to see this done by less costly means, such as publications and annual meetings. In time,

however, Hedge reconsidered, supported creation of the institute and agreed to take part.

Letter, Frederic Henry Hedge to Reverend James de Normandie, 9 January 1877, Bellows Collection, Massachusetts Historical Society, Boston, Massachusetts. Letter, Frederic Henry Hedge to Henry W. Bellows, 18 January 1877, Bellows Collection, Massachusetts Historical Society, Boston, Massachusetts.

96. "Biographical Sketch of Frederic Henry Hedge," The Christian Register, 28 August 1890, 551; Long, **Frederic Henry Hedge**, 48. For text of speech see Frederic Henry Hedge, "Commemorative Address," in **Commemoration of the 400th Anniversary of the Birth of Martin Luther by the Massachusetts Historical Society** (Boston: Massachusetts Historical Society, 1883), 17-39.

97. Frederic Henry Hedge, **Atheism in Philosophy, and Other Essays** (Boston: Roberts Brothers, 1884), 3.

98. Ibid., 4.

99. Long, **Frederic Henry Hedge**, 52-53.

100. Long, 43; Pochmann, 584. Edition used: Frederic Henry Hedge, **Hours with German Classics: Masterpieces of German Literature Translated into English** (New York: The German Publication Society, 1913).

101. "Biographical Sketch of Frederic Henry Hedge," 551; Wells, 98.

102. Frederic Henry Hedge, **Martin Luther and Other Essays** (Boston: Roberts Brothers, 1888).

103. Frederic Henry Hedge and Annis Lee Wister, **Metrical Translations and Poems** (Boston: Houghton Mifflin Company, 1888).

104. "To Frederic Henry Hedge," 12 January 1888, **Autobiography, Diary, and Correspondence**, ed. Edward Everett Hale (Boston: Houghton Mifflin Company, 1892), 389.

105. Lyon, 9; Perry, 281.

106. Allen, "A Memory of Dr. Hedge," 266.

107. Frederic Henry Hedge, **Sermons** (Boston: Roberts Brothers, 1891).

Chapter Three

A POSITIVE STATEMENT ON TRANSCENDENTALISM

American Transcendentalism was first and foremost a religious movement. Perry Miller warned that failure to recognize that point could lead to a misunderstanding of its direction, while another critic noted that religion was so important to Transcendentalism "that one is tempted to regard it not only as fundamental but all inclusive." [1] It developed in the 1830s from within Unitarianism as a revolt against the "mere tissue of pale negations" of that denomination. [2] Seventeen of the Transcendental Club's twenty-six members were Unitarian ministers, and they hoped to use their belief in the intuitive perception of spiritual and moral truth to restore Unitarianism's idealism and pietism without losing its freethinking and individualism and without resorting to the excesses of emotional revivalism. [3]

Frederic Henry Hedge led attempts to fuse native and foreign elements of American Transcendentalism. He was among the first Americans to adopt Transcendentalism's most basic tenets. His article, "Coleridge's **Literary Character**," which appeared in the March 1833 issue of the Christian Examiner, was the first attempt at positively explicating Transcendentalism in a major American publication. [4] Hedge's contemporaries considered the article "seminal" to the American Transcendental movement, [5] while Perry Miller hailed it as responsible for bringing the movement into being. It was "the point at which Transcendentalism went over to the offensive." [6]

Forty-four years after publication of "Coleridge's **Literary Character**," Hedge maintained that he did not believe his article had actually established American Transcendentalism, since some around him were already "predisposed to the rejection of the old sensualistic ideas" and receptive to the suggestions of Transcendentalism in already published writings of Coleridge and Carlyle. [7] If not an original impulse, then, most still agree with Miller that the article organized a yet disparate movement and gave it intellectual support and philosophical construction. [8] "Coleridge's **Literary Character**" was Hedge's earliest published statement on Transcendentalism, and it provides a clear view of his intellectual relationship to the movement and to its German exponents.

Ostensibly a review of Coleridge, Hedge seized the opportunity to introduce major elements of German Transcendentalism and to discuss his own views on the matter, especially as to the "divine intuitive impulse within us." [9] His credentials to do so were already well established by his studies in Germany and years of intellectual leadership at Harvard College and the Divinity School. [10]

In this article, Hedge labeled Coleridge at best a "somewhat original thinker," who was "inclined to comment upon the sayings and doings of others, rather than to say or do himself." He believed Coleridge's strength lay in his understanding and judgment, not in his creative genius. He was most valued for his systematic and definitive approach to concepts largely the product of other creative minds, mostly German, rather than for the creation of new ones. Further Hedge believed that Coleridge failed to consider Transcendentalism's "most basic speculations," and it was with these that Hedge launched into a presentation of the major German Transcendentalists. [11]

Hedge quickly moved to the heart of his argument. He criticized those who denounced as obscure, mystical, or extravagant whatever was supersensual and that could not be made plain by images addressed to the senses. [12] This denied the higher powers of man, contradicted Transcendental epistemology and most importantly, made Transcendental philosophy untranslatable. One could not understand Transcendentalism with such basic assumptions:

> Mere translations, however perfect, are inadequate to convey a definite notion of Transcendentalism to one who has not the metaphysical talent necessary to receive and reproduce in himself a system whose only value to us must depend upon our power to construct it for ourselves from the materials of our own conscience, and which in fact exists to us only on this condition. [13]

Francis Bowen served as a major spokesman for those critics to whom Hedge referred. Bowen saw Kant as an "original, bold, and systematic spirit," but he resisted attempts by post-Kantians to extend man's powers beyond those so formulated in Kant's pure and practical reason. Such a tendency, Bowen attributed to, at best, a "revival of the old Platonic School," or, at worst, as the product of a "diseased admiration for everything from the German source." [14] Further, he felt it had been done under false pretense by introducing new and incomprehensible philosophical nomenclature which "tends to heat the imagination and blind the judgment." [15] In 1837 Bowen made the following observation:

> [Transcendentalism] rejects the aid of observation, and will not trust experimentation. . . . General truths are to be attained without previous examination of particulars, and by the aid of a higher power than the understanding . . . pure intelligence usurps the place of humble research. [16]

Hedge believed it was impossible to understand Transcendentalism without the endowment of and use of powers of abstraction and synthetic generalization beyond those of sensibility and understanding. This epistemological power, which he felt Kant and the post-Kantians possessed "in so eminent a degree," represented the "Transcendental point of view." It relied on the "interior consciousness," and was distinguished from the common consciousness by its status as an active, not a passive, state. In Hedge's language it was "free intuition," attained by a vigorous effort of the will. [17]

In "Coleridge" Hedge made clear the purpose he saw for Transcendentalism, focusing on that which attracted him and others in New England to it. He felt that it was for those minds that sought "with faith and hope a solution to questions which philosophy meddles not with,--questions which relate to spirit and form, substance and life, free will and fate, God and eternity." If one had no interest in such questions, or did not believe that it was possible to solve them, he or she should abstain from approaching Transcendentalism as a field of inquiry. This predisposition indicated that such a person had no talent or call for it. [18]

Hedge's view of the centrality of intuition to Transcendentalism can best be seen in his treatment of the movement's object. He saw the aim of Transcendentalism as an attempt "to discover in every form of finite existence, an infinite and unconditioned ground of its existence, or rather as the ground of our knowledge of its existence, or to refer all phenomena to certain noumena, as bases of cognition." Transcendentalism sought not to explain the existence of God and creation, objectively considered, but to explain our knowledge of their existence. Importantly, it was not a skeptical philosophy, but a positive one, a philosophy that sought to build rather than to destroy. [19]

In "Coleridge's **Literary Character**" Hedge explained the synthetic nature of the intuitive process. The process proceeds from a given point, the lowest that can be found in our consciousness, to the whole of intelligence, with the entire system of its representation. The correctness or philosophical propriety of the resultant construction which is to be based on this given point, this absolute thesis, has to be assumed at first, until proven by the successful completion of the system which it is designed to establish. [**20**]

The test Hedge put forth to identify the completion of this intellectual construct, as well as its correctness, was "continuity and self-dependence." The key to "continuity and self-dependence" is the last step in the process, the deduction of time, space, and variety, or, in other words (as time, space, and variety include the elements of all empiric knowledge), the establishing of a coincidence between the facts of ordinary experience and those which we have discovered within ourselves and systematically derived from our first and fundamental position. When that step is accomplished, the system is complete, the hypothetical framework falls away, and the structure supports itself. [**21**]

Having established his own perspective, Hedge moved to review similarities and dissimilarities between his Transcendental vision and that of Kant and the post-Kantians. Like Bowen, Hedge emphasized the limits of Kantian philosophy, but he also titled him "father of critical philosophy." Further, although he agreed with Bowen that Kant had not created a "system," he did feel Kant had "furnished the materials from which all the systems of his followers have been framed." [**22**]

Hedge clearly indicated what held Kant close to his heart. Kant and Hedge shared a common assumption, which was diametrically opposed to that of the prevailing Lockean sensualism. Whereas currently prominent empiricism assured that man's cognitions are determined by the objects they represent, therefore denying an a priori view of objects, Hedge found in Kant confirmation of his own assumption that objects outside of us are determined by our cognitions. Therefore the world depends on the nature of our intuitions, which realizes "the great desideratum--a priori knowledge." He did not assume Kant's characterization of a priori knowledge; neither did he assert his own at this point. Like other American Transcendentalists, he rested on the assumption that it exists, and that it therefore allows the return to man of powers capable of dealing with the ultimate. Man once again becomes the absolute self as unconditionally existing, incapable of being determined by anything other than himself, and determining all things through himself. [**23**]

Like other American Transcendentalists, Hedge sought confirmation of his own Transcendental concepts, which were largely an extension of Kant's, in the post-Kantians. He, as they, picked, sampled, isolated, and assumed what he could use from them to go beyond those limits set by Kant. Thus although his insights into the post-Kantians were insightful and penetrating, he stressed what he wished and made little effort at being complete. In "Coleridge," in fact, Hedge spent much of his time denouncing what he saw as incorrect among the post-Kantians, often in terms similar to those employed by critics such as Bowen or Andrews Norton.

For example, in Fichte, Hedge saw a system based on Kant. He called Fichte "the idealist" but found he went too far "seeking the last result of the subjective path." Fichte suggested that all knowledge of the absolute, indeed the basis of reality, is limited to the self's own subjective knowledge. [24] This was confirmed elsewhere where Hedge noted that "under Fichte's stern rule, a ruthless idealism exploded all the realities of being. The actual world vanished with a breath from the great professor's mouth . . . In all Germany, there was only 'I,' no you nor he nor she nor it, but only 'I'. . . . " [25]

In Schelling, Hedge found a more "kindred spirit." He took a more objective direction than Fichte, and as compared to other "like-minded" Germans, Schelling established an intellectual philosophy "more ripe, more substantial, more promising, and, if we may apply such a term to such speculation, more practical than any of the others." Although a post-Kantian, Hedge saw Schelling as starting a new period of philosophical inquiry and referred to him as "the founder of a new school." [26]

Yet Hedge could be critical of Schelling as well, especially as to the extremes to which Schelling's philosophy could lead. In the same passage as the one noted above on Fichte, he continued:

> Then came Schelling, and "I" was dethroned . . . reduced to a mere function, a mode of the great "Identity," a pole of the one indivisible subject-object in which all is compressed. The Absolute this time was posited as identity of matter and spirit, of subject and object. To love one's self in the "universal world-consciousness," was not the correct thing. [27]

What appealed to Hedge was not only Schelling's epistemology, but his ontology. Specifically, he referred to Schelling's Transcendentalen Idealismus as establishing an ontological base that treated the external world as of the same essence as the thinking mind, but as being different manifestations of the same divine principle. Knowledge results from the disagreement between the outward and inward, the object and the subject, or nature and intelligence, as both rely on processes of their own. The first begins with nature and proceeds upward to intelligence. The other begins with intelligence and ends with nature. The first is natural philosophy, the second Transcendental philosophy. It is a systematic reconciliation of two schools to restore what Hedge saw as the balance of nature and man. He rejected it in the end, only when its path led unalterably to pantheism. [**28**]

As stated earlier, "Coleridge" was the first positive statement on German Transcendentalism in America. More importantly, however, for our purposes, it established Hedge's Transcendentalism. It pointed to his decided preference for German philosophers over all other foreign sources. He wrote that "German Transcendental metaphysicians had done more than ever before accomplished for the advancement of the human intellect." Yet he was just as clear in distancing himself from any one in particular. Finally, he continuously suggested that the major element in New England Transcendentalism was the intuitive method. This he saw as the major accomplishment and only common point of agreement for the group. [**29**]

Having established that there was no further structure built upon the Transcendental method on which Transcendentalists agreed, Hedge concluded his article by discussing how it had been applied and indicating his decided agreement with its original purpose. He began by confirming an earlier statement that Transcendentalism was foremost an intuitive method applied to religion. In the case of Germany, he praised Transcendentalism not only for its "dauntless spirit of inquiry, amazing erudition, and quickening power," but most importantly for its having "saved the religion of Germany" from both "fanatic extravagance" and "speculative infidelity."

In "Coleridge," Hedge asserted that Transcendentalism had reestablished "the spiritual in man and the ideal in nature." As such, he felt Transcendentalism had commended itself by its "fruits," for "it lives in its fruits, and must ever live, though the name of its founder be forgotten, and not one of its doctrines survive." [**30**] What remains is to see how he used the basic concepts of Transcendentalism toward the same end in his own intellectual construct.

NOTES

1. Perry Miller, **The Transcendentalists: An Anthology** (Cambridge, Ma.: Harvard University Press, 1960), 8. Henry David Gray, **Emerson: A Statement of New England Transcendentalism as Expressed in the Philosophy of its Chief Exponent** (1917; rpt. New York: Frederick Ungar Publishing Co., 1958), 7.

2. **The Development of American Philosophy: A Book of Readings,** eds. Walter G. Muelder, Laurence Sears, and Anne V. Schlabach (Boston: Houghton Mifflin Company, 1960), 109.

3. Paul Boller, Jr., **American Transcendentalism, 1830-1860: An Intellectual Inquiry** (New York: G. P. Putnam's Sons, 1974), xix. Octavius Brooks Frothingham, **Transcendentalism in New England, A History** (1876; rpt. Gloucester, Ma.: Peter Smith, 1965), 114. William G. Mc Loughlin, **Revivals, Awakenings, and Reform, An Essay on Religion and Social Change in America, 1607-1977** (Chicago: The University of Chicago Press, 1978), 102.

4. Frederic Henry Hedge, "Coleridge's **Literary Character,**" Christian Examiner, 14 (1833), 108-129; Caroline H. Dall, **Transcendentalism in New England: A Lecture Delivered Before the Society for Philosophical Enquiry, Washington, D.C., May 7, 1895** (Boston: Roberts Brothers, 1897), 14-16; Henry A. Pochmann, **German Culture in America: Philosophical and Literary Influences: 1600-1900** (Madison: The University of Wisconsin Press, 1957), 582.

5. Joel Porte, **Representative Man: Ralph Waldo Emerson in His Time** (New York: Oxford University Press, 1979), 55; Nelson R. Burr, **A Critical Bibliography of Religion in America** (Princeton, N.J.: Princeton University Press, 1961), 242.

6. Miller, 67.

7. Dall, 15.

8. Miller, 67.

9. Stanley M. Vogel, **German Literary Influences on the American Transcendentalists** (New York: Archon Books, 1970), 116.

10. Dall, 15.

11. Hedge, "Coleridge," 110, 118.

12. _Ibid._, 117.

13. _Ibid._

14. Ronald Vale Wells, **Three Christian Transcendentalists: James Marsh, Caleb Sprague Henry, Frederic Henry Hedge** (1943; rpt. New York: Octagon Books, 1972), 5, 6; Francis Bowen, **Modern Philosophy, From Descartes to Schopenhauer and Hartman** (New York: Charles Scribner's Sons, 1887), 158; Francis Bowen, "Transcendentalism," _Christian Examiner_, 21 (1837); see also Francis Bowen, **Critical Essays** (Boston: Roberts Brothers, 1842).

15. Francis Bowen, "Locke and the Transcendentalists," _Christian Examiner_, 23 (1837), 179, 181.

16. _Ibid._, 372.

17. Hedge, "Coleridge," 119.

18. _Ibid._, 120.

19. _Ibid._, 121.

20. _Ibid._

21. _Ibid._

22. Hedge, "Coleridge," 122-123. See also Frederic Henry Hedge, **Prose Writers of Germany** (New York: C. S. Francis, 1856), 25.

23. Hedge, "Coleridge," 124. See also Hedge, **Prose Writers of Germany**, 58-60; Ralph Waldo Emerson, "Nature," in **Anthology of American Literature: Colonial through Romantic**, ed. George McMichael (New York: Macmillan Publishing Co., Inc., 1980), 1018.

24. Hedge, "Coleridge," 116.

25. Hedge, **Prose Writers of Germany**, 57; Frederic Henry Hedge, "Arthur Schopenhauer," _Christian Examiner_, 76 (1864), 50. A criticism also made by Francis Bowen in Bowen, **Modern Philosophy**, 310.

26. Hedge, "Coleridge," 125; Hedge, **Prose Writers of Germany**, 57.

27. Hedge, "Arthur Schopenhauer," 50.

28. Hedge, "Coleridge," 125. Francis Bowen led American critics in their attack on Schelling as a pantheist. See Bowen, **Modern Philosophy**, 345.

29. Hedge, "Coleridge," 125-126.

30. _Ibid._, 125-127.

Chapter Four

DIVINE IMMANENCE

Frederic Hedge tied Transcendental ideals to traditions of the Christian Church. This placed him in the company of figures such as Caleb Sprague Henry and James Marsh, often referred to as "Christian Transcendentalists," and in conflict with those whose Transcendental views led them beyond the church, such as Ralph Waldo Emerson and George Ripley. [1] One critic has quoted Hedge to show why he joined the two forces:

> Everything in religion which denounces nature and insults life must be abandoned for principles which show the present worth of nature and dignity of man. This will be nearer the true religion of Jesus, a religion of life, humanity, nature,--a religion of the present . . . without it religion will not grow and it will give way to philosophy and lyceum. [2]

The phrase "Christian Transcendentalist" can be seen as redundant when considered in terms of the origins of Transcendentalism itself. Transcendentalism was, after all, the product of a reaction against the deadening influence within that faith. But neither does the phrase give the true significance of the connection Hedge made between Transcendentalism and Christianity.

Hedge's Transcendental impulse, that which he shared with other Transcendentalists, was his belief in intuitive method. He indicated a belief in the existence of innate ideas in the Kantian sense of a priori categories of the understanding and in Transcendental concepts of time and space. But it was his belief in man's intuitive capacities that served as the driving force in his Christian Transcendentalism. As such Transcendentalism was more than a theory of knowledge, as it tended to be for Transcendentalists such as Emerson. [3] It was a reassertion of an element of religious faith that Hedge felt had been recently cast into doubt by critics such as Andrews Norton. Norton had written:

> There can be no intuition, no direct perception of the truth of Christianity, no metaphysical certainty . . . of the facts on which religion is founded . . . except that derived from the testimony of God from the Christian revelation [in this case meaning scripturally revealed miracles]. [4]

According to Hedge, man's intuitive insight provides truths which lie beyond the understanding. These truths, especially moral law, are drawn from within and are a priori in the sense that they not only precede experience but are derived without it. Further, these intuitive insights, he believed, are drawn directly from the divine in man--in every man--and thus are from God. This faith reestablished for Hedge, as well as for other Transcendentalists, not only man's divinity, but also, the indisputable nature of this source of knowledge. Emerson indicated the importance of this conclusion when he referred to it as Transcendentalism's "one sublime idea."

In addition to moral law, Hedge included knowledge of the existence of God and belief in Him among those concepts not the product of ratiocination. As substance, God is not only inscrutable but inconceivable to the understanding. At best man can see design and infer intelligence. But even in these instances he is relying on sensual perception of a multitude of secondary agents and antecedents. Man cannot know the omnipresent and immediate will of God or the "one divine cause." [5]

Among the proofs of God's existence that Hedge dismissed for their a posteriori dependence on sensual data were the cosmological proof and the physico-theological case. The cosmological proof, which he attributed to John Locke and Gottfried Leibnitz asserts that all sensible phenomena and all finite experience must be referred in the end to an infinite and immaterial Being, as their first cause. Since all phenomena have causes, and since those causes are the effects of other antecedents, man is led to an infinite regression, which Hedge considered absurd, or to the acceptance of an ultimate first cause. Such a first cause must be a Being outside of this series, from Whom the series originated. The Being must be omnipotent, because It is the source of all creation and power, and all wise, since It is the source of worldly intelligence. [6]

The cosmological proof leaves unanswered the question of what caused the first cause. To Hedge, the only deductible answer was that the first cause caused itself; it was both cause and effect. But he could not conceive of a self-existent being outside the universe any more than he could believe in an original "unerected universe." [7]

The physico-theological proof, which Hedge associated with William Paley and John Bridgewater, is the argument from design: "Whatever is by its constitution adapted to a particular end supposes a contrivance, and hence a contriver." Since the means by which the design is created must exceed that of its creation, the power of the creator must exceed all human power and skill, and, in fact, be infinite. This theory asserts that man sees what appears to be design everywhere he looks in nature, and only infinite power and skill can account for its plan and execution. [8]

Hedge identified the argument from design as purely subjective and therefore invalid. It applies man's idea of human workmanship to what he perceives in nature. If man does not believe in God first, Hedge asserted, he cannot consider either the idea of first cause or contrivance in nature. Instead, he accepts nature as self-constituted. Thus, both the cosmological and physico-theological proofs merely justify man's a priori assumption of the existence of God. They do not ascertain it as a previously unknown fact. [9]

Hedge rejected what he termed the a priori, ontological argument for the existence of God as well. The ontological proof depends on the demonstration of God from Himself or the nature of this idea. St. Anselm, René Descartes, and Baruch Spinoza espoused this view. It holds that man believes in God as something than which nothing greater can be conceived. That than which nothing greater can be conceived cannot be of the intellect alone. It cannot be a mere thought of the mind, for if it were only a thought, it might also be conceived as existing, and to exist is greater than merely to be thought. If man insists that that than which nothing greater can be conceived is of the mind alone, the mere conception that that very thing exists is something greater and, thus, contradictory. [10]

Hedge rejected this proof because he believed it also presupposes a belief in God. It is a proof only to the believer, not to the nonbeliever. "All that it really proves is, that given the idea of God, it is that of a necessarily existing being. The idea is presupposed as something given by religion. The argument rests on the postulate of faith." [11]

Hedge saw a fourth attempt to prove God's existence in Kant's **Critique of Practical Reason.** In this proof Kant did not assume the existence of the external world. Instead he viewed the phenomenal world as a sequence of mental experiences--seeing, hearing, feeling, tasting. He was then led to consider the ultimate grounds of these experiences. Kant wrote that his "consciousness" told him he was not the author of these experiences but the receiver. Further, he asserted that in some instances he was entirely passive, and in those instances in which he was active, receipt of the experience was not dependent upon that action. Therefore, Kant turned to an external cause. [12]

Kant's external cause had to be "adequate to the effect in matter," which by his definition is inert and powerless. Matter cannot of itself produce an effect. Therefore, the cause must be a power equal to man's "uttermost experience." Since on comparing his experience with others Kant found an almost uniform agreement (i.e. what is white, square, hot, etc.), he inferred the unity of power which creates these experiences in different minds. Therefore, Kant came back to the proof of God's existence in a manner and by definition similar to that of the physico-theological argument. [13]

Hedge found Kant's proof of God's existence subject to weaknesses similar to those already stated for other arguments. As in the argument from design, he felt Kant's proof did not escape reliance on the certainty of the existence of things and his observation of them to prove God's existence. But more importantly, he believed Kant's proof continued to rely on his a priori belief in God's existence. Without such a presumption, Hedge asserted, Kant could not have identified God as the source of his sense impressions. [14]

The common point in Hedge's rejection of the philosophical arguments discussed above is his assertion that in each case belief in God precedes and underlies all attempts to prove God's existence. This a priori concept vitiates the reasoning in such demonstrations. Thus, he concluded, philosophical demonstrations may serve to defend belief in God's existence, but they do not discover it. Those who do not have the idea will not find it following these methods. [15]

Hedge therefore offered his own proof of God's existence: "We know God, if at all, not by inference or demonstration, but by direct intuition." [16] Knowledge of God is the first product of man's divinely inspired intuitive power. It is the strongest of man's convictions and, therefore, necessary and universal. Because it is the product of his intuition, it is uncontradictable and not subject to verification by the understanding. The roots of Hedge's proof lay in Channing's concept of man's "likeness to God." [17] It was reaffirmed in Theodore Parker's statement: "The idea of God is a fact in the consciousness of man." [18] Hedge wrote:

> God is his own witness; and his writings of himself in every unsophisticated mind and every sound heart is the surest and most satisfactory proof we can ever have of this primary truth. If God exists, it is incredible that the Being so named should not give assurance of himself to intelligible thought, should not bear witness of himself in intelligent minds. [19]

Hedge referred to knowledge of God's existence as "an idea preexisting in the mind" and as "an intuition of the moral sense." It is a concept given in the nature of man, or the product of God's self-revelation from within each man to those who are ready to receive Him. It is an idea existent in all men that rises to consciousness in a manner similar to that which man uses to attain truths of moral law. Without it he can neither conceive of the existence of God nor feel the inadequacy of a world without Him. [20] With it both are undeniable, and man is led to believe in Him.

Hedge insisted that belief in God is not born of the understanding. If it were, the matter of religion would be in the range of "scientific" philosophy and demonstration and no longer would be a matter of debate. Instead, it is the product of the "Word" from within, and, as such, it is unarguable fact, to be honored even in the face of demonstrable contrary or contradictory proofs of the understanding.

The medium of Hedge's intuitive method was what he referred to as the word of God. The word of God, received intuitively, is man's highest authority because it is direct knowledge. It brings new truths to man, or confirms those revealed to him from without and by others, thus serving as a necessary stage in confirmation of the will. [21] It is revelation, but of a personal sort:

> Revelation is not a voice without but a voice within, not a prodigious communication out of the skies, a doctrine appended to the tail of some portent, but the intuition of a rapt soul that has met the Spirit of God in its meditation. [22]

Hedge believed that without the power of divine intuition man can know nothing beyond the surface of the sensible world. Without this power he can know nothing of what Hedge termed Transcendental concepts (an extension of Kant's Transcendent concepts)--the substance of the universe and its origin, the eternal or its cause, the purpose of man's existence, the laws of man's behavior, and the means of his salvation. [23] Further, by asserting the divine element in man as that which serves as the connection between the natural and spiritual worlds, Hedge established God's omnipresence. God is immanent rather than removed and, as such, the source of man's continuous revelations. He referred to the divine element in man as the "soul" and to its substance as "the Holy Spirit," which are typically Christian terms. [24]

In terms of the Kantian scheme, Hedge's concept of divine intuition extended beyond the limits of pure and practical reason, in a way similar to that of the post-Kantians and of other American Transcendentalists. The soul as the divine in man is a special faculty, which serves not only as pure reason to supply innate concepts for the understanding but also a practical reason giving man moral law. Further, it provides knowledge of God's existence, access to Hedge's Transcendental concepts, and the certainty of divine originating authority. [25]

Elsewhere Hedge discussed the importance of certainty in divine originating authority. Without this "condescending word," which is "peculiarly Christian," he asserted, the name of God would be only a name, "a vague distinction having no relation to the heart or life." [26] With it man has not only the motivation for salvation, but also the method of discovering the truths that the truly motivated seek. [27]

Hedge's Transcendental epistemology raised the power of man's perception to a higher plane, but it also placed Hedge in conflict with faiths around him. Most Unitarians opposed him, although as a denomination they had not yet fully defined a comparable doctrine. Those who postulated man's knowledge of God's law on the unaided human mind opposed him, as did those who based faith solely on historical Christianity, external revelation, or apostolic miracles. Yet Hedge maintained:

> The heart demands a present God--a God who is never far from any one of us; a Will working in every event that takes place. It needs, therefore, to know that it is not abandoned to hard, inevitable laws, and processes that act with unconscious necessity. [28]

Hedge noted how this basic Transcendental precept led to conflict with others of the Unitarian faith:

> They [more Orthodox Unitarians] did not consider that every soul is heaven born, that human nature has no moral limits, that God, as spirit, is in men as well as out of them. Unconsciously biased by the sensuous philosophy of Locke, himself a Unitarian, they conceived of God as wholly external--an individual in space; of heaven as topographically distinct from earth; of the human mind as receiving all its impressions from without. [29]

Hedge tied his belief in intuitive method to his conception of God's immanence. Without God's immanence he saw no basis for intuitive certainty, and, as will be seen, no way for man to effect his own salvation. Without God's immanence man would be totally dependent on God's intervening will or upon conformity to the laws of an indifferent, mechanized universe. God's reinvolvement would contradict the basic definition of God. Would God, the perfect creator, find it necessary to intervene in a universe he had established on immutable laws? [30]

Hedge needed to know more than that God is merely an omnipotent force or that He can create and destroy, or, for that matter that the world is of God's handiwork. He sought to prove that God is immanent and diffusive within man, not an isolated, incommunicable individuality. [31] By doing this, he reestablished God as the origin of truth, especially moral law, and moral law as the source of man's love and redemption. Truth or moral law, then, is not external, but internal; it is never inferred from visible creation, but revealed to man by God's voice from within. In Hedge's words, "Until God is known as a moral ideal, He in not known at all." [32]

God's spirit being within all men, Hedge suggested that there is nothing between man and salvation, or between man and God, but the measure of that spirit. That measure is reflective of the degree of consciousness of God in the soul. It differentiates man from the rest of the animal kingdom and raises him to the highest stage of human development. [33] This construct became the origin, proof, definition, and use of Hedge's Transcendental intuitive method. It grew out of William Ellery Channing's doctrine of the "essential sameness" of God and man, but Emerson gave it its fullest application: "Everyman is a divinity in disguise." [34] Hedge remained somewhere in between.

Hedge extended his concept of the divine presence beyond man through nature, allowing that "all the energies of nature are methods of divine authority," and that "the phenomena of nature are phases of the one eternal presence." This concept satisfied him by its simplicity and by avoiding such paradoxes as an active universe and an inactive God; intense divine activity at one time and quiescence thereafter or "a sabbath longer than the term of labor"; two divinities, nature and God; coexistent self-subsisting energies and external motivating forces; and a double providence, one for every day use and one for special occasions. Finally, he believed it satisfies the heart by bringing God nearer to man in the world around him. [35]

Hedge's God is "cause, creator, essence, animator, shaper, and sustainer." He dwells "in the highest laws and in the lowliest particles," and from Him flows "all truth, beauty, and goodness."

This placed Hedge at one with other Transcendentalists who identified their God as Supreme Soul, Oversoul, Creator, Original Cause, Universal Power, Higher Law, Supreme Mind, Eternal Reason, Universal Consciousness, and Universal Spirit. Because Hedge's God also transcends nature, however, he avoided charges of Pantheism, leveled at many of these same figures. He remained a recognized theist. [36]

By reasserting the theme of man as God-made and God-like, Hedge established certainty for man's intuitive method and man's rank as first among God's creatures. What remained was to determine man's relationship to Christ. This relation can best be described as the final element in what Hedge called "the eternal circle of divine evolution." This cycle began with, as Hedge put it, "God active," and will end with "God reflective." He also referred to the relation as having begun with "God imagining" and as ending with "God imaged." [37]

At one point or another, Hedge discussed all four of the most widely accepted theories of Christology. He dismissed all but one, which he modified and adopted as his own. The first was held by Jews contemporaneous with Jesus, later Socinians, and many Unitarians, including Transcendentalists such as Theodore Parker. They defined Jesus as mere man, possibly adopted as a son by God at his death, and distinguished from other men only by his moral elevation or character, his wonder working powers, and his martyr death. [38]

The second view, held by more orthodox Christians, arose after the destruction of Jerusalem, when the historical Jesus had receded into the distance. His image as an actual person had grown dim, and the "tendencies of the Gentile mind to deify illustrious and extraordinary men began to react on the simplicity of the gospel." Christianity was no longer satisfied with historical fact. It exalted Christ above earthly limitations into something superhuman and divine. This, Hedge believed, made Christ pure spirit, assuming the likeness of man but divested of all natural belongings, including flesh and blood. He became a divine apparition. [39]

The third Christological interpretation, the Arian perspective, established Christ as neither God nor man. In this case, Christ is a superior creature to man, of special creation, established between man and God. [40] He is not equal to the Father, but rather, as the son, created by the Father for the salvation of man. He is not God, nor is he man. Further, he has not always existed. This theory developed during the later third and early fourth centuries. It was effectively restrained by Athanasius at the Council of Nicaea in 325 and by others in the Church thereafter, but some Unitarians, including William Ellery Channing, continued to accept it in the nineteenth century.

Hedge rejected the first Christological concept for several reasons. First of all, he could not accept Christ as merely man because this idea failed to explain the status to which he had risen in the eyes of the Christian world. Secondly, if this interpretation were adopted, the gospel would become a "barren tale," and its import would be lost forever from our eyes. [41] Further, this view did not satisfy what Hedge saw as man's need for an immanent God. It established a removed and transient one. [42]

Hedge saw acceptance of this first Christological viewpoint as glorifying the human spirit, without the divine element, and placing it improperly in a place for our devotion. He felt this smacked of saint worship, hagiology, or of Romanizing. [43] Finally, he insisted that such an interpretation was inconsistent with the word of Jesus and his Apostles. Their word declared Christ "a representative personality,--a revelation of God in man, a manifestation or showing forth of the divine, by which mankind are to be taught and won, redeemed from evil and united to God." Without such a personality, man is denied the power of self-redemption. [44]

Hedge found the concepts of Christ as pure God or of special creation equally difficult to accept. As noted above, neither concept secures the continued immanence of God nor the purpose of "representative personality." The first asserts God's presence only with Christ. It may serve the need of apprehending God in human form, but Hedge felt it "smacked of idolatry," reminiscent of earlier times which "gave birth to graven images of wood and stone." [45] He believed that both concepts leave man only with vicarious atonement, which he emphatically denied. [46] Finally, he asserted that if Christ as pure deity runs the paradox of the Godhead in two natures, Christ as special creation raises the question of the nature "of a creature with a substance separate from both God and man." [47]

Hedge was aware of the difficulty of "construing the veritable image of Jesus" from the written word. He held that references to Christ's image in the four gospels are often conflicting, as to history or legend. Yet he studied these, as well as discussions at the fourth and fifth century councils at Nicaea, Constantinople, Ephesus, and Chalcedon, and concluded that Christ is both God and man. [48] This is consistent with a commonly held fourth Christology. Hedge found this concept inconsistent with Judaism and Islam, both of which denied the dual nature of God/man, even among their prophets, on the basis of their definition of the Godhead; but he saw similar concepts in both Hinduism, Buddhism, and, of course, Christianity. [49]

As to scripture, Hedge saw the first three gospels as maintaining the Judaic tradition. Christ is the national messiah, with no suggestion or hint of divine incarnation, human deification, or union of God and man in Christ. In John, however, God was made flesh in Christ. Hedge saw this as an amalgamation of the Jewish tradition and that of the Greeks, who allowed for mid-stages of deification. From this concept Catholicism, and ultimately Christianity, drew its incarnated Christ. The union of the human and divine remains and is made partaker of eternal life, as does the principle that only through this special nature is man redeemed from the power of sin and death. [50]

Hedge's Christ contains both a human and a divine nature, and both natures exist without conflict or confusion. Each does its own work; each possesses its own property; both combine in one appearance and one effect, "a coordination and conjugation of the two in one person. The person is one, the natures are two." [51] Such a view acknowledges the divine origin of Christian dispensation, but, by acknowledging his humanity, it also makes evident our sharing of Christ's basic capabilities. Christ is not a cross between Deity and humanity but "perfect God and perfect man." He became so because Jesus surrendered himself entirely to the truth. "With the same divine element that Christ shared with all men, He gave himself without measure to the Spirit, and therefore without measure the Spirit was given to him." [52]

Hedge's Christ is God/man, born of man yet one in substance with God, or consubstantial with the Father. As Hedge quoted St. Paul on man: "For in him dwelt all the fullness of the Godhead, bodily." [53] If man differs from Christ, he does so in respect to degree alone. Hedge agreed that the degree to which Christ had attained his divine nature had gone unequaled, but he insisted that what Christ possessed by nature, man possesses, if in less developed form. "Whatever was true of Jesus historically is theoretically and prospectively true of Christianized man." [54] This was the basic Transcendental impulse, the word of God from within, and Christ was Hedge's "representative man." [55] What, then, of Christ's crucifixion and atonement?

If, as Hedge believed, the meaning of Christ's life is the redemption of human nature, his atonement represents the reconciliation or reunion of man and God, in whose image man was formed. Atonement, by Christ's example, reestablishes the power of the divine in man. Without it man is left with vicarious atonement and continued utter dependence, as exemplified by Calvinist and Orthodox Christian dogma. With it mankind is redeemed through its own God-given capacities.

Hedge denied the Calvinist view of Christ's crucifixion as an "expiatory sacrifice," for the remission of sins. It was not "to settle a debt due to divine justice, which had the right to demand the everlasting perdition of the human race as the penalty of Adam's sin." [56] But Hedge's concept of atonement was not devoid of any element of Christ. This would deny all value to Christ's death, beyond the evidence it furnished of his sincerity, and the consequent presumption it afforded of his divine authority. [57]

Hedge's God is a loving God, and He is ready to forgive man his sins. Christ's mission was to point the way to salvation. His atonement was the supreme act of mediatorial agency. It brought man by faith and obedience into right relation with God. It was an efficacious influence on man achieved by Christ's character, life, and death, based on the attraction of truth. Christ is embodied truth, and man is irrestibly attracted to truth. [58]

Hedge also believed that Christ's atonement represents self-renunciation: "Self-renunciation is the very meaning of the cross." Reminiscent of Transcendentalism's Puritan ancestry, Hedge insisted that man's salvation depends on self-renunciation, which results in man's reconciliation with his natural, selfish, carnal pleasures. This can be accomplished only by reproducing Christ's sacrifice in his life. As Christ's crucifixion was not without pain, neither is man's salvation. Once again, Christ is man's special benefactor; man is saved by Christ's example. The example of Christ's crucifixion is so essential to man's salvation that Hedge occasionally refers to the atonement in more orthodox terms of sacrifice and expiation, but it remains salvation by Christ's example and through man's divine power. [59]

Hedge summarized his view of Christ's atonement as that which draws man away from active rebellion toward God and from resistence to His word. When this takes place, atonement is furthered yet another step by man's own example:

> We are not only partakers in the great historical atonement in Christ, but we, too, according to the grace that is given us, atone for others, and, as far as our influence extends, become a sacrifice and propitiation for the sins of man . . . the symbol of the cross triumphs, and the true higher nature of life begins. [60]

Hedge's quarrel was not with the assertion of the divine in Christ, but with its limitation to him, excluding the rest of mankind. He felt this denied Christ's very words: "That they all may be one in us." [61] By establishing the presence of God in all men, Hedge established the basis for man's knowledge of God's will, his conscience, and his salvation. These concepts remain to be considered.

NOTES

1. Ronald Vale Wells, **Three Christian Transcendentalists: James Marsh, Caleb Sprague Henry, Frederic Henry Hedge** (1943: rpt. New York: Octagon Books, 1972), 146; Joseph L. Blau, **Men and Movements in American Philosophy** (New York: Prentice-Hall, Inc., 1952), 117; Nelson R. Burr, **A Critical Bibliography of Religion in America** (Princeton, N.J.: Princeton University Press, 1961), 242.

2. Wells, 132-133.

3. Ibid., 46-47.

4. Andrews Norton, "A Discourse on the Latest Form of Infidelity," in **The Transcendentalists: An Anthology**, ed. Perry Miller (Cambridge, Ma.: Harvard University Press, 1960), 211.

5. Frederic Henry Hedge, **Reason in Religion** (Boston: Walker, Fuller, and Company, 1865), 36.

6. Frederic Henry Hedge, "The Way of Religion," in his **Ways of the Spirit and Other Essays** (Boston: Roberts Brothers, 1877), 45-49.

7. Ibid., 49.

8. Frederic Henry Hedge, "Critique of Proofs of the Being of God," in his **Ways of the Spirit**, 153-154.

9. Hedge, "Critique of Proofs of the Being of God," 157-158; Frederic Henry Hedge, "Natural Religion," Christian Examiner, 52 (1852), 129.

10. Hedge, "Critique of Proofs of the Being of God," 171; Hedge, "Natural Religion," 129.

11. Hedge, "Critique of Proofs of the Being of God," 171.

12. Ibid.

13. Ibid., 180.

14. Ibid.

15. Hedge, "Critique of Proofs of the Being of God," 185; Hedge, "Natural Religion," 134-135.

16. Hedge, "Critique of Proofs of the Being of God," 188.

17. William Ellery Channing, "Likeness to God," in **American Philosophic Addresses: 1700-1900,** ed. Joseph L. Blau (New York: Columbia University Press, 1947), 570; William Ellery Channing, "Self-Culture," in his **The Works of William Ellery Channing** (New York: Burt Franklin, 1970), 13.

18. John White Chadwick, **Theodore Parker: Preacher and Reformer** (Boston: Houghton Mifflin and Company, 1900), 186; John Edward Dirks, **The Critical Theology of Theodore Parker** (New York: Columbia University Press, 1948), 78.

19. Hedge, "Critique of Proofs of the Being of God," 188.

20. Hedge, **Reason in Religion,** 13, 36, 66; Hedge, "Critique of Proofs of the Being of God," 144; Frederic Henry Hedge, "The Natural History of Theism," in his **Ways of the Spirit,** 122-125.

21. Frederic Henry Hedge, "Authorities and Scribes," in his **Sermons** (Boston: Roberts Brothers, 1891), 22.

22. Ibid., 24.

23. Hedge, **Reason in Religion,** 13. See also Elizabeth Flower and Murray G. Murphy, **A History of Philosophy in America** (New York: Capricorn Books, 1977), I, 9.

24. Wells, 148.

25. Hedge, **Reason in Religion,** 291.

26. Ibid., 297.

27. Wells, 128; Frederic Henry Hedge, "Antisupernaturalism in the Pulpit, An Address Delivered to the Graduating Class of the Divinity School, Cambridge, July 17, 1864," Christian Examiner, 77 (1864), 156.

28. Hedge, **Reason in Religion,** 76.

29. Frederic Henry Hedge, **Theological Progress During the Last Half Century** (Providence: Knowles, Anthony and Co., 1878), 65.

30. Hedge, **Reason in Religion,** 75-77.

31. Ibid., 27.

32. Hedge, **Reason in Religion,** 57. See also Wells, 106.

33. Hedge, **Theological Progress,** 65-66; Frederic Henry Hedge, "Parker's Reminiscences of Rufus Choate," Christian Examiner, 68 (1860), 262.

34. Channing, "Likeness to God," 570; Flower and Murphy, 406; Ralph Waldo Emerson, "History," in his **Essays** (New York: E. P. Dutton and Co., Inc., 1947), 23.

35. Hedge, **Reason in Religion,** 80.

36. Paul Boller, Jr., **American Transcendentalism, 1830-1860: An Intellectual Inquiry** (New York: G. P. Putnam's Sons, 1974), 61; Vivian C. Hopkins, **Spires of Form: A Study of Emerson's Aesthetic Theory** (New York: Russell and Russell, 1965), 61.

37. Frederic Henry Hedge, **The Primeval World of Hebrew Tradition** (Boston: Roberts Brothers, 1870), 25.

38. Frederic Henry Hedge, "Incarnation and Transubstantiation," in his **Ways of the Spirit,** 348-349; Frederic Henry Hedge, **The Atonement in Connection with the Death of Christ** (Boston: American Unitarian Association, 1866), 4; Hedge, **Reason in Religion,** 231-232. See also Joseph Henry Allen, **Our Liberal Movement in Theology: Chiefly as Shown in Recollections of the History of Unitarianism in New England** (Boston: Roberts Brothers, 1892), 6; William R. Hutchison, **The Transcendentalist Ministers: Church Reform in the New England Renaissance** (New Haven, Ct.: Yale University Press, 1959), 61, 106, 201; Henry A. Pochmann, **German Culture in America: Philosophical and Literary Influences: 1600-1900** (Madison: The University of Wisconsin Press, 1957), 218.

39. Hedge, "Incarnation and Transubstantiation," 349; Hedge, **Reason in Religion,** 232; Frederic Henry Hedge, "The God of Religion, or the Human God," in his **Ways of the Spirit,** 215.

40. Hedge, **Reason in Religion,** 230.

41. Hedge, **The Atonement,** 4.

42. Hedge, **Reason in Religion,** 232-238.

43. Ibid., 257.

44. **The Atonement,** 4.

45. Hedge, "The God of Religion," 215.

46. Frederic Henry Hedge, **Conservatism and Reform** (Boston: Charles C. Little and James Brown, 1843), 80.

47. Hedge, **Reason in Religion,** 256.

48. Hedge, **Reason in Religion,** 227, 230, 235. See also John White Chadwick, **Old and New Unitarian Belief** (Boston: George H. Ellis, 1901), 4.

49. Hedge, "Incarnation and Transubstantiation," 344. See also Chadwick, 4.

50. Hedge, "Incarnation and Transubstantiation," 347-348.

51. Frederic Henry Hedge, "Dr. Huntington on the Trinity," Christian Examiner, 68 (1860), 263.

52. Hedge, "Authorities and Scribes," 27-29.

53. Hedge, **The Atonement**, 4.

54. Hedge, "The Way of Historic Christianity," in his **Ways of the Spirit**, 90-91.

55. Hedge, "Incarnation and Transubstantiation," 350.

56. Hedge, **The Atonement**, 3-4; Hedge, "The Two Religions," in his **Ways of the Spirit**, 289.

57. Hedge, **The Atonement**, 3.

58. Hedge, **The Atonement**, 3-5; Hedge, **The Primeval World**, 122-123; Frederic Henry Hedge, "The Religion of the Resurrection," in his **Sermons**, 251.

59. Hedge, **The Atonement**, 8-11; Hedge, "The Religion of the Resurrection," 253.

60. Hedge, **The Atonement**, 10-12.

61. Hedge, "Incarnation and Transubstantiation," 352.

Chapter Five

THE WILL TO ACTION

By recognizing the dual nature of Christ and man, and by viewing Christ's atonement as reestablishing the efficacy of the divine in all men, Hedge not only established Christ as the most fit object of man's love and worship, but he identified Christ as the "Word." "The Word was made flesh," and it "lighteth all who come into the world." The "Word" is the spirit of God, and it is in all men. It allows man to transcend the limits of sensibility and understanding. [1]

One further conclusion drawn from Hedge's theology is that "there is nothing between God and man but man's self-alienation through waywardness and sin." [2] The "Word," which brought about the redemption of Christ, serves as the agent of knowledge and, therefore, of salvation for mankind. It is the highest expression of knowledge available to man, and if he is willing to accept it, it becomes "the ground" of faith, the basis for a reformed character, and the path to salvation. [3]

Hedge's "Word" resembles seventeenth and eighteenth century Calvinist concepts of "supernatural grace," in that it is a divine gift without which man cannot be saved. The key to salvation is man's obedience to moral law, and moral law is available to him only through the "Word" within him. If Hedge's redemptive power is extended to all men, in contrast to the Calvinist belief in "particular redemption," why then is alienation evident or even possible? If Christ's example is an "encouragement of human frailty," or "a pledge of human destiny," or "a call to glory and immortality," why are not all men anxiously seeking and rapidly becoming sons of God? [4] A closer analysis of divine intuition, human will, and conscience is required.

In a manner similar to Channing, Emerson, Ripley and Brownson, Hedge described divine intuition as "a breath, vision, or whisper in the heart." Divine intuition is a "subtle influence," which not only informs the mind, but also directs the life by inspiring the will. It unites "knowing with being." It supplies the ideas of moral good, which have no prototype or symbol in nature. It is the consummate use of the "Holy Spirit," in traditional Christian theology. Divine intuition is only a "pledge" of divine communication, however, and its efficacy is in proportion to the individual's measure of faith:

> The communication with the Godhead, and the wonder working power of the Spirit, are always equal to man's receptivity, and the measure of man's receptivity is his obedience. [5]

Hedge believed that receptivity of the wonder working spirit is ultimately subject to God's will, but, as noted above, God has willed that no man will be deprived of it. Man can strengthen it by use or diminish it by abuse. "Unconditional surrender to the truth and the leadership of the spirit" becomes man's essential condition, because the "Word" will not come to those who do not seek it. Reflecting his studies of Oriental and Western mystics, especially Emmanuel Swedenborg, Hedge wrote:

> Revelation is a product of the human soul musing till the fire burns. And what kindles that fire is the Spirit of God that with lightning flash as on Sinai, or of the soft auroral light as in Nazareth, comes to the musing, patient, unselfed soul. In the measure in which that soul, by purification, humiliation and perfect obedience, attempts to see God [the soul] is made receptive of His Spirit, the revelation born of it. [6]

Hedge identified the stages through which the soul must pass in order to attain its mystical union with God. Stage one begins when the mind is no longer content with knowing "the obvious relations of things." At this point the "brooding mind" ascends from forms to principles, from the visible manifestation to the invisible power. Man begins to mature spiritually and loses himself in the contemplation of "one pervading intelligence." This intelligence is infinite, and it possesses every form of finite being as well as constitutes the life and essence of all created things. Hedge referred to this state as contemplative mysticism and noted that its object is to interpret all things in terms of the spiritual nature of the universe. [7]

In Hedge's second stage the mind returns from the universal to the particular, from abstract essences to determinate forms. Having initially ignored the information made available by the senses, the mind devises principles of its own. Hedge referred to these principles as intuitional insights, which can be differentiated from those of the senses by their more ethereal origins. [8]

Hedge considered the first two stages of the mystical experience essential to man's receptivity of God's word. He saw its third stage as ruinous and pointed to Swedenborg as an example of how this path of spiritual development could end in corruption. In the third stage of the mystical experience, mysticism turns to "enthusiasm." Having completed its creative process and "constructed its theory of temporal and spiritual things," the mind seeks to express its findings in outward acts. In this state, man leaves the "mother church" and "riots in ascetic enormities." "Inflamed with the fierce zeal of proselytism, [he] waxes intolerant of received opinions, and snatching the word of persecution attempts to force [his] heresies upon the world." He feels divinely commissioned to interpret divine truth for other men, and his powers of intuition run rampant. **[9]**

Hedge did not deny the existence of passive insight or uninitiated revelation. He clearly indicated, however, that in nearly every case, the receipt of direct knowledge depends on the active involvement of the individual, the pursuit of the divine within oneself. Hedge felt he reflected the Pauline sense of scripture on this point. American Transcendentalists generally agreed, George Ripley being among the most vocal. **[10]**

Hedge correlated active pursuit of the "Word" to prayer. He accepted the traditional view of the efficacy of prayer, namely that it is man's only way to "lay hold of God," or to sway the Omnipotent, but his definition of prayer went beyond mere words. He defined prayer as "an earnest desire and fervent affection." It is "the use of the divine within us to commune with God." When man prays he actively seeks the voice within, and having found it, enters into personal conscious and mutual relations with God. He communes with a spirit above the level and order of nature, and he finds certain direct truths. All God asks of him in prayer is "simplicity and singleness of purpose, without preoccupation and conceit." **[11]**

As noted earlier, Hedge believed that each man is capable of reaching the same height of spiritual development. The quickening spirit overrules social rank and intellectual disparities. As he put it in the democratic spirit of his age: "More than any scheme of human polity, it levels society by raising the lowest to an equality with the highest in that which in all is highest and best . . . [and] without which all other equality is futile and vain." **[12]** Yet, not all men begin from the same point nor develop at the same rate. All is arranged in stages of development. **[13]**

Hedge's stages of human spiritual development are not necessarily biogenetic or historical; they are not repeated in every life or seen as following the broad and continuous historical evolution of society. He tied his explanation of the discrepancy in point of departure to what he observed as differences in moral endowment. Although a full explanation will be presented when consideration is given to his concept of immortality, it is necessary here to state that Hedge saw man as born to relative stages of goodness. This initial state influences the degree of progress the individual makes in his spiritual journey. [14]

In Hedge's scheme some people are born with souls more disposed toward the reception of God's word and its quickening influence than others. Those persons of comparatively greater disposition toward goodness are subject to fewer inward contradictions. They find it easier to resist conflicting external forces and to accept God's grace or word. This inability in turn makes the task of self-discipline and obedience to God's word, or moral law, even easier. [15]

Hedge's concept of the first stage of man's moral development is one of childlike, passive reception and implicit faith. It is the stage of authority. In that stage man receives without question and without hesitation what his teachers write in books or establish as popular tradition. These teachings may be of human creation or the product of revelation. In biblical times these revelations may have been outwardly revealed to the senses or internally received by intuition. Hedge believed people of that age were more impressed by external events and more likely to deem them divinely caused than people of the nineteenth century. These earlier occurrences became the source of many scriptural passages. He suggested that in his more "sophisticated" century, intuitively received revelations were more common. [16]

Hedge insisted that as long as man relies on teachers, his belief is acquiescence, not conviction; he accepts rather than comprehends. This is followed by the assertion of the understanding, but because the understanding lacks conviction, its operation is exaggerated and often hostile. It results in doubt, contradiction, and denial. [17]

As the number of generations separating man from sources reporting their divine experiences increases, or as man grows older and more independent in his thoughts, the degree of confusion described above also increases. In time, Hedge believed, such external authority no longer suffices in itself. Man seeks his own divine communication. Such knowledge is certain, and it satisfies his need for conviction (listed earlier as an innate drive in man). It removes contradiction and replaces analysis and "groping inquiry." The result is not what the understanding calls a doctrinal system or dogma, but instead, spiritual truth or vision. Finally, Hedge asserted that divine communication does not dictate truth but makes it more attractive to man by elevating him through sensual impulse to spiritual truth. Spiritual truth is the moral archetype or ideal, that law which functions within man, as physical law operates without. [18]

Hedge referred to the representative of the first stage of spiritual development as "natural man." At the later stage, he becomes "spiritual man." Both are different manifestations of the same dual nature. In the first, the roots of the spiritual have not yet developed. In the second, examples of which Hedge variously referred to as Christ or the saints, man has developed his innate capacities and cultivated his spiritual life in a way consistent with his natures. But if both capacities are of the same creature, which takes precedent when truth derived from insight conflicts with that of human understanding and demonstrable proof? [19]

Hedge took several approaches to the idea of conflict between intuition and understanding. First, he saw little chance of such contradiction. Truths developed in one system are necessarily outside the realm of inquiry of the other, as those of Kant's pure and practical reason lie outside sensibility and understanding. Further, there is only one truth, and the discoveries of one system should verify or complement those of the other, if properly understood.

The question arises as to how truths of the intuition can be differentiated from those of the understanding. Hedge provided three guidelines. He began by asserting the practical character of intuition in that it deals with the deepest questions and dearest concerns of the soul in a popularly acceptable way. The truths of revelation are not philosophical conceptions, labored inductions, or analytic subtleties, which can be expressed only in abstruse, scholastic phraseology. Instead, they are "plain, emphatic enunciations of truths concerning God and man, duty, destiny, and human well-being, such as the humblest and most uncultured can appreciate and appropriate and turn to use." Further, all of intuition's utterances "have a moral bearing." [20]

Secondly, "real insight," or divine intuition of the truth, gives an individual certain authority beyond that of the scholar. "It is genius adopted by the spirit of God into heavenly fellowship, and consecrated to heavenly uses," or "genius with moral intensity." This may, in the biblical sense, announce God as a "reputed worker of miracles," or one as walking in the ways of God. [21]

Finally, truths of the understanding or of intuition should be judged by their results. As Hedge put it: "Philosophy founds schools; revelations churches." What is at first internal, having been derived intuitively, becomes external. It becomes that upon which churches are formed and by which men live. [22]

Hedge urged that all intuitive beliefs be closely and continuously scrutinized by the understanding. However, within their sphere and in matters of undeniable importance (for example, moral law), man's intuitive beliefs must take precedence over all others. Like William James in his "will to believe," years later, he insisted that this should be the case even when demonstrable proof or the understanding seems to fly in the face of man's revelations. It should be remembered, however, that Hedge's trust in that idealized "one universal truth" practically precludes this situation from occurring. Contradictions usually result from misinterpretation. Instead, in nearly every case, he saw the coordination of understanding and intuition for maximum growth of the mind. [23]

Because Hedge based his view of intuition on voluntary submission to the divine presence, and because the most important element received from intuition is moral law, he had to consider the importance of the will. Basic to his scheme was the assumption that the divine presence does more than inspire divine knowledge and moral truth. Like seventeenth and eighteenth century concepts of supernatural grace, intuition quickens moral and spiritual life and enhances the will toward good. As he concluded: "To know the truth, it is necessary to will the truth." [24]

Hedge assumed that man's will is influenced by his perceptions, especially of moral law, which he derives from intuition. Further, he believed that, unless countered by some other external force, such perceptions lead to practice of that law. His idealism was based on the proposition that truth is not received except by those who genuinely seek it, and that they are then more likely to act on its behalf. [25]

Hedge made the analogy that the spirit is to the mind, what light is to the eye. As the light shows truth to the eye, so the spirit to the mind. "Let the eyes be open, the heart free, and the understanding will be full of light." [26] Doubt or unbelief vanish and the spirit guides man to truth. It becomes his moral guide, stimulating his will and encouraging him to seek yet further truths and to act in their direction. In the end, all knowledge and spiritual truths, as well as moral action, partake of this process. [27]

In the case of knowledge of God's law, Hedge held that man's mental faculties are but secondary agents, referred to also as mere organs. Knowledge is inspired by God and received through man's divine intuition. Because aspiration toward good generally follows such knowledge, both knowledge and the will to act are held as God given. As previously established by Edwards and Channing, however, Hedge believed that reception of divine truth is not mechanical or coercive. It merely supplies man's capacity and impulse to do good. As he noted: "We are moved, yet we move freely." Free will remains, but through it, man naturally accepts divine influence, ties it to his destiny, and chooses the spirit of God to reign in his will. [28]

For Hedge, freedom of the will exists. Such freedom allows for our fallibility and avoids recourse to a mechanized universe. God does not act on the mind mechanically, but morally. He does not compel belief, but persuades. Thus, acceptance of the word of God remains elective and is not the inevitable result of mechanical compulsion on the mind. It is liable not only to willful opposition, but to error. The first case will be dealt with in the next chapter. The second results from man's failure to surrender to the leadership of the spirit within him. The failure to surrender gives man the experience of error, but it also allows correction and thus furnishes the discipline man needs to effect the means of his growth. [29]

Hedge insisted that freedom of the will does not mean "absolute disengagement from all rule" or "lawless roving." He did not agree with the commonly held Arminian concept that man can will what he wills. Instead, he held that free will consists of "free consent with legitimate sway, in free cooperation with the Superior Will." As in the case of Channing or Schelling, Hedge asserted that freedom of the will is man's ability to align his will with that of God. Liberty is the ability to act accordingly to its dictates. The first is supplied by the divine presence, the second is dependent on man's peculiar external circumstances. [30]

Because the degree of divine presence increases and the control over man's external circumstances improves as he ascends the scale of life, each successive order of beings is freer than the one beneath it. The brute is thus freer than the plant and man freer than the brute, even though those laws which govern him, such as evil and social laws, become more complex. Plants and animals can obey no laws but those of their own nature, those which dictate their very existence. They cannot understand or even be conscious of them. [31]

God's law is a restriction of man's will only for those who resist its control. The way to surmount this restraint is by perfect obedience, by accepting the law so entirely, by so identifying his will with the Supreme Will which ordains it, that he becomes himself a party to the law. Then God's law ceases to be restraint and becomes his own volition. Hedge wrote: "Man is free when he freely obeys the law in his mind. Resist the law of duty, and it galls you with an iron grip; seek to evade it, and it pursues you with a merciless lash." Assent to it and God's Law becomes part of man's own nature--the spontaneous expression of his will. [32]

Hedge asserted that there are two opposite currents of influence in the world, but he did not title them good and evil. The one current leads the individual toward God; the other ends in death (to be explained along with immortality). To move with the former brings moral freedom and is man's natural impulse. To be carried by the other is to contradict his own nature and is, therefore, bondage. Yet, man has the choice. [33]

Hedge concluded that the world itself is conditioned by God, and it, in turn, conditions man. Although man might sometimes weary of such conditions and see them as bondage, such bondage can be escaped only by his submission to it with mind and heart. Because the current is man's natural way, to oppose it is to seek the unnatural. Free will is divinely circumscribed by a universal will; free will seeks to resolve itself into the universal. Thus, to find freedom is to first find the given pattern for man's lives, and this man finds within himself. Man's will becomes his necessity, and he possesses himself. [34]

To possess himself completely, which is the best life can yield, Hedge asserted man must secure himself from all inward and outward annoyance. This is the reward for moral obedience, while in such obedience, man emphasizes the divine within him and increases the amount of being in him of the Godhead. The greater his moral refinement, the clearer is his conception of God. The clearer his conception of God, the more attractive is God's word. When man accepts more of God's word, his moral refinement grows, beginning the process once again. Hedge used Christ as the supreme representation of this obedience, self-emancipation, and highest cultivation of the divine through "a liberated life, whose freedom came from acceptance of the humblest conditions into which he brought divinity." [35]

Hedge did not believe that man's willful opposition can change the purposes of God or avert His grace. Man cannot alienate His love or render Him less willing to aid or bless. God remains true to man, however man might turn from Him. Man's deepest and indestructible tendency is Godward, and his insatiable thirst is for the living God. Man's soul longs for an infinite good, loyalty to an invisible supreme God, grace, a spiritual world, and everlasting life. [36]

Yet, because man is free, he is capable of destroying the efficacy of the divine within him. He can alienate his heart from spiritual truth, both by not seeking it and by turning away from it, once revealed. This is the source of moral corruption and the counterforce to the will. Yet, man is still not lost, because his conscience, which Hedge defined as man's basic sense of God, higher order, or supreme moral law, cannot be made entirely inactive. [37]

Even if neutralized for the moment, the conscience remains within man and holds him accountable. Hedge called conscience man's "true custodian" of individual well being. It holds him accountable in three ways: moral perception, moral obligation, and moral retribution. In the first case conscience distinguishes between right and wrong. In the second it commands right and forbids wrong, independent of any gain or loss accruing from one or the other. In the third case it punishes disobedience with suffering more or less acute, according to the moral development of the individual. Those with the highest state of moral development suffer most for their transgressions. [**38**]

Finally, once sparked, Hedge believed the conscience leads to a joining of truth and will. This, in turn, raises man's moral vision to yet higher truths, conscientious and beneficent actions, and, ultimately, to a higher spiritual plane of life. Herein lay a scheme for self-perfection, which he shared with other American Transcendentalists, but Hedge's belief in human perfection remains to be considered.

NOTES

1. Frederic Henry Hedge, "Cause of Reason, the Cause of Faith," Christian Examiner, 70 (1861), 317; Frederic Henry Hedge, **Reason in Religion** (Boston: Walker, Fuller, and Company, 1865), 333-334.

2. Hedge, **Reason in Religion,** 232, 238.

3. Ibid., 284.

4. Hedge, **Reason in Religion,** 241, 242, 250, 256, 353, 354, 397; Frederic Henry Hedge, "The Doctrine of Endless Punishment," Christian Examiner, 67 (1859), 103; Frederic Henry Hedge, "The Way of Historic Atonement," in his **Ways of the Spirit and Other Essays** (Boston: Roberts Brothers, 1877), 98; Frederic Henry Hedge, "The Two Religions," in his **Ways of the Spirit,** 286. See also George H. Williams, **Rethinking the Unitarian Relationship with Protestantism: An Examination of the Thought of Frederic Henry Hedge** (Boston: The Beacon Press, 1949), 26.

5. Hedge, **Reason in Religion,** 283, 343; Frederic Henry Hedge, "Ethical Systems," in his **Martin Luther and Other Essays** (Boston: Roberts Brothers, 1888), 232; Frederic Henry Hedge, "Natural Religion," Christian Examiner, 52 (1852), 122. See also William Ellery Channing, "Self-Culture," **The Works of William Ellery Channing** (New York: Burton Franklin, 1970), 30; Ralph Waldo Emerson, "The

Divinity School Address: An Address Delivered Before the Senior Class in Divinity College, Cambridge, Sunday Evening, July 15, 1838," in **Anthology of American Literature: Colonial Through Romantic**, ed. George McMichael (New York: Macmillan Publishing Co., Inc., 1980), 1037; George Ripley, "The Latest Form of Infidelity Examined," in **The Transcendentalists: An Anthology**, ed. Perry Miller (Cambridge, Ma.: Harvard University Press, 1960), 215; Orestes A. Brownson, "Two Articles from the Princeton Review," in Miller, **The Transcendentalists,** 215; Elizabeth Flower and Murray G. Murphy, **A History of Philosophy in America** (New York: Capricorn Books, 1977), 1, 10; Ronald Vale Wells, **Three Christian Transcendentalists: James Marsh, Caleb Sprague Henry, Frederic Henry Hedge** (1943; rpt. New York: Octagon Books, 1972), 148.

6. Frederic Henry Hedge, "The Theism of Reason and the Theism of Faith," in his **Personality and Theism: Two Essays** (Cambridge, Ma.: John Wilson and Son, 1887), 38.

7. Frederic Henry Hedge, "Emmanuel Swedenborg," Christian Examiner, 15 (1833), 204.

8. Ibid.

9. Hedge, "Emmanuel Swedenborg," 195-196, 204; Frederic Henry Hedge, "Antisupernaturalism in the Pulpit, An Address Delivered to the Graduating Class of the Divinity School, Cambridge, July 17, 1864," Christian Examiner, 77 (1864), 150.

10. Hedge, **Reason in Religion,** 58; Hedge, "Natural Religion," 122; Ripley, "The Latest Form of Infidelity Examined," 219.

11. Hedge, **Reason in Religion,** 58, 294; Frederic Henry Hedge, "Authorities and Scribes," in his **Sermons** (Boston: Roberts Brothers, 1891), 25; Hedge, "The Theism of Reason," 36-37; Wells, 128-129.

12. Hedge, **Reason in Religion,** 287.

13. Frederic Henry Hedge, "The Lesson of Flowers," in his **Sermons,** 47. See also Wells, 120.

14. Hedge, **Reason in Religion,** 290.

15. Ibid.

16. Frederic Henry Hedge, "The Spirit's Rest," in his **Sermons,** 239.

17. Hedge, "The Spirit's Rest," 239; Frederic Henry Hedge, "The Way of Religion," in his **Ways of the Spirit,** 46; Hedge, "Cause of Reason," 226.

18. Hedge, "The Way of Religion," 46; Hedge, "The Cause of Reason," 226; Frederic Henry Hedge, "The Deluge," in his **The Primeval World of Hebrew Tradition** (Boston: Roberts Brothers, 1870), 202; Wells, 116.

19. Hedge, "The Way of Religion," 46; Hedge, "Cause of Reason," 226. See also Wells, 106.

20. Hedge, **Reason in Religion**, 59.

21. Ibid., 62.

22. Ibid., 64.

23. Horace Howard Furness, **Records of a Life Long Friendship, 1807-1882** (Boston: Houghton Mifflin Co., 1910), 36, 51; Paul F. Boller, Jr., **Freedom and Fate in American Thought from Edwards to Dewey** (Dallas, Tx.: Southern Methodist University Press, 1978), 168.

24. Hedge, **Reason in Religion**, 5.

25. Ibid., 288.

26. Ibid.

27. Ibid.

28. Hedge, **Reason in Religion**, 286, 288; Hedge, "Two Religions," 302-303; Channing, "Self-Culture," 15; Flower and Murphy, 43.

29. Hedge, **Reason in Religion**, 205.

30. Hedge, **Reason in Religion**, 288; Frederic Henry Hedge, "Arthur Schopenhauer," Christian Examiner, 76 (1864), 76; William Ellery Channing, "Spiritual Freedom," in his **Works**, 174; Boller, ix.

31. Hedge, **Reason in Religion**, 190.

32. Ibid.

33. Ibid., 288.

34. Hedge, **Reason in Religion**, 192; Frederic Henry Hedge, "Personality," in his **Martin Luther**, 192. Frederic Henry Hedge, "The Way of Historic Christianity," in his **Ways of the Spirit**, 67; Wells, 118.

35. Hedge, "Personality," 304; Wells, 118; Joseph Henry Allen and Richard Eddy, **A History of the Unitarians and the Universalists in the United States** (New York: The Christian Liturgy Co., 1894), 70.

36. Hedge, **Reason in Religion**, 14; Hedge, "The Doctrine of Endless Punishment," 113.

37. Hedge, **Reason in Religion**, 29, 30, 31; Hedge, "Ethical Systems," 235; Frederic Henry Hedge, "The Pure in Heart Shall See God," in his **Sermons**,

75; Frederic Henry Hedge, "The Gospel of Manual Labor," in his **Sermons**, 115; Frederic Henry Hedge, "Conscience," in his **Sermons**, 316. Hedge often cited Goethe's Faust as an example in this case. See for example: Frederic Henry Hedge, "Brooks' **Faust**," Christian Examiner, 63 (1857), 16.

38. Hedge, "Conscience," 315-316, 324; Wells, 115, 117.

Chapter Six

PERSONAL PERFECTION AND IMMORTALITY

One could reason from Hedge's writings that if Christ and man are of a similar, dual nature, and if Christ attained divine status through the perfection of his nature, then man might do the same. Yet there is no other known historical example of such perfection. Did Hedge allow for such perfection, or did he perceive human limitations with which Christ did not have to contend?

To begin to answer this question, it is necessary to recall Hedge's premise that man is of a dual nature: one human, one divine. But as there is promise in such a nature, there is also limitation. As seen earlier, the continued unfolding of the divine spirit is the true progressive development of man. If man were of a spiritual nature alone, as certain American Transcendentalists such as Emerson and Parker believed, spiritual unfolding could lead to the "leavening" of the whole, but Hedge did not believe this to be the case. [1]

For the total "leavening" of the spiritual nature of man, his human nature would have to be eliminated. This is impossible. Hedge was well aware of those such as Channing who preached that man "should hate his animal life in comparison with the intellectual and moral life which is to endure forever." [2] But he felt the elimination of either nature would deny the basis of self. The perfection of man, then, if that were to be allowed, would be in terms of both natures inviolable. The result would not be divinity alone, as Hedge put it, but man as "one with God in Christ," or "the stature of a perfect humanity." It would be "neither flesh nor spirit, but where flesh is sublimated into spirit, and spirit is realized in flesh." [3]

Hedge further offered that even if man were to reach a perfected state on earth, as previously defined, he would remain man. He could cultivate his divine intuition to its greatest receptivity of God's word; he could attain the highest spiritual nature possible to man; he could draw as close as possible into consciousness with God by whose spirit he was continually nourished; he could even move entirely from the stage of Adam to that of Christ; yet, he would remain man, albeit at the highest stage of his divine evolution. [4]

Hedge's basic guide was that "the vessel must conform to the mold." Man has been placed in a framework of laws which prescribes the dimensions and the plan he will fulfill. He is constituted and maintained by physical and moral laws, to which he must submit as the sure and only good. These very limits, however, allow his perfection. If no one of man's propensities exceeds its due, each can be developed in harmony with the rest until all are perfected within the limits set for them. If this were accomplished, he would represent the image of Christ or the perfect image of God in which his being is cast. [5] As Hedge suggested:

> Let us not chafe, but glory in these bonds, and welcome every law which we find in our condition and in ourselves as the finger of God in the mainstream of life, pointing out the path which alone can bring us the satisfaction we seek. [6]

Hedge asserted that the fact of man's conscious intelligence implies the conscious intelligence of the creator. God, according to Hedge, is perfect and, therefore, "must will the recognition of that perfection" in man as the "only supposable end of moral creation." [7] Thus, the stage is set for human perfection, even if in terms of the limitations discussed earlier. But Hedge, unlike Emerson and Parker, resisted faith in such perfection. [8] He indicated in at least two places that there is little hope for human perfection in life. In one case he noted: "From whatever point we set out, the goal of perfection is equally remote, and in this we must be reconciled." [9] In another he insisted that man is basically fallible and, therefore, cannot act infallibly. [10]

Hedge did imply, then, that although man has the means to approach perfection, he cannot reach its outer limits while he is man. He explained this in the following terms: "To reach the outer limits of perfection we must know God." But this is not possible, because any God that man could know as man would be no God. "Only that can be defined which is finite," and God, according to Hedge, is infinite. [11] Once again, however, Hedge insisted that man should not despair, even though his destiny does not correspond with his desire. He asked man to realize that he has limits and to accept them. Further, he saw these limits as large in scope and not the source of a fretful spirit.

Rebellion is useless, yet painful, for it is against man's very lot in creation. [12]

Hedge's true perfectibility lies in immortality. Immortality, he noted, is commonly supposed to be a specialty of Christian doctrine. Yet, he saw no explicit declaration of this in the gospels. Instead, he cited inferences from the life and sayings of Christ. For example, Hedge used a biblical quote: "God is not a God of the dead, but of the living, for we all live unto him." He also used the example of Christ's resurrection. In his reasoning, Christ's example would have served no purpose if resurrection of the dead in general were not allowed. [13] Finally, reminiscent of an earlier stand by Channing, Hedge insisted that the strongest proof of man's immortality lies in the fact that man believes in it. It is a pledge from that power that made man of immortality as a possibility of the human condition. [14] He observed that whereas immortality is inferred, however, it is not regarded as a natural consequence of the nature of the soul. It is something to be achieved, or communicated, by God through Christ. [15]

Hedge did not view immortality or life hereafter as the dissolution of the continuity of life. Such dissolution, or even the transition from one state to an entirely different one, "would destroy our identity and would therefore be something with which, as conscious beings, we could have no concern." [16] Instead, he saw immortality as a "spiritual new birth, life more abundant, intenser action, endless progress,--the mortal life quickened into life eternal." [17] Even in death man's life is a "linked succession or series of steps, each necessarily connected with the preceding one." Man's passage from one link to the other is so gradual a process that he may not know at what precise moment he leaves one life for another. Man loses his conscious self "by degrees," but "by degrees he finds it again." [18] Moreover, Hedge's eschatology did not conceive of a simultaneous resurrection of the dead, physically or spiritually, at the end of the world, based on a general judgment fixing the condition of all souls for all coming time. [19] Instead, his immortality is based on the highest aim of the individual soul in its highest devotion.

Hedge believed that the soul's highest state of devotion is not, as he felt Calvin implied, escape from damnation, but instead repose in God. The soul seeks nothing else. Its whole being is consecrated in the one desire, "Thy will be done." Because man has it in his power through his divine self, to know God and enjoy God's spirit within him, he does not need to pursue God beyond himself or beyond the earth. By seeking himself, man seeks God. If heaven is defined as man's enjoyment of God's spirit and its presence within him, as Hedge believed, then heaven is as near to man as his own soul. In Hedge's words: "Heaven is as near to our souls as this world is to our bodies." As man seeks the spirit within him, he unites with God and the Kingdom of God is within him. [20]

Yet, to Hedge, the idea of immortality is a spiritual one, defined by man's alliance with moral law. The spirit lives, while the body dies. He cited St. Paul on this topic: "As in Adam all die, so in Christ all be made alive." [21] Once again, however, the rule of degree applies. All souls are immortal in some sense. None is annihilated at death along with the body. The soul, or the divine presence, is the foundation and cause of man's organism, not its result. It is the central force of the system it inhabits, not its subject. The soul always exists, ready to lead man to moral law through divine intuition, but the degree of its efficacy is in proportion to the degree of his acceptance of its message. The greater man's acceptance of God's message, the greater the soul's central force, and the more immortal the soul. [22]

Hedge allowed for the existence of a soul throughout the animal kingdom. In a sense reminiscent of Leibnitz's monadology, he described the soul in terms of indestructible atom-like units, although in no sense did he indicate that it is not a purely spiritual entity. The point here is that the soul is indestructible. It is life force. In the simplest of creatures of the animal kingdom the "central principle" of the soul, (its spiritually efficacious nature) is weak. It is compensated for by increased vitality. Further, instead of a single regent soul, animal forms are pervaded by a multiplicity of inferior, unconscious souls. [23]

The unconscious vitality of the section of the animal kingdom outside man is great, even to the point of reproduction and replacement of perished members. But the soul remains discretely multiple and unconscious. There is, therefore, little or no voluntary action. Hedge cited the example of the snail and earthworm, which cannot define their own individuality by an act of consciousness embracing the entire organism, distinguishing it from other bodies. In this case, then, immortality cannot be predicated on any other grounds than the indestructibleness of those elements of the soul. In death, they return to the generally diffusive soul, similar to the Oriental or Emersonian oversoul, and are redefined and reestablished in yet another organism, in each case supplying the vitality of life. [24]

The soul of man, unlike that of lower animals, is capable of individual and insoluble immortality. This is immortality, as Hedge saw it, in the gospel sense. Generally, the soul survives the dissolution of bodily death, except in cases of extreme deprivation and limitation. Such deprivation or limitation results from the alienation of man from God's word and from the divine within him. When this happens, man's soul grows closer to that of the lower animals in fate.

Drawing from early Christian Gnostics and Jacob Boehme, Hedge believed that in bodily death the alienated soul cannot recover itself intact from the mortal shock and take up once again conscious life elsewhere. It lacks sufficient force to remain intact or to recollect a "new system of particles," or a new body in which it can reign as consciousness and central, life-giving power. It ceases to be a "conscious individuality" or "moral agent." It then becomes either part of insensate spirit (matter) or becomes a constituent and subordinate part of another soul. Its independent, conscious individuality is lost to it, as is the life force it once projected. [**25**]

The key to survival of the human soul is adherence to moral law, or the "lessons of the soul," as conveyed through divine intuition. [**26**] The result is not a natural but moral growth; not a universal, but a special one; not a heritage, but an acquisition. Without such development, dependent on the will, immortality cannot be attained, or even sought, in this world, nor conferred in the next. [**27**]

Hedge further asserted that through the exercise of man's will, his soul rises on the scale of being. As this occurs the soul grows more intact, central, and individualized. One "monarch" soul possesses and dominates the entire frame. It subjects and subordinates all cross currents filling the body with vitality in a higher sense of immortality than mere indestructibleness. When the soul is reestablished in its new form, it begins its pursuit of moral law again from the point at which it left off in its preceding embodiment. This accounts for Hedge's assertion of the discrepancies in moral state and allows for the continued growth of the soul from one lifetime to the next. [**28**]

Hedge did not believe that the superiority of man's nature guaranteed his immortality. The soul has to earn its deathlessness. Sluggishness can prevent it from being active and from "collecting itself in a vigorous effort of self-communion." It can remain cold and indifferent to the supreme good, shutting itself off from the influx of God's spirit. In such a state, the soul does nothing with the germ of everlasting life that it has; it is only of this world. [**29**]

It is man's voluntary submission to his spiritual or divine nature that allows the infusion and growth of the Holy Spirit within him. It is only with this growth that direct knowledge of God, divine intuition, occurs and leads man to a higher moral plane or spiritual existence. This allows him to partake of an immortality essentially different from that of the brutes, for the brutes do not share in the capacity to ignite the spark of the divine within. Christ is the prototype for this immortality. He was its "first fruits," but the same capacity lies within all men for "in Christ all shall be made alive." [30]

It should be noted that Hedge did allow for environmental influence on the progress of the soul. As will be seen later, this provided one motive for his social gospel. In particular, he referred to the case where the child is born to "Christian parents, well circumstanced," and provided with the "best education for moral well being." Hedge felt this child would have greater opportunity for growth than one born into the "bosom of want and vice," or into a "squalid" home where the child is in "daily contemplation of evil examples." The first, by accident of birth is destined to life-long progress, the second to "infamy, shame, depravity, and ruin." As seen earlier, however, Hedge insisted that efforts of the will can overcome such circumstances for better or worse. [31]

One question remains at this point: If Hedge's scheme of immortality allowed for the transferral of the developing soul from one body to another, what of the experiences of one life and another? If moral and spiritual growth were allowed from one life to another, what of accumulated memories, lessons, and emotional ties?

The answer to this question lies in Hedge's belief that human experience is not "coextensive" with man's being, and that his memory does not comprehend it. In Hedge's words, "We bear not the root, but the root us." In this case the root is the soul, but the soul, properly speaking, is not man's. It is not a part of him as much as he is a part of it. The soul is the source of man's individuality, but it is larger than he is and, as seen earlier, older. That is, the soul is older than the conscious self. [32]

Hedge observed that the conscious self does not begin until some time after the birth of the individual. Thus, he opened himself to the popular controversy over the existence of the individual and the soul--whether a new soul is furnished to each new body, or the body given to a pre-existing soul. He saw no certainty for either view. He allowed for both, as long as the preexistence or immortality of the soul is basic to both. [33] The logical extension of Hedge's definition of the soul as vital life force leads to the assertion that the soul is naturally part of the body from its inception. Its rise to consciousness can be explained in terms of the cultivation of those peculiarly human-divine elements of will, conscience, and divine intuition. He saw no need, however, to involve himself in this controversy.

Why, then, can man not remember pre-life existence? First, according to Hedge's scheme, it may not have been a conscious existence, and therefore, would have had no conscious experience. Secondly, even if conscious, experience cannot be preserved. It is effaced by the new. As he explained, memory depends on continuity of association, and death breaks that continuity. This may be for the best, Hedge added, because the memory of past life would only prejudice a subsequent life's affairs. Man would dwell in the past instead of the future. [34]

Yet, as noted earlier, the soul does not totally begin again. It retains the "effect of its previous existence." It does not assume its present condition as though it had never before existed. Its past experiences essentially modify it, and it takes its character from its former state. Again in a manner similar to the Hindu concept of the transmigration of the soul, Hedge held that the soul takes into the present certain tendencies and dispositions, or growth or lack of it, in a previous life. If moral growth occurs, the moral nature of the soul asserts itself in a degree transcending the limits of a single experience, reaching from one life to the other. The continuity of the "pilgrim soul" is maintained. [35]

Finally, if the soul is immortal, what of heaven or hell? What of the traditional Christian ideas of heaven or hell as the translation of earthly souls by death to a spiritual life in a place separate from this world? Hedge considered this view "a preposterous idea of human destiny." [36]

To consider Hedge's view of hell, it is necessary to recall his belief that in bodily death the alienated soul cannot recover itself intact from the mortal shock. It cannot take up once again conscious life in another bodily form, and thus it loses its "conscious individuality." It returns to the generally diffusive soul and then becomes a subordinate part of another individual soul. Hell, or eternally tormenting damnation, as traditionally defined, is an impossibility. When the soul is so depraved as to be "damned," it succumbs and ceases to exist. It is no longer an entity in itself. [37]

Hedge's concept of hell is consistent with his denial of "the doctrine of endless punishment." He held that belief in such a doctrine leads people to attach supreme importance to the penalties of God's law, "as if the penalty makes the obligation, or could justly enhance the sense of accountableness in rational souls." Under "the doctrine of endless punishment," man's main objective becomes escape from damnation rather than the ideal of self-perfection and everlasting life. It breeds "selfish fear," rather than "exceeding love." As Hedge concluded:

> Conviction of sin is an indispensable step in the reformation of the sinner. But this conviction is to be effected, not by forcing the eye inward, but by that enlightening and quickening of the conscience which comes through adequate exhibition of moral truth in [awakening] the sense of present defilement, of an insupportable burden to get rid of for its own sake, not for the sake of what may hereafter come of it. The sinner should be taught to dwell on the sin itself, and not on the penalty incurred by it. [38]

As to Hedge's view of heaven, it is necessary to recall his concept of the continuity of the soul. All souls are of divine origin, and their striving assures continued moral and spiritual growth and their share of immortality. Hedge simply placed heaven as the end product of this striving. His heaven is a moral state based on the soul's destiny. It is the stage at which God's goal for the soul is realized. [39]

Hedge did not consider earth and heaven as two distinct places. They are, instead, two levels of human experience. Man is born into one. He reaches the other through the development of his spiritual nature. Once there man finds "the right place and connection and nurture for every soul He has caused to be." The soul's seeking ends in the finding of a life richer than all its experience or even its fondest dreams. [40] As Hedge put it:

> I see no reason for this translocation to "heaven" in death; no reason for supposing that the sphere of planetary attraction ceases with the dissolution of the animal frame, no reason for supposing that the planet's hold of its own is bounded by the animal life. On the contrary, it accords of reason to believe that the soul--which makes the individual and which must not be confused with the accompanying spirit, which is not the individual--is a part of the planetary life, and can never, while that life endures, be divorced from the system to which it belongs. . . .
>
> I am persuaded that dying is not migration, that this earth is man's future and eternal abode, and that in the course of human development the time will come when death shall no longer occupy the place it now does in the human economy. . . . We do not go to heaven, but heaven comes to us. They whose inner eye is opened see heaven, and they who see it are in it, and the air to them is thick with angels, like the background of Raphael's <u>Mother in Glory</u>. [41]

Not only is the germ of such a perfect state within each man, but all earthly conditions, commonly defined as good and evil, exist for the perfection of his character. [42] Man's model is Christ, and his ministry and death attract man by their supreme example, bringing him into right relation with God. As the son of God, Christ represents the Divine. As the son of man he represents the ideal, the visible bodying forth of the perfect and divine humanity, in which all men share. [43]

Heaven, or everlasting life, as Hedge preferred to call it, is an earthly condition without its power of sin. The way to heaven is heaven, and heaven is nothing but a way or a method of the soul. It depends on direct knowledge of the transcendent and that is achieved through perfection of the soul. Perfection of the soul results from the "flowering of character through its growth in life." [44]

Hedge's views on immortality and the hereafter were among the most elaborately drawn of American Transcendentalists, although as noted earlier other thinkers shared in particulars of its various aspects. In the creation of these views, he drew from sources of the East and West, from Hindu mysticism and liberal Christianity, and from philosophers as diverse as Boehme and Leibnitz. Yet his basic Transcendental belief in man's divine nature and intuitive insight into God's moral law remained at their center. He viewed immortality and life hereafter as the fruition of man's journey toward perfection. The journey depends on man's divine capacities, which were given in God's creation, led by Christ's example, and found through the human will.

NOTES

1. Donald N. Koster, **Transcendentalism in America** (Boston: Twayne Publishers, 1975), 44; Henry A. Pochmann, **German Culture in America: Philosophical and Literary Influences: 1600-1900** (Madison: The University of Wisconsin Press, 1957), 191.

2. William Ellery Channing, "Spiritual Freedom," in his **The Works of William Ellery Channing** (New York: Burt Franklin, 1970), 173.

3. Frederic Henry Hedge, **The Leaven of the Word** (Boston: Dutton and Wentworth, 1849), 5-6; Frederic Henry Hedge, **Reason in Religion** (Boston: Walker, Fuller, and Company, 1865), 89; Frederic Henry Hedge, "The Soul's Deliverance," in his **Sermons** (Boston: Roberts Brothers, 1891), 93.

4. Hedge, **Reason in Religion,** 29. See also Ronald Vale Wells, **Three Christian Transcendentalists: James Marsh, Caleb Sprague Henry, Frederic Henry Hedge** (1943; rpt. New York: Octagon Books, 1972), 107.

5. Hedge, **Reason in Religion**, 188.

6. *Ibid.*, 189.

7. Hedge, **Reason in Religion,** 53; Frederic Henry Hedge, "Personality," in his **Martin Luther and Other Essays** (Boston: Roberts Brothers, 1888), 279-280.

8. Koster, 44; Paul F. Boller, Jr., **Freedom and Fate in American Thought from Edwards to Dewey** (Dallas: Southern Methodist University Press, 1978), 74; Henry Steele Commager, **Theodore Parker** (Boston: Little, Brown and Company, 1936), 153.

9. Hedge, **Reason in Religion,** 181.

10. Frederic Henry Hedge, "Cause of Reason, the Cause of Faith," *Christian Examiner,* 70 (1861), 213.

11. Frederic Henry Hedge, "The Theism of Reason and the Theism of Faith," in his **Martin Luther**, 326.

12. Hedge, **Reason in Religion**, 181.

13. *Ibid.*, 320.

14. Hedge, **Reason in Religion,** 163; Frederic Henry Hedge, "Self-Culture," in his **Works,** 14.

15. Hedge, **Reason in Religion**, 370

16. *Ibid.*, 154.

17. *Ibid.*, 371.

18. *Ibid.*, 154.

19. *Ibid.*, 371, 373.

20. Hedge, **Reason in Religion,** 109, 387; Frederic Henry Hedge, **Theological Progress During the Last Half Century** (Providence: Knowles, Anthony and Co., 1878), 71.

21. Hedge, **Reason in Religion,** 375.

22. *Ibid.*, 373.

23. *Ibid.*, 376.

24. Hedge, **Reason in Religion,** 376; Koster, 40; John S. Harrison, **The Teachers of Emerson** (New York: Haskell House, 1966), 78-80.

25. Hedge, **Reason in Religion,** 328; Frederic Henry Hedge, "The Doctrine of Endless Punishment," Christian Examiner, 67 (1859), 126.

26. Hedge, **Reason in Religion,** 380.

27. Ibid., 382.

28. Ibid., 376.

29. Ibid., 109, 377.

30. Hedge, **Reason in Religion,** 25, 280, 378; Hedge, "The Doctrine of Endless Punishment," 113.

31. Hedge, **Reason in Religion,** 359-360, 364.

32. Frederic Henry Hedge, "The Human Soul: Its Origin and Destination," in his **Ways of the Spirit and Other Essays** (Boston: Roberts Brothers, 1877), 360.

33. Ibid.

34. Ibid., 357-360.

35. Hedge, "The Human Soul," 360; Hedge, **Reason in Religion,** 164.

36. Hedge, "The Human Soul," 361.

37. Hedge, **Reason in Religion,** 414-415.

38. Hedge, "The Doctrine of Endless Punishment," 99-101, 108, 121.

39. Hedge, "The Human Soul," 364, 367; Perry Miller, **The Transcendentalists: An Anthology** (Cambridge, Ma.: Harvard University Press, 1960), 108.

40. Hedge, "The Human Soul," 364, 367; Hedge, **Reason in Religion,** 378.

41. Frederic Henry Hedge, "The Way of Historic Atonement," in his **Ways of the Spirit**, 112-113. See also Hedge, "The Doctrine of Endless Punishment," 128.

42. Hedge, "Personality," 305. See also Wells, 118, 119, 122.

43. Frederic Henry Hedge, **The Atonement in Connection with the Death of Christ** (Boston: American Unitarian Association, 1866), 5, 7.

44. Frederic Henry Hedge, "Emerson's Writings," Christian Examiner, 38 (1845), 90-91. See also Wells, 118.

Chapter Seven

REVELATION, RATIONALISM, AND HISTORICAL CHRISTIANITY

Frederic Hedge's epistemology placed him in an uncomfortable position in his polarized religious community. On the one hand, he asserted the existence of continuous revelation, based on man's divinely inspired intuitive powers. This led to criticism by more conservative figures, such as Andrews Norton and Francis Bowen, who questioned man's fitness for such an exalted position. They preferred to find God's will through rational powers of the understanding or through faith in the Bible and its historically recorded revelation. [1]

On the other hand, Hedge did not totally exclude rationalism and faith in biblically recorded miracles as sources of man's knowledge of the divine. This placed him in conflict with more radically individualistic Transcendentalists, such as Ralph Waldo Emerson and Henry David Thoreau, who sought to assert man's totally exclusive dependence on intuition for matters of a spiritual nature. If unpopular, however, Hedge's formulation was entirely consistent with his view of man, evolution, and the role of the church. It was not an attempt at compromise for its own sake, nor did it change substantively from its earliest conception. [2]

Hedge's emphasis on continuous, personal revelation did not lead to his denial of biblically recorded revelations, or miracles, or of their efficacy, as Andrews Norton feared. [3] He consistently asserted that sufficient knowledge of God leading to faith does not consist solely of that gained through the individual mind. Not everyone, after all, is granted the same extent or degree of such knowledge. Even if all souls have the same capacity, only those who genuinely surrender to God are graced with this "Word." These people become the specially "elect" through their own efforts. They are chosen by God as his oracles or organs of truth. They become seers or prophets, and their comparatively small number makes their position all the more important for others.

Those who surrender to God reflect the infusion they gain from Him in their oral and written word and in their exemplary lives. Hedge saw such teachings or examples, whether or not they become the basis of religious institutions, as "the Holy Spirit made concrete." They are an important element in man's faith, and they are to be worshipped in proportion to their proximity of the direct word. For example: Was the word recorded by the person who received it or by someone at a later date? How much time has passed since its reception? Were they "pretended revelations" claimed by enthusiasts in an uncritical age? Although the message is never totally wrong, revelations, even those recorded in scripture, are given for specific times and places in the evolution of man. In time, their relevance, as well as the degree of their accuracy, may be lost. [4]

Hedge pointed out that revelations of such intensity as to issue in a church, "to furnish the ground of a new dispensation," or even to give one a "sufficient vision of God," have been the experience of only a few individuals. Therefore, "the mass of mankind has had to receive them on historical authority, as they have received the greater part of all their knowledge." This is done mainly through scripture, church, or preacher. All are "mediators" or "interpreters" from God to man. Moreover, they are valid, if unequally efficient to intuition, as ways which God uses to make Himself known. [5]

Hedge believed that tradition results from revelation. This tradition is based on spiritual insight and is valid in proportion to its fidelity to the message received. Originally received directly, as revelation, it becomes indirect in its extension, mostly in the form of church doctrine. Yet for those who criticized faith in such doctrine, such as Emerson, Thoreau, and the Free Religionists (to be discussed), Hedge offered the following:

> Men may rail as they please at the letter, and disparage what is outward in religion, but those churches are the strongest that have the most of it, strongest not only in the way of efficient action and ecclesiastical power, but strongest in spiritual vitality. Out of them have come the sublimest examples of spiritual life; while those churches which have thought meanly of the letter, and sought to dispense with it, have languished and died out. [6]

Hedge insisted that the fault lies not in the letter of church doctrine because it comes of spirit. Difficulties arise from the want of continued spirit by which to "interpret its import," and to "reproduce it in our lives." Established doctrine needs the spiritual life that continuous revelation offers. Without it, doctrines once received first hand, and even the institution they establish, lose their "infused spirit." [7] He concluded:

> Much of the complaint we hear of the coldness of the letter and much of the impatience with rites and scriptures, so far from betokening larger spirituality, is often but a proof of weakness of faith, a want of power to penetrate into the soul of these things, to interpret their deeper import, and recover their latent life. [8]

Hedge felt revelations received through the external senses, commonly referred to as miracles, had lost their importance. They were necessary in pre-Christian times, but not thereafter. They assumed in man "no other agency than obedient reception of some truth or command conveyed without by an audible voice or visible sign." In pre-Christian times perceptive minds necessary to receive the word from within had not yet been cultivated. It was Christ's gift to man, however, that he would develop that mind, seek God's word from within, and become truly in the apostolic sense, the "son of God." [9]

The highest form of divine knowledge, then, is direct revelation, internal in nature. Direct revelation includes the active involvement of the individual as well as divine inspiration. Thus, it makes the mind an active, cooperating power, rather than just a passive recipient. It is human coagency with the divine. Man may not always understand the divine nature of such revelations, but they are "breathed" into him, leading to an exaltation of the mind and quickening of the will. [10]

Hedge thus sought to combine acceptable elements of historical Christianity's supernaturalism with those of Transcendental intuition. If his adherence to the latter caused difficulties with more conservative Unitarians, his insistence on the former led to disagreement with those of the same faith who denied supernaturalism altogether. If any form of supernaturalism was sufficient to drive Emerson from the church, a partial acceptance was required by Hedge to define his relationship to Christianity. [11]

Hedge, like other Transcendentalists such as Theodore Parker or George Ripley, consistently opposed those supernaturalists who sought to use miracles as proof of divine authority and evidence of Christian truth:

> Miracles are valueless as proofs of divine authority, because, with our views of such matter, it is easier to believe in the thing to be proved than it is to believe in the alleged proof. It is easier to believe that a teacher is divinely inspired, than it is to believe that he exhibits any prodigy which contradicts, or seems to contradict, the possibilities of nature. [12]

Hedge believed miracles performed by God or Christ were not intended solely to confirm missions of the prophets or of Christ. They were not meant to force conviction, or, as Andrews Norton asserted, to serve as the basis for the truth of Christ or Christian doctrine. Norton insisted that denial of miracles as recorded in scripture is "to strike directly at the root of faith in Christianity." He believed miracles attested to the divine mission of Christ and if they are denied "nothing is left that can be called Christianity." Internal evidence is insufficient. [13]

To Hedge, scripturally recorded miracles had "beneficient ends" of overcoming natural obstacles by the willing of that faith to which nothing is impossible. They were works of love, yet they cannot convince man if his heart is not so disposed. [14] As he noted, for example, "I accept the miracles recorded in the Gospel, because I find in them no difficulty so great as encountered if I reject them." [15] In the case of Christ, he wrote that he "did not seek to overwhelm the senses to force compliance. The senses are suborned to the will, and refuse to testify truly and the understanding can always argue invalidation or evade proper conclusions." In sum: "Faith is not the offspring of miracles, but miracles, of faith." [16]

Hedge's stand on miracles led him to investigate critically and to dismiss miracles that contradicted historical findings or the understanding, especially at the hands of Higher Criticism and science. He did so in the spirit of "intellectual progress" and the "conscientious love of truth." If, as he saw it, historical and scientific researchers at times lacked Christian devotion and even honesty, or if they occasionally exercised a "negative spirit" or "self-willed approach," few "preachers of the Gospel" could be credited with "entire intellectual sincerity." Both groups had their ulterior motives and prejudices which bound or determined their conclusions. [17]

Hedge did not feel Higher Criticism would "greviously harm" Christianity, unless Christianity's faith was inappropriately based on the historical accuracy of biblical narration. In that case faith was bound to falter and end in "hypocrisy" or "illusion." [18] He believed Higher Criticism had already revealed certain historical inaccuracies, which had little affected Christianity's fundamental principles. Where demonstrated fact had contradicted scriptural text, the text had given way, but no harm had been done to Christianity's basic truths. [19] He referred to Ferdinand Baur and quoted David Strauss for:

> Christ's supernatural birth, his miracles, his resurrection and ascension, remain eternal truths, however their reality as facts of history may be called in question. [20]

Hedge saw a positive side to Higher Criticism. He cited Strauss' **Das Leben Jesu** (1835) as an example of positive "elucidation and restatement," leading its readers to "aspire to the ideal Christ." [21] Hedge, like Ripley, felt such works would lead to a better understanding of Christian truths by purging traditional Christianity and scripture of its "falsifications," "corruptions," and "spurious additaments, interpolations, and misinterpretations," and by leaving the "oriental genius of the Gospel." [22] Man would have to readjust to meet new facts and to seek the personal character of Christ, but he felt the result would "enable and spiritualize the faith of the many." On this point he quoted Baur's plea that Higher Criticism would lead man to "abandon the letter which killeth for the spirit which giveth life." [23] Hedge concluded:

> The real question is not whether Jesus said or did precisely this or that in each particular instance, but whether Christianity is true and divine, the power of God and the wisdom of God unto salvation; whether this light, which for so many centuries had irradiated the world, and given us such guidance as we have had in spiritual things . . . is true. [24]

Hedge was even less troubled by the role of science. Indeed, in opposition to fellow Transcendentalists like Emerson and Thoreau, he espoused science and urged Christians to wake up to its teachings. [25] He urged the church to adopt some of science's investigative spirit in its own considerations. [26] It should be recalled here that when Hedge entered Harvard he considered a career in science.

Hedge believed that in at least one sense science was an implementation of charitableness. It brought material progress and, with that, comfort to the inflicted and destitute. To this Hedge merely added a warning that material comfort is the "destiny" only of those who fail to accomplish their true end as defined by their nature. These people are or remain "children, beggars, and slaves." [27] What he mostly concerned himself with was the challenge scientific discoveries and pretenses pose to religion.

Hedge believed that religion and science, like Kantian reason (intuition) and the understanding, were gifts of God to work hand-in-hand for the greater knowledge and service of God. Both use different, even conflicting, methods and have separate fields of inquiry, but are meant to complement rather than compete with one another. He asserted that science was born of the spirit of the Protestant Reformation, as truly liberal Protestantism was the latest development in the incorporation of science into religion. Protestantism, especially Unitarianism, should therefore "rejoice" with science in all its discoveries and thank science for every fact which it adds to the sum of human knowledge. [28] At one point, for example, Hedge referred to science as "a minister of God, an evangelist whose mission is to 'show the Father,' and regenerate the world." [29] If difficulties arise, they are due in part to the unjustified fears of theologians or the "air of superiority" of science. [30]

To Hedge, science, like Higher Criticism, had not yet proven anything that religion could not deal with, or even incorporate into its theology, and he was confident it would not do so in the future. He admitted that in the present day the popularity of science had eclipsed that of religion, but he insisted that, in time, the "mistress of the house" (religion), would reassert itself "by divine right" over its "uncontrollable child." [31] Science, after all, like the understanding, has its limits, and those limits preclude its dealing with issues essential to man, including knowledge of God, ultimate causes, the moral law, man's origin, and his destiny. Hedge, like Emerson, believed these areas of knowledge had always been and would remain the uncontradictable province of divine intuition, and thus, of religion. They are unknowable and undemonstrable in the world of science. [32] Emerson wrote, for example, that although science is aimed to find "a theory of nature," it had not yet even "a remote approach to an idea of creation." [33]

A revealing example of Hedge's attitude toward science was his consideration of the theory of evolution. Unlike many others, including nonministerial leaders such as American naturalist Louis Agassiz, he did not consider evolution a threat to belief in the sacredness of human life or in God's role in creation. In its details he saw nothing that withstood reconciliation with the biblical account of creation. In its broader lines it only confirmed American Transcendentalists' faith in man as the ultimate product of creation, and in their own evolutionary theories of history and nature of man. [34] Hedge would have agreed with a later scholar who concluded that the doctrine of evolution did not come to the United States through Darwin but through New England Transcendentalism. [35]

Hedge saw Darwinian evolution as only a theory during

his lifetime, but if it were proven, he believed it would give scientific support to his own concept of evolution. If Darwin's was a linear concept, his was teleological. Otherwise, Hedge believed Darwin had merely given evidence of what lay in his own scheme between God's creation and man's final reconciliation and reunion with God. He did not deny evolution; he asserted that it began with God and would end with Him. Darwin had described part of its observable. earthly process.

What Hedge, as well as other American Transcendentalists and even Asa Gray, the acknowledged American interpreter of Darwin, denied, were the Darwinian concepts of random mutation and natural selection. He denied the idea of survival of the fittest and its implication as to change. His scheme was evolutionary, but like Gray's it was based on an orderly universe and a divine preconceived plan, allowing for purpose and direction, but still dependent on human will. [36] Elements of Hedge's response to Darwin have been seen in earlier materials on the divine element in man, free will, and immortality, but its basis lies in his concept of creation.

Hedge discussed seven popular "cosmogonies" to explain his theory of the creation of the universe. The first involves creation by chance. He called it Epicurean. It assumes an infinite number of "atoms and motions." The atoms, having "mutual affinities," inevitably combine. "As good luck would have it," after numerous failures, the atoms "blunder into right relations and behold a world." Hedge rejected this theory because he felt it presupposed the existence of a Supreme Will that established the "mutual affinities" between atoms and initiates their motion. [37]

The second cosmogony holds for a secondary agent, a creator divorced from the Godhead. Derived during biblical times, this theory serves as an answer to the problem of "impure creation from pure majesty." The secondary agent's personal interest is divorced from God's, and therefore allows for man's seeming inability to quite satisfy "the highest and finest aspirations of the soul." [38] Hedge could not accept a divided Godhead.

The third concept asserts a separation of God and nature. It adds the "essential depravity of matter," including Manicheanism. Attributed to Gnostics of the first three centuries A.D., it differs from the second theory in that God did not will this creation. Matter is interpreted as a punishment for man, that if overcome leads to redemption. In redemption, man will return to his original spiritual state and matter will be reconfined in its original bounds. Hedge saw this theory as establishing yet a third divinity between God and the Devil, or, as he referred to it, "theosophic foolery." [39]

The fourth theory insists that God created from pre-existing "substance without quality." According to the ancient Greeks, this substance had no attributes but extension. This is the nebular hypothesis, and Hedge rejected it because it did not answer the question of who created the pre-existing matter. [40]

Hedge attributed the fifth view to St. Augustine, but not to scripture. It is the Christian view, and it suggests that God created from nothing. This theory attempts to answer Manichean and Gnostic dualism, which, as seen above, "ascribed independent eternity to matter, and made it the source of all natural and moral evil." Hedge did not dismiss this theory outright, but instead extended it to two other formulations: creation out of spirit and ideal creation. [41]

Creation out of spirit is largely based on Leibnitz's "monadology." It relies on the "fulguration," or sparking-off, of monads from God or the divine monad. These monads are of the same substance with God, and can be distinguished from Him only in their possessing a lesser quantity of the same substance. Their creation is therefore an emanation from God. This theory does not account for differences of conscious and unconscious existence, so Hedge rejected it and turned to ideal creation. [42]

Hedge held for the theory of ideal creation. He found creation from nothing inconceivable, even by God. Creation from some foreign material would necessarily be of some "eternal, self-existing, matter, distinct from God, unconscious, inert, merely passive to divine operation." He therefore believed that God's creation must be the "going forth," self-manifestation, or "projection and reflection" of God Himself. The universe is of one and the same substance of God, and as such it has no independent existence. [43]

According to Hedge, God created a universe of spirits. These spirits were emanations of Himself, which remain naturally attracted back toward their original source. This instilled an evolutionary process as the soul strives toward immortality. God's spiritual creation has free will, however, and some of these spirits exercise their free will to "estrange themselves from the Fountain Spirit," and lose their self-possession, or their conscious life. Hedge felt this theory accounts for unconscious being (matter) as well as conscious existence (soul), the difference measured in their relative states of consciousness, which in turn reflects their place in the evolutionary scale. [44]

Hedge asserted that creation was as old as God. If evolution had its point of departure, it therefore began in the eternal past. God, according to Hedge, is all loving and cannot abide in Himself alone or in the solitary contemplation of His own idea. He needed to create an object to rejoice in and bless. If this need and stimulus occurred to Him at any time, it must have occurred to Him in the very beginning of His existence in the eternal past, for His needs were always the same and no antecedent, external influence was possible. [45]

If creation began in the eternal past, however, Hedge nowhere implied that all forms of life originated at that point. Instead, he suggested that the appearance of individual species occurred over the ages, with each appearance representing a higher rung on the evolutionary ladder. Each further-evolved bodily manifestation appropriately reflected the improved state of the soul to vitalize it. Man, of course, stands as the final product of God's creation. He houses the soul which stands ready to return to its source, immortalized.

Hedge reconciled various scriptural details with those elements of the evolutionary process with which he agreed. These included the stories of Adam and Eve, creation in seven days, and God's placing of the soul in man at creation. In the first instance, he simply suggested more than one pair of Adam and Eve at various times and locations. This allowed for variations in race and place of origin. He saw the seven days of creation as possibly representing seven epochs or seven eras of direct family lines. As God placed the conscious soul in man with man's creation, He must have done so when man evolved to that point where he headed all earthly forms. God then placed in him a conscious soul, separating him from brute creation and its particular unconscious life force or soul. Hedge saw this as the true creation of man in the "image of God" as literally represented in the Bible. [46]

Finally, it should be noted that Hedge's view of nature led him to oppose the Calvinistic concept of nature as corrupt or as the source of evil. He, like Emerson, found nature to be of divine origin and a blessing to man. He suggested that from it man learns the sacred significance of beauty. He sees that the world is more than a system of bare necessities and dry utilities, and that civilization is based on love of beauty more than on the grosser satisfactions of life. [47] Only his strong theistic insistence on a transcendent God as the emanating source of nature spared him the pantheist label, something he vigorously rejected, and which was often tied to Emerson. [48]

With Hedge's attitude toward Higher Criticism and science, it is clear that he saw little sense in binding himself to rationally discredited beliefs through blind faith, even if recorded in scripture. He insisted that man is not bound to a "vigorous construction of the letter of the narrative in every case." Such bondage is indefensible and can only lead to "monstrous superstition": [49]

> What is written is open to criticism, for the soul is greater than any scripture, and nothing can be more foreign from the spirit of Christianity than a slavish interpretation of its records. [50]

Yet Hedge did not dismiss the entire written record. Miracles, for example, are within the realm of an omnipotent God, Christ, or even of the divine in man, if fully developed. He opposed the common objection to miracles, which is based on the idea that miracles are contrary to the "order of nature." This he saw as arising from an a priori assumption based on common experience translated into natural law. He argued that natural law exists and that it should be used in the scrutiny of recorded miracles, but he added that all such laws are not known and those that are remain subject to man's faulty observation. If set prematurely, what man holds as laws of nature limits his experience and incorrectly precludes the miraculous. As Hedge noted: "Miracles should not break the law, but we know not if they do." [51] Elsewhere he added:

> I can believe in any miracle which does not actually and demonstrably contravene and nullify ascertained laws, however phenomenally foreign to nature's ordinary course. [52]

Specifically, Hedge asserted that many miracles in the New Testament were indeed possible. They transcended human experience, yet they had not been disproven. By eliminating them man would lose the past, violate historical evidence, and undermine all history. He concluded with the following in reference to those miracles not contradicted by understanding or intuition.

> I believe in them because I believe that spiritual powers are superior to physical, and may hold them in subjection; because I believe that the soul is stronger than material nature, and may command it when it truly commands itself; and because I see in the person of Jesus a greater miracle than any of the works recorded of him. [53]

Hedge identified this as the true area of faith.

Neither did Hedge dismiss the accuracy of other elements of historical Christianity. He believed historical documentation had proven Christ's existence and that he was put to death under the order of Pilate. [54] Further, he asserted that the establishment of the church in the first century, its subsequent universal diffusion, and its beneficent effect on the human condition affirmed the ministry of Jesus, the strong impression of this word and character, his purity of manners and moral greatness, his life of beneficent action, his martyr death, and his manifestation to his disciples after his death (either as subjective experience or objective reality). [55]

Yet Hedge continued to insist that Christianity assures the truth of the facts noted above, and not the facts that prove Christianity. As with miracles, to base the truth of Christianity on the credibility, in every particular, of the Gospel record, to measure the claims of the religion by the strict historic verity of all the narrative of the Christian testament, is to prejudice the Christian cause in the judgment of competent critics. It is to challenge the "cavil and counter demonstration of unbelief." [56]

Hedge concluded that history and Christianity assure the truth of certain facts of historical Christianity, but by no means all the facts affirmed by writers of the New Testament. He asserted that some segments are allegorical, others of myth and legend, while still others are errors of translation or transcription, or yet again, the result of overzealous visionaries. Put another way, he insisted that "the truth of Christianity is not identical and coterminus with the literal truth of its record." [57] Faith in Christianity as divine dispensation, therefore must not depend upon belief in the veritable history of all that is recorded in the Gospel. "Not the historic sense, but the spiritual import; not the facts, but the ideas of the Gospel, are the genuine topics of faith." [58] Hedge wrote:

> The record to me is a literary relic of inestimable value, an original memorial of the dearest and divinest appearance in human form that ever beamed on earthly scenes. . . . But all this is important only as it draws its inspiration from and leads my aspiration to the ideal Christ. [59]

In sum, Hedge, on the one hand, spoke out against blind acquiescence in authority, whether of institutions, men, or written law. Blind faith alone leads to "a pantheon of questionable divinities, a pandemonium of unquestionable fiends, an overshadowing theocracy for civil rule, a dispensation of dark ages without end." [60] Human understanding, as far as it reaches, has provided the "light." "If any prefer the darkness to the light, the darkness they have chosen is their own." [61] What remains is to "seek meaning beyond detail giving honor to the written word without doing unnecessary violence to reason and common sense." [62]

Yet, on the other hand, unrestrained rationalism, Hedge believed, could lead to "unbelief." It needs the "nutriment and impulse" of faith, for "the world of rationalism is ringed and washed by a sea of wonder, navigable only to faith." Without faith, rationalism alone will lead to "a world without a God, bodies without spirits, earth without heaven, a day without a morrow, a way without a goal." [63] As Hedge put it: "Criticism is indispensable, but faith is equally so." There always exist "dark passages in life through which man has to walk with faith." The light of man's understanding in these cases does him no good. [64]

Hedge believed that the only way theology can advance to new and more adequate solutions to its problems, is by the joint action of both factors, understanding and faith, each supplying what the other lacks. Yet both have to be guided and determined by an all-controlling love of truth and by man's divine intuition, which, in the end, is the supreme arbiter. [65]

Once again, divine intuition is the supreme arbiter, because its realm is outside that of the understanding or of written law. Hedge saw intuition as the "fruit of Christ's example," and its function is to keep religion true and pure by eliminating from the code of elemental beliefs the human additions and corruptions of history. If faith is to be established in areas of spiritual truth and moral law, it must be on the personal and continuous revelations of divine intuition. [66] Put another way, Hedge stated:

> Not by reason alone did my soul arrive at Transcendental truth; not from beneath, but from above,--not by intellectual escalade, but by heavenly condescension, . . . the fountain of all our ideas of spiritual things, the well from which reason draws. [67]

Products of divine intuition are the final arbiter because they are direct impulses of God. They are "insusceptible of proof" except for their own "interior light." They transcend demonstration, logic, or experience. In the past, Hedge asserted, Christianity had been injured by its defenders who failed to recognize this. They had futily sought to ground their authority on external proof, rather than a "higher authority." Such proof, he believed, is the equivalent of proving the existence of light: "It proves itself by shining, so moral light shines into the soul that is willing to receive it." Intuitive truths, divinely illuminated truth, cannot be reasoned. [68]

Frederic Hedge favored the use of divine intuition in matters of religion, but he refused to exclude rationalism or historical Christianity. All were God given, and although the first serves as final arbiter, all are to serve the purpose of religion, which remained uppermost in Hedge's mind. Thus he stood in sympathy with, yet in opposition to radical Transcendentalists, orthodox Unitarians, and rationalists, each of whom refused to acknowledge the authority of the others. To Hedge, all these options can be used to reach and unlock the divine spirit within human nature. That spirit lies "deeper than any system," and "stronger than any faith." When reached it quickens the "natural proclivities of the soul" towards its highest "moral fruits." [69]

NOTES

1. Francis Bowen, "Transcendental Theology," Christian Examiner, 30 (1841), 214.

2. Herbert W. Schneider, **A History of American Philosophy** (New York: Columbia University Press, 1963), 242; Joseph L. Blau, **Men and Movements in American Philosophy** (New York: Prentice-Hall, Inc., 1952), 122; Ralph Waldo Emerson, "Nature," in **Anthology of American Literature: Colonial Through Romantic,** ed. George McMichael (New York: Macmillan Publishing Co., Inc., 1980), 997; Sherman Paul, **The Shores of America: Thoreau's Inward Exploration** (Urbana: University of Illinois Press, 1958), vii.

3. William R. Hutchison, **The Transcendentalist Ministers: Church Reform in the New England Renaissance** (New Haven: Yale University Press, 1959), 54.

4. Frederic Henry Hedge, "Natural Religion," Christian Examiner, 52 (1852), 118; Frederic Henry Hedge, **Reason in Religion** (Boston: Walker, Fuller, and Company, 1865), 202, 288.

5. Hedge, **Reason in Religion,** 64; Frederic Henry Hedge, "Antisupernaturalism in the Pulpit, An Address Delivered to the Graduating Class of the Divinity School, Cambridge, July 17, 1864," Christian Examiner, 77 (1864), 15.

6. Hedge, **Reason in Religion,** 306.

7. Hedge, **Reason in Religion,** 65, 66, 303, 308; Hedge, "Antisupernaturalism," 151; Frederic Henry Hedge, "Dr. Furness's Word to Unitarians," Christian Examiner, 68 (1859), 433.

8. Hedge, **Reason in Religion,** 308.

9. Ibid., 65, 278.

10. Ibid., 58.

11. Hedge, "Antisupernaturalism," 148. See also Paul Boller, Jr., **American Transcendentalism, 1830-1860** (New York: G. P. Putnam's Sons, 1974), 24.

12. Hedge, **Reason in Religion**, 264. See also Hutchison, 57, 86; George Ripley, "The Latest Form of Infidelity Examined," in **The Transcendentalists: An Anthology**, ed. Perry Miller (Cambridge, Ma.: Harvard University Press, 1960), 216-217, 225; Joseph Henry Allen, **Sequel to "Our Liberal Movement"** (Boston: Roberts Brothers, 1897), 33; Henry A. Pochmann, **German Culture in America: Philosophical and Literary Influences: 1600-1900** (Madison: The University of Wisconsin Press, 1957), 218.

13. Andrews Norton, "A Discourse on the Latest Form of Infidelity," in Miller, **The Transcendentalists**, 210-211. See also "Of Cousin and the Germans, Princeton Review," Christian Examiner, 28 (1840), 389.

14. Hedge, **Reason in Religion**, 63, 268, 424.

15. Frederic Henry Hedge, **An Address Delivered Before the Graduating Class of the Divinity School in Cambridge, July 15, 1849** (Cambridge, Ma.: John Bartlett, 1849) 23.

16. Hedge, **Reason in Religion**, 267.

17. Hedge, "Antisupernaturalism," 145, 149, 159; Hedge, **Reason in Religion**, 431-432; Frederic Henry Hedge, "Dr. Ferdinand Christian Baur," Christian Examiner, 64 (1858), 11; Frederic Henry Hedge, "Cause of Reason, the Cause of Faith," Christian Examiner, 70 (1861), 223; Pochmann, 29-31.

18. Frederic Henry Hedge, "Tischendorf's Plea for the Genuineness of the Gospels," Christian Examiner, 80 (1866), 304; Frederic Henry Hedge, "The Mythical Element in the New Testament," in his **Ways of the Spirit and Other Essays** (Boston: Roberts Brothers, 1877), 316.

19. Hedge, "Cause of Reason," 218.

20. Hedge, "The Mythical Element," 317; Hedge, "Tischendorf's Plea," 304; Hedge, "Dr. Ferdinand Christian Baur," 34.

21. Hedge, "The Mythical Element," 340.

22. Hedge, "Antisupernaturalism," 156; Pochmann, 212.

23. Hedge, "Dr. Ferdinand Christian Baur," 38-39.

24. Hedge, **Divinity School Address**, 24; Hedge, "The Mythical Element," 316.

25. Pochmann, 246; Alexander Kearn, "The Rise of Transcendentalism, 1815-1860," in **Transitions in American Literary History**, ed. Harry H. Clark (New York: Octagon Books, Inc., 1967), 283.

26. Frederic Henry Hedge, "The Religion of the Present," Christian Examiner, 67 (1859), 50; Frederic Henry Hedge, "Remarks Made at the Thirty-Sixth Anniversary Meeting of the American Unitarian Association, May 24, 1861," The Monthly Journal of the American Unitarian Association, 2, No. 7/8 (1861), 318-319. See also Ronald Vale Wells, **Three Christian Transcendentalists: James Marsh, Caleb Sprague Henry, Frederic Henry Hedge** (1943; rpt. New York: Octagon Books, 1972), 125.

27. Hedge, "Cause of Reason," 219; Frederic Henry Hedge, "The Nineteenth Century," Christian Examiner, 48 (1850), 375.

28. Frederic Henry Hedge, **Theological Progress During the Last Half Century** (Providence: Knowles, Anthony and Co., 1878), 63; Frederic Henry Hedge, "The Way of Religion," in his **Ways of the Spirit**, 56; Frederic Henry Hedge, "The Way of Historic Atonement," in his **Ways of the Spirit**, 114; Frederic Henry Hedge, "The Theism of Reason and the Theism of Faith," in his **Martin Luther and Other Essays** (Boston: Roberts Brothers, 1888), 306-310; Frederic Henry Hedge, "Martin Luther," in his **Martin Luther**, 36; Hedge, "Cause of Reason," 219; Frederic Henry Hedge, "Romanism and Its Worship," Christian Examiner, 56 (1854), 243; Frederic Henry Hedge, "Science and Faith," in his **Martin Luther**, 181-183.

29. Hedge, "Cause of Reason," 219.

30. Pochmann, 174-175.

31. Frederic Henry Hedge, "The Destinies of Ecclesiastical Religion," Christian Examiner, 82 (1867), 7.

32. Hedge, "Historic Atonement," 114-117; Hedge, **Reason in Religion**, 36-38, 45-47, 95; Hedge, "The Theism of Reason," 308; Hedge, **Divinity School Address**, 19; Hedge, "Antisupernaturalism," 155; Frederic Henry Hedge, "Science and Faith," in his **Martin Luther**, 177-179; Frederic Henry Hedge, "Remarks, Made at the Thirty-Eighth Anniversary Meeting of the American Unitarian Association," The Monthly Journal of the American Unitarian Association, 4, No. 7/8 (1863), 319; Hedge, "Remarks, Made at the Thirty-Sixth Anniversary Meeting of the American Unitarian Association," 318-319; Emerson, "Nature," 998; Herbert Hovenkamp, **Science and Religion in America, 1800-1860** (Philadelphia: University of Pennsylvania Press, 1978), 216. See also James Loewenberg, "Darwin Comes to America, 1859-1900," Mississippi Valley Historical Review, 28 (1941), 339-368.

33. Emerson, "Nature," 998.

34. Frederic Henry Hedge, "The Brute Creation," in his **The Primeval World of Hebrew Tradition** (Boston: Roberts Brothers, 1870), 72; Frederic Henry Hedge, "Nine Hundred and Sixty-Nine Years," in his **Primeval World**, 145; Hedge, **Reason in Religion**, 47, 212; Frederic Henry Hedge, "Science and Faith," in his **Martin Luther**, 181-183; Frederic William Conner, **Cosmic Optimism: A Study of the Interpretation of Evolution by American Poets from Emerson to Robinson** (Gainesville: University of Florida Press, 1949), 2.

35. Morris R. Cohen, **American Thought: A Critical Sketch** (Glencoe, Il.: The Free Press, 1954), 69.

36. Frederic Henry Hedge, "Man in the Image of God," in his **Primeval World**, 25-26; Richard Hofstadter, **Social Darwinism in American Thought** (New York: George Braziller, Inc., 1965), 18; William H. Lyon, **Frederic Henry Hedge: Seventh Minister of the First Parish in Brookline, 1856-1872** (Brookline, Ma.: First Parish in Brookline, 1906), 335; Frederic Henry Hedge, "Introduction," in his **Atheism in Philosophy and Other Essays** (Boston: Roberts Brothers, 1884), 3.

37. Frederic Henry Hedge, "On the Origin of Things," in his **Ways of the Spirit**, 192.

38. Ibid., 193.

39. Ibid.

40. Ibid., 195.

41. Ibid., 200.

42. Ibid.

43. Frederic Henry Hedge, "The World a Divine Creation," in his **Primeval World**, 15-16.

44. Hedge, "Origin of Things," 189, 200.

45. Hedge, "The World a Divine Creation," 17-18.

46. Hedge, "Man in the Image of God," 27, 32, 34; Frederic Henry Hedge, "Man in Paradise," in his **Primeval World**, 46, 48.

47. Frederic Henry Hedge, "The Lesson of Flowers," in his **Sermons** (Boston: Roberts Brothers, 1891), 37; Emerson, "Nature," 997-1024.

48. Hedge, "The World a Divine Creation," 17-18; Boller, 67; Vivian C. Hopkins, **Spires of Form: A Study of Emerson's Aesthetic Theory** (New York: Russell and Russell, 1965), 61.

49. Hedge, "Cause of Reason," 210-215; Hedge, **Reason in Religion**, 201.

50. Hedge, **Reason in Religion**, 279.

51. Hedge, **Reason in Religion**, 62-63, 271-272; Hedge, "The Mythical Element," 324; Hedge, "Antisupernaturalism," 149.

52. Hedge, "The Mythical Element," 324.

53. Hedge, **Reason in Religion,** 278-279.

54. Hedge, "The Mythical Element," 317.

55. Hedge, "The Mythical Element," 317-318; Frederic Henry Hedge, "Emerson's Writings," Christian Examiner, 38 (1845), 95.

56. Hedge, "The Mythical Element," 318.

57. Ibid.

58. Hedge, "The Mythical Element," 318, 333; Hedge, **Divinity School Address,** 25-26.

59. Hedge, "The Mythical Element," 335.

60. Hedge, "Cause of Reason," 215; Hedge, **Reason in Religion,** 198; Allen, **Sequel to "Our Liberal Movement,"** 54-56; Hedge, "Theism of Reason," 31-32.

61. Hedge, **Reason in Religion,** 214; Hedge, "Cause of Reason," 214.

62. Hedge, **Reason in Religion,** 198, 210, 279; Hedge, "Cause of Reason," 208, 211, 223; Hedge, "Theism of Reason," 309; Joseph Henry Allen, **Our Liberal Movement in Theology: Chiefly as Shown in Recollections of the History of Unitarianism in New England** (Boston: Roberts Brothers, 1892), 17.

63. Hedge, "Cause of Reason," 208, 215; Hedge, "Introduction," 1; Hedge, **Divinity School Address,** 18-19; Hedge, "Remarks, Made at the Thirty-Eighth Anniversary of the American Unitarian Association," 320; Frederic Henry Hedge, "The Universal and the Special in Christianity," in **Unitarian Affirmations: Seven Discourses Given in Washington, D.C. by Unitarian Ministers** (Boston: American Unitarian Association, 1890), 6.

64. Hedge, **Reason in Religion,** 205; Hedge, "Theism of Religion," 315; Hedge, "Antisupernaturalism," 155.

65. Hedge, "Antisupernaturalism," 159; Hedge, **Reason in Religion,** 203-204, 263-264; Hovenkamp, 153-154.

66. Hedge, "Cause of Reason," 206, 215; Hedge, **Reason in Religion,** 207; Frederic Henry Hedge, "The Spirit's Rest," in his **Sermons,** 240; Wells, 128-129.

67. Hedge, "Cause of Reason," 215. See also Boller, 202.

68. Hedge, **Reason in Religion,** 276-277.

69. Hedge, "The Two Religions," in his **Ways of the Spirit,** 314-315; Hedge, "Historic Atonement," 119; Frederic Henry Hedge, "Bellow's Suspense of Faith," Christian Examiner, 67 (1859), 287.

Chapter Eight

ECUMENICITY AND ITS LIMITS

George H. Williams pointed out that Frederic Henry Hedge may have been the first American Christian to use the word "ecumenical" in what Williams regarded as the modern sense of "a regathering of Christendom." [1] Whether or not this is the case, it is certain that Hedge was a leading nineteenth century ecumenic, whose ideas on the subject were considered well into the twentieth century. He saw the goal of Christianity as a "Broad Church" or as "a gathering of all men through the universal divine presence." [2] This, he believed, would be the natural end of Christianity.

He believed Christ's name had the power to organize history, "to thread the nations and the ages on the string of an idea, and to bind them in ecumenical relations to the throne of God." [3] The union of all churches, true catholicity under "one federal Head who is invisible," however, would be realized only through the influence of some body of Christians who would "consistently maintain the catholic ground, and act out, in all senses and bearings, the catholic spirit." This body, he believed, would be Unitarians. [4]

Hedge was well aware of the historical process of sectarianism that followed the Reformation and that appeared to deny any sense of reunion. Protestantism in its attempt to deny existent beliefs in earthly authority and human limitations had spawned a centrifugal force fracturing all of Christendom. He believed that force had "assured a hue of the same word to all," but it had also denied the full property of that faith to any one denomination. [5] He regretted the resultant loss of uniformity and solidarity, including evangelical "uncharitableness," which sought denominational dominance rather than truth, but he saw its necessity for Christianity to encompass diverse cultures, thought, and temper. Moreover he insisted that all Christian denominations had remained faithful to the essential role of Christ, and from that point "many paths lead to the same goal." [6]

Finally, Hedge held that there was reason to believe that the centrifugal force of separation had ceased and that "in the order of the spirit's progressive life . . . centripetal affection [would] again prevail." [7] As he put it:

> There is a spirit at work in the affairs of men, mightier than all ecclesiastical establishments and sectarian combinations. The old laws are everywhere disappearing, old sects are breaking up. The tide of humanity is sweeping away their petty barriers, and bearing us and our institutions to a higher mark and a better day. [8]

Hedge saw Unitarianism as the latest and "penultimate development" in Christianity, as well as the catalyst to effect universality in the Pauline sense. [9] He, as William Ellery Channing before him, hoped the very name would come to signify the "unity of churches in spirit." [10] To do so Unitarians would have to forego any expectation of, or desire for, denominational as well as doctrinal affirmation or rejection. This would be done not out of indifference but out of faith in a future theological synthesis. Unitarianism would, instead, plant its principle of liberality, not to gather converts for Unitarianism, but to modify their communions by its example. In this way Unitarians would see "their principles extend more widely than their name," and they would represent, "in spirit and doctrine, a truly catholic church, a church of scope so ample as to embrace all faiths and all souls." Hedge thus sought to avoid "self-defeating sectarianism," but he spurned "spurious universality" as well. [11]

Hedge believed that the Broad Church would be realized through the continued unfolding of the divine presence in man. It would exist when the divine nature of man had been so fully developed that the bonds of traditional institutions would no longer be needed. But, until that state existed, institutions would necessarily remain and be means to that end.

Because Hedge considered Christianity as that institution which was effecting the kind of change described above, he defended it against its opponents. Christianity had given believing souls "peace in its doctrine and salvation in its cross," as well as a "guide in life and a stay in death." It had "molded humankind, and changed the fact of the world," and he expected this course of development to continue. Providence would not introduce Christianity into the world and bring it to this point without committing itself to its continued growth and final end. [12]

Hedge explained that "action of the Holy Spirit was the fundamental postulate, the organic hypothesis of Christian church history." It directed the order of events so that nothing was fortuitous. It was "the instrument employed," and the result was necessary. He concluded that although history seems capricious, it was the "rational idea of Divine revelation." Such purpose cannot be demonstrated. It is a pure intuitive hypothesis, which only the connection of all things can verify, but he felt belief in it is necessary. [13]

Belief in the purpose of historic Christianity rationalizes "the portents and enormities of history," bringing them into harmony with an intelligible, conceivable order of the universe. Hedge believed that to deny historic Christianity or the divine order is to "suppose Christ to be defeated by Anti-Christ." Revelation would be supposed a failure and the word of God "returning unto Him void, not having accomplished the thing which He pleased, not prospered in that whereunto He sent it." The idea of historical and continuous divine revelation, which Hedge shared in part with orthodox and Transcendentalist Unitarians, necessitates the corollary of providential oversight of that revelation, of order in historical development, and of continuous development for the future. [14]

From the above it is clear that Hedge's concept of the Broad Church was based on the continued unfolding of divine inspiration through the progressive minds of Christianity. Further, those who hold this balance for the future are to remain within the church. The free functioning of divine intuition is essential, but the blessings of ecclesiastical continuity and its contraints are not to be forgotten. This leads us to his position in the movement toward doctrinal identification within Unitarianism in the late 1860s. [15]

The ostensible purpose of the doctrinal movement in Unitarianism in the 1860s grew out of the expected surge in religiosity following the Civil War. Growth in American Unitarianism had remained static in the two decades preceding the war, but some Unitarians felt that if the denomination's various independent congregations could be joined in a postwar missionary front it could forward "the religion of free America." Hedge agreed with this. There were, however, a sizable number of those within Unitarianism who also felt the church needed greater organization, with or without the missionary objective, to ward off what they perceived as further decay and degeneration resulting from its laxity. [16]

At annual meetings of the American Unitarian Association in 1863, 1864, and 1865, the National Conference of Unitarian Churches was formed and proposals were made for the Conference's first meeting at Syracuse in 1866. A general statement of purpose was agreed upon, but it was to be reconsidered for final adoption at Syracuse. Henry Bellows, who was responsible for the original statement, believed it contained little doctrine and was not intended to exclude anyone within the widest definition of Christianity. Rather he saw it as a point of definition for Unitarianism, with which Unitarians could identify. He believed it would eliminate intradenominational confusion and "finger pointing," and end what he saw as a "state of degeneration." [17] Radical Unitarians, however, disagreed.

By 1865, Hedge's liberal views on doctrinal subscription were well established. In 1861 he wrote:

> We do not expect or desire complete uniformity of administration and rite, or even of doctrinal type. There must always be differences of administration, of worship, and of doctrine. Catholicism does not consist of uniformity of articles, but in unity of spirit,--not in a common exposition, but a common confession and mutual good will . . . we may hope for so much of that spirit as shall serve to secure a full recognition of the Christian name for all who honestly claim it, and a friendly co-operation of Christians of every type for practical Christian ends. [18]

Elsewhere Hedge insisted that "God had not willed that men think alike." It was, therefore, futile, if not destructive, to seek a uniform faith. As a result, he asked Unitarians to

> embody a Christianity so dissolute of dogma, and at the same time, of moral quality so stringent, as to hold all creeds in solution, and by a generous abandonment, on our part, of all doctrinal defenses and theological ramparts, to conquer, if possible, an antisectarian peace. [19]

Hedge urged this even though he knew lack of creedal unity weakened ecclesiastical consciousness and strength and hindered the extension of the Unitarian communion. Creeds, he believed, were of theology, and theology was the offspring, not the mainspring, of religion. Creeds were of the understanding, not of the heart or spirit. [20]

This is not to say that Hedge felt all doctrines were equally true. They needed to be scrutinized. Neither does it deny that he considered some form of demonstration of polity, if even in its broadest form, or that he did not have a limit to his universalism. At one point, nearly ten years before the Syracuse controversy, he wrote to Bellows suggesting that he would like "some kind of demonstration" by which it would appear that a large and respectable portion of the Unitarian body was "not disposed to relinquish the results of fifty years of struggle," and that would "repudiate any attempt to coalesce with orthodoxy on a doctrinal basis." [21]

Later that year Hedge wrote to Bellows again and continued to insist that the future of Unitarianism lay in "radical complexion" or "ultra-liberals" of the Unitarian ministry under age forty, such as Octavius B. Frothingham. [22] Yet in both letters, and elsewhere, he reneged on pursuing any such demonstration further. Any association based on a "regular constitution," for example, would lead to "exclusiveness," "iniquities," "oppression," and "violence to humanity and truth." [23] Yet he was already hinting that a "crisis" might call for such an organization. In such case, he urged that lines be drawn under the "principle of wide hospitality" with only the "Christian confession" as its limit. [24]

By 1865, Hedge had shifted his consideration of doctrinal subscription from fear of liberal backsliding to that of radical dissolution. In **Reason in Religion**, generally considered to be the major statement on liberal religion of the period, Hedge noted the limits within which Unitarianism must function. Once again he insisted that Christianity be of the spiritual unfolding established by St. Paul, and he quoted St. Paul, that empty formality according to the letter of the law could kill religion. [25] This clearly established Hedge's belief in the Christian Church as a spiritual society. But he also made his point that the church was associated for spiritual ends and that it needed "a mutual understanding as to aim and action." Agreement on this point was essential to the church's very being. He warned that "if all propositions were allowed, and if everyone was allowed to inscribe his own form of faith," Christianity

> would soon become extinct, overlaid with speculations of all who incline to speculate, with the vision of all who dream . . . that harlot of every reformer who might wish to dally with her . . . a pantheon for all divinities . . . pandemonium for every abortion of the human mind. [26]

With this perspective, Hedge arrived at the Syracuse Convention in 1866.

Specifically, Hedge opposed two changes, offered by the Reverend Francis Abbott, in the constitution proposed at the A.U.A. convention in 1865. The constitution, worded by Henry Bellows, had been affirmatively voted by a large majority, but, final adoption was delayed until 1866. Abbott, on behalf of those who shortly organized the Free Religious Association, urged that the phrase "Lordship of Christ" be eliminated from the constitution and the title "National Conference of Unitarian Churches" be changed to the "National Conference of Unitarian and Independent Churches." Abbott explained that this would commit the National conference to "perfect freedom of thought" and the nonexclusion of anyone who was in "general sympathy" with their "purposes and practical aims," yet could not agree to the exalted position established for Christ. Abbott and those he represented preferred to see Christ as "among the leaders of humanity." Hedge voted with the two-thirds majority that defeated the first proposal and adopted the compromise title "National Conference of Unitarian and other Christian Churches." He was seen as a reconciler at this meeting, but in his mind freedom of religion was not the issue as much as was the Christian basis of Unitarianism. [**27**]

Clearly, Hedge had drawn the line. He was one of the most liberal and broad minded ministers at the Syracuse Convention. He had hoped difficulties could be resolved without resorting to doctrinal statements. Following the Syracuse Convention, he voted for the adoption of progressively more liberal measures and against attempts to more closely define the National Conference's statement of faith. But he could not deny what he saw as the "only test of apostleship and salvation for mankind" that Christ demanded, belief in one God and in Jesus Christ as His son. [**28**] Like others who had voted in the negative, he saw Abbott's proposal as possibly being "construed" as "hauling down the Christian flag." [**29**] Hedge had voted for the same stand when the A.U.A. had considered it in 1853, and there is no evidence that he every reconsidered the position. Although he regretted the loss of many whom he earlier considered to represent the future of Unitarianism, he insisted that any minister who denied the tenet should be excluded from the Unitarian pulpit. [**30**] Emerson's negation of this Unitarian idea, for example, was the basis upon which Hedge refused to invite Emerson to enter his pulpit in Bangor, when his friend visited him there. He also felt that Theodore Parker's denial of this point placed him outside the Christian ministry. [**31**]

Hedge explained his position on Emerson in an article for the Christian Examiner in 1845. He found Emerson not to be a Christian "in the usual and distinctive sense of the term," because he failed to allow for the "Lordship of Christ." Hedge wrote that Emerson did not believe in "a special and miraculous revelation" and that he held Christ to be "a mere teacher of moral and religious truths--a reformer, not distinguished from other teachers and reformers, except by the greater number of followers that have chanced to rank under his name, and longer continuance and wider spread of his doctrine and influence in the world." He concluded that "on this point we are at issue with him, and the difference between us is heaven-wide." [**32**]

It should be noted that although Hedge insisted on keeping

Unitarianism within the Christian fold, as defined by the belief in the Lordship of Christ, he did not believe that such a "confession" should "bound" Unitarians' religious sympathies. As he put it, "All religions that devoutly aspire, all religions that diligently labor, all religions that minister to human weal, deserve our sympathy and claim our respect." But he continued to insist that "Christianity is more than a religion; it is history's highway, humanity's thoroughfare. The paths that diverge from it will return to it again, or lose themselves in nothingness." [33]

Finally, Hedge's lingering denominationalism did not contradict his ecumenicity. Instead, his ecumenicity grew out of what he saw as the purpose of denominations. If, as he believed, all churches were created by God, through His revelation in man's mind, an individual could be confident in choosing the denomination that best fits his temperament. He affirmed, then, his obligation to perfect that portion of the infinite truth that his denomination was given, to unfold it, and to contribute it to Christianity as a whole, in its seeking as the universal faith. [34] Unitarianism needed a Christian definition, if it was to have the organic strength it needed to play that part or even to survive. [35]

The Syracuse affair points up the dualism of Hedge's approach to the Broad Church. The Broad Church was dependent on the human spirit and the unleashing of the divine element, divine intuition, within man. It would be achieved, however, within the context of ecclesiastical continuity. Hedge wrote that "progress consists in development. And development supposes instead of an abrupt renunciation of the old, an unbroken and organic connection with it. Who would build permanently must build on the past." [36]

Hedge believed that the Free Religionists had failed to see the ecclesiastical continuity of history. Further, he insisted that they had overlooked the point that "only a new church can supplant the old." He explained that any new church destined to endure "must be the offspring of the past" and "related to the past by natural descent." Moreover, any new church would not be "an association of thinkers and critics . . . planting themselves on abstract theism." Such associations had existed at various times and places, but they had never succeeded in "planting a church or in supplanting one." [37]

To understand Hedge's concepts of the unfolding divine spirit and ecclesiastical continuity is to understand his basic Christian Transcendental impulse and his method of history. These concepts, in turn, were the key to his faith in the future invisible church made visible, or the Broad Church. The Broad Church, he believed, will be the product of an evolutionary process mating the undeniable forces of human progress, time, and place.

It will be based on a "religion free as human thought, where the present predominates over the past, and the future over the present," and in which "vision outruns tradition." [38] But Hedge warned:

> Mankind does not consciously and willfully foreshape their own future. . . . History is not the product of human foresight, but divine ordination, education. . . . We are under tutelage, one school master after another having charge of the race for a season, and, in fulness of time, delivering up his charge to the next. The school master for the time being is not an institution, but an idea, a system of ideas, to which the institutions of the time owe their birth. . . . We cannot escape it. The individual may think he is rid of it, but his fancied emancipation is only the flight of the aëronaut, floating above the earth in a balloon but still subject to gravity. [39]

Hedge's Broad Church will be in the Pauline sense a communion of saints drawn by the power of the Holy Spirit, in a manner similar to that operating within the individual. [40] The church that results will bring "the embodiment of a spiritual force, which, sallying from the heart of God (and operating in the hearts of all men), creates a vortex in human society that compels the kingdoms, compels the aeons, in its conquering wake, and tracks its way through the world with a shining psychopomp of saintly souls." [41] As the spirit goes forth from God, calling forth a response from the soul, the Broad Church will draw upon this response in the souls of all men in the godward relation. Christ promised such a church and served as "the wisdom and the power" to effect it. [42]

According to Hedge, the growth of the divine impulse in man, or divine education, is ineradicable. It flows continuously to man in varying dispensations. If it sometimes is "caught in the doldrums of stagnant sacerdotalism," it is never lost, never immovably fixed. It flows from one generation and civilization to another. It is identical with none, but it is generally identified with one group or another at each stage of its course. At that time, Hedge felt it was identified with Christianity, the chief minister of human progress for this millenium. [43]

Hedge's concept of the evolution of a universal church involves a continued resolution of the contradiction of the Christian ages through the dialectic of old and new, institution and vision, conservatism and liberalism. Further, it presupposes a contradiction to the commonly held glorification of the Apostolic Age and to the consequent belief that every subsequent age is a wider departure from the truth, establishing a steady progress in corruption. He believed quite the opposite. [44]

Hedge recalled the writings of Abbot Joachim of Floris, a twelfth century mystic. Joachim divided the history of the world into three ages of dispensation from God, corresponding to the three persons of the trinity, which Hedge believed only in the symbolic sense of the three aspects of God, not as three persons. [45]

Joachim's first age was that of God the Father. It was of the dispensation of law and relied on bondage and fear. It was recorded in the Old Testament. The second age was of Christ, revealed in the New Testament. It was an age of instruction and dispensation of doctrine and discipline, but also of freedom. It began with Christ and remained as Hedge's age. [46]

Joachim's third age would be of the Holy Ghost and of the future. It would be an age of knowledge and spiritual emancipation, as well as a time of dispensation of liberty and love, based on the revelation and embodiment of the Holy Spirit in rational minds. It would be the end of all God's doing and the final revelation of all of God's law in Hedge's Broad Church. [47]

Specifically, Hedge believed that the Broad Church will evolve through two stages: Intradenominational ecumenicity and interdenominational ecumenicity. The first will fulfill the prophecy of temporal and spiritual unity in the future church as seen in Luke 13:29: "And men will come from east and west, and from north and south, and sit at table in the kingdom of God." In this case the points of the compass are not only geographical directions or global sections, but the Christian qualities dominant in those areas. The east represents stability and conservatism; the west, mobility and progress; the north, internal activity or the inner life, idealism and mysticism; and the south, exterior productiveness, ritualism, symbolism, and ecclesiastical organization. [48]

Hedge insisted that the Broad Church will have its east, or its propensity for steadfastness and fixity, especially as to the figure of Christ: "God's Christ, and our Christ, the same yesterday, today, and forever, the spiritual sun of our human world." The idea of Christ, not as moral teacher or philosopher, but as the son of God, is fundamental and indispensable, and it lies ineradicably in the hearts of men. As noted earlier, Hedge believed it to be the binder in "ecumenical relations to the throne of God." [49]

Those concepts necessarily connected with the idea of Christ will also be preserved through the influence of the east. These include belief in man's nature, calling, and destiny, as well as reconciliation and atonement in Christ. Hedge believed that although these concepts are not identical with all denominations, they underlie all Christian dogma. Further, they are original constituents of the Gospel, and, thus, necessary elements in a true Christian church. Finally, they will serve as guides for those "whose dominant sense has no intuitions of its own," and as well for those whose minds have been awakened, but remain inconstant. [50]

From the west the Broad Church will gain its forward-looking perspective. The west will add sufficient flexibility in doctrine and discipline to allow growth beyond its immutable truths. It will challenge conservatism with examination, reason, and speculation, for Hedge believed that Christianity is not an established system of views, institutions, and immutable forms, but a "flowing demonstration of the spirit in such forms of thought, aspects, and embodiment as each successive age requires, or is fittest to comprehend and to profit by . . . a progressive revelation of God in Christ." [51]

The northern element of the church, represented by Emmanuel Swedenborg and Jacob Boehme, offered Hedge his mystical element. He quickly added that Puritanism had no such affinity. Mysticism, to Hedge, is a "feeling after God," without which the church would be in danger of losing its "consciousness of God." "God in Christ" would no longer be its "home, government, and head." He used Catholicism "with Rome for its heaven and a pope for its God," as an example of a church resistant to its northern influence. [52]

Hedge's southern perspective adds "an organic body" and "articulated forms." It began with the establishment of a religious commonwealth immediately following the withdrawal of Jesus from his followers. This religious commonwealth allowed the Holy Spirit, which was too pure or ethereal without an organized social power or visible church, to take form, to be perpetuated, and to grow from one generation to the next. Without it the Broad Church, based upon the word of God, can never be realized. It is the basis of Hedge's ecclesiastical organization and continuity, and Hedge recognized its existence as a positive quality of Roman Catholicism. [53]

The second stage of Hedge's scheme for his Broad Church, "interdenominational work in practical Christianity," is based on cooperative denominational work in practical Christianity. He believed this stage could begin in his lifetime and that it would focus on "life and work." Christianity, to Hedge, is "a practice, not a speculation," and "practical reform, the regeneration of society in the image of Christ, the putting away of sin and social evil from the world, is its end, as well as its center or nucleus of Christian union." As he put it: "The test of a true spirit is its productiveness." [54]

Hedge's concept of practical Christianity became the basis of his social gospel. Although his social gospel will be discussed later, suffice here to say it was based on the doctrine of atonement, which was closely tied to that of incarnation. [55] Christ is a manifestation of the union of the human and the divine, or a divine humanity. This infers a call to man to aspire to that divine humanity and to remove all social evils and abuses, "in a word, reform, the regeneration of society in the Christian image." All Christians, Hedge believed, could unite in this, and in fact, must, "if ever the ends for which Christ lived and died are to be accomplished on earth." [56]

As will be seen, Hedge saw interdenominational Christianity, based upon the concept of the social gospel, as the one distinct contribution of the American character to Christianity and its evolution toward universality. It is the practical, social, and humane perspective rather than the theological. Character is more important than creed. [57] This assures the Broad Church's "gracious, healthful, and humane" character, as it arises from a Christianity which will be "eyes to the blind, glad tidings to the poor, and resurrection to the dead, helping, healing, saving, sin-remitting, wonder-working." [58]

In sum, the final realizaiton of Hedge's Broad Church, the invisible church made visible, lies in fully realized man in his divine nature, the efficacy of Christ's atonement, and in the union of all such men on earth. It will be the culmination of the progressive earthly life in the personal and collective sense. It will involve the joining of the spiritual and temporal in a perfect state on earth:

> Atonement will not be complete until the distinction of sacred and profane, temporal and spiritual, business and religion, church and world, is practically neutralized; until these dislocations of human nature are healed, these several parts and processes atoned in one undivided and absolute life. [59]

The Broad Church will be joined in what Hedge defined as man's entrance into "heaven." It will be the realization of the heavenly kingdom on earth with perfected man, laboring in the spirit of Christ. [60] Further, it will be a time of true and meaningful ecumenicity with one priesthood of the wise and good, and one standard of law, namely the spirit and life of Christ. All men will be one in Christ and one with God in a church combining the greatest liberality with the greatest union. [61]

NOTES

1. George H. Williams, **Rethinking the Unitarian Relationship with Protestantism: An Examination of the Thought of Frederic Henry Hedge** (Boston: The Beacon Press, 1949), 3.

2. William R. Hutchison, **The Transcendentalist Ministers: Church Reform in the New England Renaissance** (New Haven: Yale University Press, 1959), 16; Frederic Henry Hedge, "The Churches and the Church," Christian Examiner, 41 (1846), 202; William H. Lyon, **Frederic Henry Hedge: Seventh Minister of the First Parish in Brookline, 1856-1872** (Brookline, Ma.: First Parish in Brookline, 1906), 17.

3. Frederic Henry Hedge, "The Broad Church," Christian Examiner, 69 (1860), 59.

4. Frederic Henry Hedge, **An Address Delivered Before the Graduating Class of the Divinity School in Cambridge, July 15, 1849** (Cambridge, Ma.: John Bartlett, 1849), 16; Howard N. Brown, **Frederic Henry Hedge, A Memorial Discourse** (Boston: George H. Ellis, 1891), 3; George E. Ellis, "Old Faith and New Knowledge," Christian Examiner, 69 (1860), 221.

5. Frederic Henry Hedge, **Christianity Confined to No Sect** (Bangor, Me.: Samuel S. Smith, 1844), 7; Hedge, "The Churches and the Church," 202; Hedge, **Divinity School Address**, 12, 14.

6. Frederic Henry Hedge, "The Universal and the Special in Christianity," in **Unitarian Affirmations: Seven Discourses Given in Washington, D.C. by Unitarian Ministers** (Boston: American Unitarian Association, 1890), 2; Frederic Henry Hedge, **Theological Progress During the Last Half Century** (Providence: Knowles, Anthony and Co., 1878), 71; Frederic Henry Hedge, **Reason in Religion** (Boston: Walker, Fuller and Company, 1865), 427; Hedge, **Divinity School Address**, 5; Frederic Henry Hedge, **On the Use of the Word Evangelical** (Providence: Knowles, Anthony and Co., 1854), 4-5.

7. Frederic Henry Hedge, "Ecclesiastical Christendom," Christian Examiner, 51 (1851), 130; Hedge, **Reason in Religion**, 220; Frederic Henry Hedge, "Cause of Reason, the Cause of Faith," Christian Examiner, 70 (1861), 225.

8. Hedge, "The Churches and the Church," 204.

9. Hedge believed St. Paul was the source of Christian universalism. Hutchison, 142; Hedge, "The Universal and the Special," 2; Frederic Henry Hedge, "The Two Religions," in his **Ways of the Spirit and Other Essays** (Boston: Roberts Brothers, 1877), 293.

10. William Ellery Channing, "Spiritual Freedom," in his **The Works of William Ellery Channing** (New York: Burt Franklin, 1970), 179.

11. Hedge, **Divinity School Address,** 12-16; Hedge, **Theological Progress,** 63; Frederic Henry Hedge, "Remarks, Made at the Thirty-Eighth Anniversary Meeting of the American Unitarian Association," The Monthly Journal of the American Unitarian Association, 4, No. 7/8 (1863), 317-323; Ronald Vale Wells, **Three Christian Transcendentalists: James Marsh, Caleb Sprague Henry, Frederic Henry Hedge** (1943; rpt. New York: Octagon Books, 1972), 134; Frederic Henry Hedge, **A Sermon on the Character and Ministry of the Late Reverend William Ellery Channing** (Bangor, Me.: Samuel S. Smith, 1842), 12; Frederic Henry Hedge, "The Religion of the Present," Christian Examiner, 67 (1859), 59.

12. Hedge, **Divinity School Address,** 8, 26; Frederic Henry Hedge, "The Way of Historic Christianity," in his **Ways of the Spirit,** 94.

13. Hedge, "Historic Christianity," 70; Hedge, **Divinity School Address,** 7.

14. Hedge, "Historic Christianity," 71, 73; Hedge, **Reason in Religion,** 341.

15. Hutchison, 139.

16. George Willis Cooke, **Unitarianism in America: A History of Its Origin and Development** (Boston: American Unitarian Association, 1902), 185; Joseph Henry Allen and Richard Eddy, **A History of the Unitarians and Universalists in the United States** (New York: The Christian Literature Co., 1894), 225-226; Edward Everett Hale, "The National Conference of Unitarian Churches," Christian Examiner, 16 (1865), 413; "National Unitarian Convention," The Monthly Journal of the American Unitarian Association, 6, No. 5 (1865), 210; Stow Persons, **Free Religion: An American Faith** (Boston: Beacon Press, 1963), 12; Frederic Henry Hedge, Letter to Henry W. Bellows, 3 May 1856, Bellows Collection, Massachusetts Historical Society, Boston, Massachusetts; Henry W. Bellows, Letter to Edward Everett Hale, 31 December 1864, Bellows Collection, Massachusetts Historical Society, Boston, Massachusetts; Frederic Henry Hedge, Letter to Reverend Charles Lowe, 24 March 1865, Frederic Henry Hedge Collection, Andover-Harvard Theological Library, Cambridge, Massachusetts; Frederic Henry Hedge, Letter to Reverend Charles Lowe, 26 January 1866, Frederic Henry Hedge Collection, Andover-Harvard Theological Library, Cambridge, Massachusetts; Frederic Henry Hedge, Letter to G. C. Smith, 5 September 1867, Frederic Henry Hedge Collection, Andover-Harvard Theological Library, Cambridge, Massachusetts.

17. Hedge, Letter to Bellows, 3 May 1856; Bellows, Letter to Hale, 31 December 1864.

18. Hedge, "Cause of Reason," 225.

19. Hedge, **Divinity School Address,** 12, 26-27; Hedge, **Christianity Confined to No Sect,** 12; Wells, 139.

20. Hedge, "Two Religions," 300-302.

21. Ironically, in 1866, Hedge opposed Frothingham and many of the others listed in this letter as his "fellow laborers in the cause," because he believed they had gone too far in becoming Free Religionists. Hedge, Letter to Bellows, 3 May 1856. See also Hedge, **Divinity School Address**, 10; Hedge, **Christianity Confined to No Sect**, 11.

22. Hedge, Letter to Bellows, 3 May 1856.

23. Hedge, Letter to Bellows, 3 May 1856; Frederic Henry Hedge, "Remarks, Made at the Thirty-Fifth Anniversary Meeting of the American Unitarian Association," The Monthly Journal of the American Unitarian Association, 1, No. 7 (1860), 303-304.

24. Hedge, "Remarks, Thirty-Fifth Anniversary Meeting," 303-304; Frederic Henry Hedge, "Remarks, Made at the Thirty-Eighth Meeting of the American Unitarian Association," The Monthly Journal of the American Unitarian Association, 4, No. 7/8 (1863), 317; Hedge, "The Universal and the Special," 23.

25. Hedge, **Reason in Religion**, 304-306.

26. Hedge, **Reason in Religion**, 425; Hedge, "Ecclesiastical Christendom," 132-133.

27. Following the Syracuse Convention, Abbott, Frothingham, and others left the National Conference to form the Free Religious Association. The association was active from 1867 to 1879 promoting "the interests of pure religion" without limit on "speculative opinion or belief" or on the "absolute freedom of thought and expression," all of which they felt had been denied at Syracuse. Emerson was counted among its members. Cooke, 203; **First Annual Report of the Executive Committee of the Free Religious Association** (Boston: W. F. Brown and Co., 1868), 16; William J. Potter, **The Free Religious Association: Its Twenty-Five Years and Their Meaning** (Boston: Free Religious Association of America, 1892), 7; Octavius Brooks Frothingham, **Recollections and Impressions: 1822-1890** (New York: G. P. Putnam's Sons, 1891), 120; James Freeman Clarke, "On a Recent Definition of Christianity," in his and Francis Ellingwood Abbott's **The Battle of Syracuse, Two Essays** (Boston: The Index Association, 1875),4, 13, 14; Persons, 17, 35-54, 75-87; Morris R. Cohen, **American Thought: A Critical Sketch** (Glencoe, Il.: The Free Press, 1954), 155-156; Hutchison, 200; John W. Chadwick, **Frederic Henry Hedge: A Sermon** (Boston: George H. Ellis, Publishers, 1890-1891), 27.

Hedge saw the Free Religious Association as "tending in a false direction." He believed it did not encourage scholarship, but instead fostered, "vulgar impatience and the sentiment of negation." In the end the association "foundered on the rocks of excessive individualism," much as Hedge predicted. Frederic Henry Hedge, Letter to Henry Bellows, 18 January 1877, Bellows Collection, Massachusetts Historical Society, Boston, Massachusetts; Frederic Henry Hedge, Letter to Reverend Charles Lowe, 26 February 1866, Frederic Henry Hedge Collection, Andover-Harvard Theological Library, Cambridge, Massachusetts.

Following the demise of the Free Religious Association most of its membership rejoined the National Conference, which had grown progressively more liberal. By 1894, the National Conference had voted in a series of amendments, which admitted anyone who, "while differing from us in belief, are in sympathy with our purposes and practical views," namely "the practical love of man to God and God to man." Octavius Brooks Frothingham, **Transcendentalism in New England, A History** (1876, rpt. Gloucester, Ma.: Peter Smith, 1965), xv.

28. One critic has asserted that Hedge would not have followed fellow Unitarians in their liberalization after 1890, and that Hedge's "direct successors" would thereafter have been found in more orthodox Protestant denominations. The point is valid, yet uncertain. Hedge grew progressively more liberal, as did Unitarianism, but it is questionable if Hedge would have followed his denomination in their turn away from the earlier stand on the "Lordship of Christ," as occurred after his death. Hutchison, 6, 142, 205; Hedge, **Christianity Confined to No Sect,** 11; Hedge, "Cause of Reason," 223; Hedge, **Reason in Religion,** 218-219; "National Unitarian Convention," 213; Brown, 5; Frederic Henry Hedge, Letter to Henry W. Bellows, 24 March 1865; Bellows Collection, Massachusetts Historical Society, Boston, Massachusetts.

29. Persons, 40.

30. Frederic Henry Hedge, Letter to Reverend Charles Lowe, 26 February, 1866, Frederic Henry Hedge Collection, Andover-Harvard Theological Library, Cambridge, Massachusetts; Frederic Henry Hedge, Letter to Caroline H. Dall, 28 September 1864, C. H. Dall Collection, Massachusetts Historical Society, Boston, Massachusetts; Merle Curti, **The Growth of American Thought** (New York: Harper and Brothers Publishers, 1943), 157.

31. Frederic Henry Hedge, "Dr. Furness's Word to Unitarians," Christian Examiner, 68 (1859), 435.

32. Frederic Henry Hedge, "Emerson's Writing," Christian Examiner, 38 (1845), 95.

33. Frederic Henry Hedge, "The Way of Historic Atonement," in his **Ways of the Spirit**, 119.

34. Frederic Henry Hedge, **The Leaven of the Word** (Boston: Dutton and Wentworth, 1849), 17; Hedge, "Ecclesiastical Christendom," 133; Hedge, **Christianity Confined to No Sect**, 4-5; Wells, 137; Hedge, Letter to Dall, 28 September 1864; Hedge, "Cause of Reason," 223; Joseph Henry Allen, **Our Liberal Movement in Theology: Chiefly As Shown in Recollections of the History of Unitarianism in New England** (Boston: Roberts Brothers, 1892), 142.

35. Wells, 136; Williams, 35; Hedge, **Reason in Religion,** 218; Brown, 43; "Our Denominational Position," The Monthly Journal of the American Unitarian Association, 7, No. 7/8 (1866), 334; Frederic Henry Hedge, Letter to Convers Francis, 14 February 1843, Washburn Collection, Massachusetts Historical Society, Boston, Massachusetts.

36. Frederic Henry Hedge, "Antisupernaturalism in the Pulpit," Christian Examiner, 77 (1864), 157.

37. Frederic Henry Hedge, "Antisupernaturalism in the Pulpit," 157; Frederic Henry Hedge, "The Destinies of Ecclesiastical Religion," Christian Examiner, 82 (1867), 2, 9, 13-14; Hutchison, 140.

38. Hedge, "Historic Atonement," 95-119.

39. Hedge, "Destinies of Ecclesiastical Religion," 9. See also Hedge, "Ecclesiastical Christendom," 128; Frederic Henry Hedge, **Conservatism and Reform** (Boston: Charles C. Little and James Brown, 1843), 13.

40. As opposed to Calvin's "particular redemption." Hedge, "Historic Atonement," 98.

41. Hedge, "Destinies of Ecclesiastical Religion," 14.

42. Hedge, **Divinity School Address,** 5.

43. This statement and others imply that another church may in time supplant Christianity. Although this logically follows, Hedge failed to confirm it. Instead, he continually asserted that Christianity was the "ultimate religion," and that only the Broad Church would follow. Actually, the possibility of another intervening church in the next millenium would hardly have bothered Hedge or interfered with his concept of the evolving Broad Church and the role of Christianity in that process. Frederic Henry Hedge, "The Way of Religion," in his **Ways of the Spirit**, 56; Hedge, "Destinies of Ecclesiastical Religion," 8.

44. Hedge, "Historic Christianity," 63; Hedge, **Conservatism and Reform,"** 4-5; Frederic Henry Hedge, **Recent Inquiries in Theology, By Eminent English Churchmen; "Being Essays and Reviews"** (Boston: Walker, Wise, and Company, 1861), xiii.

45. Hedge, **Reason in Religion,** 285.

46. Ibid.

47. Ibid.

48. Hedge, "The Broad Church," 57.

49. Ibid., 59.

50. Hedge, "The Broad Church," 59; Hedge, **Conservatism and Reform,** 5, 7.

51. Hedge, "The Broad Church," 61; Hedge, **Conservatism and Reform,** 20-21.

52. Hedge, "The Broad Church," 62; Frederic Henry Hedge, **Mohammedan Mysticism** (Boston: American Unitarian Association, 1888), 412.

53. Hedge, "The Broad Church," 64; Hedge, "The Churches and the Church," 202; Frederic Henry Hedge, "The Lot of the Called," in his **Sermons** (Boston: Roberts Brothers, 1891), 125.

54. Hedge, "The Churches and the Church," 203; Hedge, **Reason in Religion**, 309; Hutchison, 142.

55. Williams, 24.

56. Frederic Henry Hedge, "The Nineteenth Century," Christian Examiner, 48 (1850), 375; Hedge, "The Churches and the Church," 203-204.

57. Hutchison, 6.

58. Hedge, **Divinity School Address**, 28.

59. Hedge, "Historic Atonement," 101.

60. Hedge, "The Churches and the Church," 203-204.

61. Hedge, "Ecclesiastical Christendom," 138; Frederic Henry Hedge, **Gospel Invitations** (Boston: American Unitarian Association, 1846), 3; Hutchison, 142; Wells, 134.

Chapter Nine

NATURE OF THE UNIVERSE AND HISTORY

It is clear that Hedge regarded his concept of the Broad Church as realizable on earth in personal and collective perfection. Personal perfection has been discussed earlier. The idea of collective perfection served as a key element in Hedge's practical Christianity and in his view of Christianity's evolution toward universality. But it was also tied to his views on human nature, atonement, incarnation, and, in the broader sense, the nature of the universe, including good and evil, and the course of history.

Hedge recognized four basic theories on the creation of the universe. The first, the theistic view, sees the universe as the "product of a single, extramundane, intelligent will." The second, the ditheistic or dualistic view, views the universe as "the joint product and battle ground of two opposing powers," usually spiritual and material, good and bad. The third, the pantheistic view, holds that the universe is the self-manifestation of a solely immanent, diffusive soul. There is no transcendent spirit. The last school believes that the universe is a self-subsisting, independent reality. It generally denies the existence of God and is considered the atheistic approach. [1]

Although Hedge believed in a universe of a divinely self-manifested, immanent, and diffusive soul, he generally held the theistic proposition as closest to his own. He avoided the pantheistic label by asserting God's transcendence, but he assumed much of pantheism's doctrine. Hedge believed that the universe is God's thought made manifest. [2] It is the natural extension of God and contemporaneous with Him. Therefore, God and all creation, both the natural and the spiritual, are of the same substance and of the same power. Specifically, nature and spirit are "parallel independent manifestations" of the divine. He explained that what is natural is "spiritual in its ascent and cause," and what is spiritual is "natural in its descent and being." Put another way, "matter is nature at rest, spirit is nature in action." As the spirit seeks reunification with itself in God, matter tends toward the spiritual. This can be seen, Hedge believed, in matter's movement from shapelessness to crystallization, from simple to complex life, and from the unconscious to the conscious, with its sense of obligation, reverence, charity, faith, and devotion. [3]

This led Hedge to consider what he saw as the three leading theories on the nature of the universe. The first supposes that general and fixed laws govern the world. These were impressed upon the universe at creation, and the universe now pursues its set course and seeks to fulfill its functions. Thus, the laws and processes of the universe are willed, but not every event. Under this system, God's design is intended to produce the greatest possible good. If man, by exercising his free will, works against God's design, he delays rather than enhances its realization. [4]

Under the second theory, the universe consists partly in preestablished, general laws and partly in occasional interpositions of divine power for the sake of certain ends not included in the original plan of creation. General laws were not intended to accomplish these specific ends. [5]

Finally, a third group of theorists believed that the universe is controlled by a present, uniform and direct action of deity. God is the sum and substance of all the agencies, processes and laws man calls nature, and by which the material world moves and subsists. "No power in nature or in works of man's device, but God--no law but divine volition. All is will by God--disaster as well." [6]

Hedge rejected the first theory because he believed it separates God from His work. It makes God a mere director or overseer of past creations, instead of present, living, in-working power. In effect, Hedge held that this theory gives man "a universe without a God," or "a soulless, unconscious mechanism, cut off by its master . . . [and] left to take care of itself." It hardly satisfies the understanding, and it fails the heart, because "the heart demands a present God and a controlling heavenly Father . . . in conscious and perpetual action." Man does not wish to be abandoned to "hard, inevitable laws." [7]

At one point Hedge even questioned if the first theory satisfies the understanding. He saw the theory as anthropomorphized, based on man's ability to make comparable earthly machines. Hedge believed this analogy fails. As he put it, "Man makes the machine, but he does not make the laws and capacities by which it acts. He avails himself of laws and capacities that are given in the substance that he employs . . . not inherent in the substance . . . [and] not attributes of matter." The machines of man's making are not self-acting, but are acted upon by intelligence, that intelligence being God through His divine action. [8]

Hedge found the second theory even more objectionable than the first. He believed it suffers from the faults of the first plus an "ineffectual contrivance" in the form of "an imperfect mechanism" by God. God's original creation is imperfect and needs constant correction in the form of partial and arbitrary intercessions. [9]

Hedge held the third interpretation as closest to his own. He felt it satisfies the understanding "by its simplicity," and the heart. God is present in Hedge's universe. He pervades all works and embraces all. Further, because of His moral nature, God's presence presupposes the good of His creations. God is man's special guardian. He spiritualizes the universe, and His acts are beneficent. Hedge believed this scheme to be one of "deepest piety," combining the best elements of pantheism with "saving graces" of theism. [10]

To follow the ditheistic or dualist view is to allow for more than one God, a dualism Hedge (as well as other Transcendentalists) found contrary to his philosophy and theology, both of which craved "unity in the origin of all of being." [11] If such is the nature of the universe, however, and if God is the omnipotent and truly loving deity that Hedge believed Him to be, how can the evil and suffering that are apparent in the world exist? How can they exist if God is immanent and diffusive, as well as transcendent?

Unlike Emerson, Hedge did not have to be taken into the slums of London by Carlyle to see evil and imperfection. He did not share in the "cosmic optimism," nor was he "blinded to the facts of evil, ugliness, and sins of the world," as critics of Transcendentalism charged to Emerson, Parker, and Alcott. [12] He believed they are "in the constitution of things" and manifest in such miseries as plagues and blights. As Hedge put it, "nature at her brightest conceals beneath that sun-beaming countenance innumerable and inscrutable griefs." [13] To ignore this, Hedge responded to Emerson, Alcott and Parker, is to "overlook great facts in stating the absolute laws of the soul and to stand accused of acting like dogs chasing their tails with pots [sin] attached. "It is of no use to run, wherever they go, the fatal pot goes with them." [14]

Hedge took issue with those who saw the apparent existence of evil as the manifestation of a separate substance or spirit in the Manichean sense or in the "pseudo-Christian" figure of the devil. If the New Testament, or even Christ himself, had employed the term, it had been used "as a given article within the mental furniture of his time." It was a rhetorical device, using an image and term generally understandable in biblical times, in a symbolic manner. As Hedge saw it, Christ by no means attempted to accent it in a way so as to authorize its acceptance as a necessary constituent of the Christian creed. [15]

Nevertheless, due to the imagination of early man, belief in Satan was fixed in the mind of Christendom for nearly 2,000 years. Further, Hedge believed, it had led to its own view of the atonement as a satisfaction of Satan, "to whom the world was supposed to have become forfeit by sin." This view had lasted for more than 1,000 years. It had not been repudiated by the Reformation. Luther, in fact, had insisted upon it, Hedge asserted, as one of the fundamentals of the Christian system. Many abuses and human injustices had resulted including witch trials as late as the closing years of the seventeenth century in America. [16]

Hedge, closer to Fuller in this instance, preferred to see what has been referred to as evil in the world as the result of the imperfection of man and of his limitations. The self is the greatest source of evil and thus of misery, through the failure of the individual to seek or to find God's moral law within which to act, or to act in concert with it once discovered. Such transgression Hedge called sin. The rest results from man's inability to deal with the more apparent "evils" of the world such as plagues and famines, the results of which threaten man's bodily existence as well. [17] If evil, then, is redefined as human imperfection and limitation, how can they be attributed to God's plan?

Hedge began by asserting that human imperfection and limitation in dealing with worldly consequences are not evils, but of "the same character as good," a point also made by Theodore Parker. Imperfection and limitation, like what is perceived as good, proceeds from God. Suffering, distress, even human transgression, emanate from and are allowed by God. They are, therefore, good in origin and purpose as to human experience, even if not perceived to be so by the individual at any one particular moment of his personal experience. [18] Such a view, Hedge allowed, is not obvious to the understanding, working from sense experience alone, but it has to be arrived at deductively beginning with man's transcendental or divinely intuitive insight into the nature of God.

Hedge believed that if man's knowledge of God is tied, in the Lockean sense, to contemplation of the world as he perceives it, with its imperfections and limitations, "inferring from the visible effects the invisible cause," man cannot reason a Being all wise and all good, either as existing or as creator. [19] Yet this is to reason from the effect to the cause, and to assume that what man perceives in the effect must begin in the cause. Hedge insisted that man reasons from the cause, which is all wise and good, to the effect. By doing so, and by assuming that what is in the cause must be in the effect, man can vindicate the goodness of God. He can conclude that all must be good in purpose in the end. [20]

Hedge concluded that evil, defined as a force in nature was not compatible with his view of God. "Either there is no God, such as we figure Him, or there is no evil." "Believing in a God on the strength of His idea in my mind, independent of the argument from nature, I say there is no evil." [21] Yet, what of the apparent human transgressions and miseries that Hedge believed abounded in the world? Called evil or not, seen as the product of a satanic force or of human imperfection and limitations, their existence had to be accounted for.

Hedge asserted that human failure and pain is "as necessary a part of the divine order as that which we call good." As seen above, if this were not the case, they would not be in the divine order at all. Further, he established that by its very definition the divine order "tends to good," continually progressing toward human perfection. Such progress is predicated on the perpetual growth in good, which in turn relies on the accumulation of "blest results." These consist not only of the unfolding divine spirit within man, but in the lessons drawn from his "conscious imperfection, want, and pain." [22]

Without imperfection and limitations man cannot have "a state of perfect blessedness," but only a state of "pleasureless torpor and measureless ennui." Without imperfection and limitations man lacks the incentive to effort and topic of action. He is "denied an essential means of growth or education" and his "health" as humanity is impaired. Without them he is denied the means of realizing Hedge's kingdom of heaven on earth. What man has formerly considered evil, then, and continues to do so at times of personal crisis, becomes in Hedge's scheme "inseparable constituent" parts of the "best possible world." [23]

In order to determine that this is the "best possible world," Hedge had to rise above the concerns of the individual and given moment, to take all creatures and ages into account. If what man popularly calls evil is "a necessary accompaniment of finite being; a condition inherent in the act of creation; a consequence resulting from the very limitations which bound individual existence," it is in the sense of the "fortunate fall," also a necessary condition of development and growth. Hedge did not believe it is the source of irreparable corruption, but of growth, "the true ideal of human life." If God had created a world without suffering, this final and greater happiness would have been denied. In imperfection and discontent lies the perfect world, "the best possible world to the sum of beings contained in it, affording the greatest happiness to the greatest number." "And that is all that reason needs to vindicate divine perfection." [24]

How, then, did Hedge account for the origin of man's imperfection and limitations? How did this account reconcile with the traditional interpretation of the Gospel's Fall? Although Hedge read and interpreted scripture according to various approaches, he viewed the narrative of the Fall as pure allegory on the origin of human imperfection, or, of "moral evil." As noted above, Hedge believed in the dual nature of man, the divine and the human, and that salvation lies in the perfection of the first in terms of the second. Yet, the existence of the second allows for a schism in man's nature which arrays the human passion against the moral sense or desire versus duty. Out of the victory of passion and desire arises moral evil. Hedge concluded that such a schism existed from the very creation of man, with his divine nature and human limitations, and that this precluded the existence of any Garden of Eden in our past. There was never such a stage of innocent perfection. [25]

This view led Hedge to assert that the serpent of the Bible was not to be interpreted as an "antecedent, extrahuman, evil power," but as a manifestation of human passion "constitutive" in man from the moment of conception. Adam's sin, or Fall, then, became the victory of that impulse over his moral sense, represented in the voice of God. [26] If, as the Bible said, God created man in His own image, Hedge believed He did so in that man is "a spiritual being, capable of conscious communion with God, and of partaking of the divine nature." Otherwise, from the very beginning, man was "a spirit incarnate in a fleshy body, bounded by an animal soul," with all the promise and limitations such a composition entails. [27] From a Transcendental perspective, Hedge saw the serpent as being represented in man's daily life as "the sensuous understanding divorced from reason and conscience, insinuating itself between the idea of good and the idea of right, separating enjoyment from duty, and urging the pursuit of the former in defiance of the latter." This is, as Hedge put it, the "fleshly wisdom, as opposed to spiritual," or "insidious reason" by which a man "deludes" himself into the belief that he is doing the best thing, consulting his own interests, when he yields to "sinful desire." [28] Such a rationalization is necessary in Hedge's scheme because he believed that no man, unless momentarily subject to the impulse of overwhelming passion, commits a sin without attempting to justify it by making it seem plausible. Thus, Hedge's conclusion that the serpent is "more subtle than all the beasts of the field." [29]

And what of Eden? It clearly did not exist in the beginning but it may be realized in the end, when man will be "better and more blest than now, in harmony with nature and at peace with himself, unvexed with care and untrammelled by sin, his creed sufficient, his being secure, and all his faculties and passions in tune." Man did not "Fall" from a golden age, but he may evolve to one. [30]

Finally, Hedge saw no "intimation" in the story of the Fall of inherited or imputed guilt. Instead, he saw Adam as a "fitting example" of mankind and the prohibition not to eat of the forbidden fruit as "his conscience or moral law within." As Hedge put it, "into every child's paradise the serpent comes," in the form of "some insidious moral mischief . . . some sinister thought that steals over the soul, tarnishing its morning bloom and deflowering its conscious innocence." [31] Against this man pits his conscience or the voice of moral law within. Prior to transgression conscience serves as warning. After transgression, which inevitably occurs, it becomes "knowledge of good and evil." If, as the Bible said, God enjoined that Adam had to die as the result of his transgression (which Hedge notes Adam did not--having lived to a "good old age"), he did so in the sense of innocence, peace, and self-content, that which necessarily follows violations of conscience. [32]

Hedge insisted that to interpret the story of the Fall in any other way is to make God an "almighty tyrant" and to make moral law "an exercise of power for the sake of power, of domination on the one hand and subjection on the other." [33] Thus, he saw the Fall not as a step out of Eden, but as one in the direction of salvation. From his loss of innocence, man gains knowledge of good and evil, and from that he gains the capacity to effect his development and destiny. Hedge quoted that portion of scripture: "And the Lord God said, Behold man is become one of us, to know good and evil." The Fall from childish innocence brought man nearer to God, for sin is the condition of penitence, and "penitence is nearer to God than innocence." Penitence was a voluntary state, innocence an accidental one. [34]

In the theoretical and long-term optimism of Hedge's view of human nature lay a practical and immediate negation; moral evil and personal transgression exist, regardless of future states. To Hedge this is a more serious concern than natural calamity, for it strikes at the heart of man and his institutions and serves as the cause of man's inhumanity to man. Such transgressions, Hedge called sin, a word he asserted was derived from the German word "Sünde," which in turn has its root in sühnen, meaning to expiate. In other words, sin is that which needs to be expiated, or that which leads to unatoned self-alienation from God. The need for expiation, Hedge believed, is self-imposed by man, the only being who sits in moral judgment of himself and, therefore, is capable of consciousness and guilt. Sin is transgression of moral law present in all men, leading to a wronged conscience, which results from man's defection from his inner holy self. [35]

To Hedge sin causes moral and social crises. The perpetuation of those crises results in a state of personal and collective arrested development, which plainly contradicts divine order. This not only results in the loss of personal beatific vision, but also in the negation of mankind's divinely appointed duty. Once again one is led to Hedge's social gospel, included in the next chapter, but first it is necessary to see how Hedge viewed human nature reflected in the course of history. [**36**]

Hedge moved easily from his faith in the individual to that of society, for he believed the latter is dependent, and naturally follows, the moral growth of the first. If, as has been seen, the destiny of the first is assured by its very nature, so is the latter, for in the end the greatness of civilization is to be measured in its virtue and wisdom, not in its numbers and wealth. If the individual is led by his divine nature from the physical level to the moral and, finally, to the spiritual level, mankind will take a similar path in the collective. [**37**]

Like George Bancroft, Hedge believed in the evolution of society based on the infusion of those same moral values attained by the individual into the common mind. Continuous revelation assures the continued quickening of the human mind. It supplies the absolute values which guide the course of the individual and serve as the basis upon which society and its institutions are to be set. As such, they are also conveyed to those who have not yet reached those laws for themselves and by doing so such persons are led to self-discoveries. Without moral principles society would not advance. Thus, although man's institutions, even if well situated, cannot originate ideas, they stimulate, shape, and modify those people who come into contact with them. In this way the progress of civilization is assured as prophesied. [**38**]

If Hedge was confident that divine guidance assures that the course of the world is "onward and irrepressibly upward" toward "the perfect order, the reign of reason, the City of God," and if it does not allow for more than temporary "fluxes" in this progress due to man's transgressions, it does not allow for revolutionary ruptures in a forward leap at the hands of man. As Hedge saw no basis for revolution in ecclesiastical continuity neither did he see it in historical continuity. Obligations to others and to the past are too great. Man cannot escape the position history places him in. He is left not to destroy or abandon, but to adopt and improve. [**39**]

Society, then, has its stages or levels that are equivalent in the collective historical sense to those of the individual. They are reflected in particular societies as well as in human civilization at large, and they represent what Hedge saw as divine necessity, or natural law in the historical process. Hedge took the rudiments of his historical construct from Giovanni Baptista Vico of Naples and his book **Scienza Nuova** (1725). In his book Vico set a pattern of stages which he saw each civilization in history as having followed. The first, or theocratic stage, is patriarchal and is marked by domestic monarchies. The second is the heroic level in which autocracy limits abuses of power which arise in level one. The third state, democracy, is reached when the idea of natural equality dominates. The first stage relies on force, the second on contract, and the third on reason. [40]

Due to man's imperfection, civilization historically has lapsed into despotism or imperial rule following the third stage, on the ruins of democracy. These ruins are bred by anarchy and corruption which historically follow democracy, and which Vico and Hedge saw as inevitable unless human character is reclaimed by a "revolution" in moral values. Barring such a revolution, civilization soon lapses into barbarism. "Faith expires, religion languishes, man grows brutal, cities decay, society becomes effete and lies supine." [41]

Hedge's optimism on the progress of history was based on two factors. The first, in contrast to Emerson's early works, insisted on historical continuity, and its evolutionary pattern necessitated his assumption that one civilization, in its rise and fall, naturally follows another on the death of its predecessor, and leads mankind to yet another on a higher plane of life. It is the debt each civilization owes to those which went before it, and the promise it offers to those that follow. Secondly, although stages have been observed, they are not inexorable. Man remains a free agent, and as such can alter the course of that society to which he belongs. Hedge attributed this second point to Gotthold Lessing, whom Hedge felt added to Vico's scheme. [42]

Hedge believed that individual free agency is constrained by given conditions, and that those conditions are constrained by the natural order of things, whether moral or physical. Further, Hedge believed that "all possible movements of the human will are comprehended in a providential sway of the parent will which works in each." Freedom and necessity, therefore, are different factors of one movement: freedom the human, necessity the divine. The contradiction between freedom and necessity disappears in Hedge's dynamic of history, where "the highest freedom is the strongest necessity." Revolutionary changes, though effected by man for his private purpose, whether he realizes it or not, contain the substance of that which is willed by the spirit of the world. [43]

The key to the progress of civilization, then, is the action of the individual in concert with natural law. The failure of such action results in the failure of civilization, or the resurgence of despotism. Reminiscent of seventeenth and eighteenth century Calvinism, Hedge asserted that society in its first stage is more liable to such failure due to the dominance of "undisciplined instincts and native passions." Want of such moral resources necessitates a fatal dependence on brute force as the final authority. [44]

Civilization's continuation depends on moral resources. From these arise "mutual attraction, friendship, and good will." They guarantee "justice and truth," and prevail against the corruption and anarchy that vice engenders. Thus, although each civilization preceding Hedge's had risen and fallen, according to an observable and seemingly inevitable pattern, he insisted that man ultimately has control over the succession of stages that follow. The terms are allowed him by God as free agent within the conditions He has set for man's survival. Moreover, as man grows through his moral education, it becomes less likely that he will choose to act in a manner opposed to God's natural order, thus failing to perpetuate civilization. The prevalent good in man and his growing knowledge of natural order insures a progressive society. Through his survival man is not reordering the course of history as much as he is acting in accordance with natural law. [45]

Hedge concluded that not only does man operate as free agent within the boundaries of natural order, but that the natural order of the world is discoverable by man. He has, after all, already discovered many elements or laws of it. Hedge quickly qualified his answer, however, by adding that much more of the divine order remains to be known, and some will remain unknown until man becomes one with God. Yet, the knowledge of natural order is essential to man and to the course of history. [46]

Hedge maintained that man, in his natural state, is totally subject to the natural order. Yet, he does not understand the laws which comprise it nor even their existence. He begins his ascent with knowledge of both and their application to his life and institutions, and when he seeks to live in accordance with them. He remains subject to natural laws, but he learns to work in concert with them. [47] From this it follows that, contrary to contemporary popular views, the savage is not freer than civilized man. He may be less bound by social conventions, but he is more the slave of his passions, more dependent on occasion, more fettered by necessity, less master of himself and the world, and therefore less free than the civilized. "Ignorance stalls progress and enhances limitations." If liberty is defined (as seen earlier) as the freedom to act in accordance with the laws of history and human progress, then liberty is not surrendered with the progress of society, it is born of it. [48]

In sum, Hedge believed that the ages of history are "genetically as well as chronologically related," giving man a rational succession of events within a divinely established natural order. Events and even ages follow each other "in such wise that one is the exponent of another, and all are moments of one process." Further, progress is the method of Hedge's history, for progress is based on the morality of man. If evil exists in the world, it remains the best possible world, and utter corruption is constantly defeated. Morality continues and, in fact, increasingly rises to the consciousness of men, displacing transgression. It establishes itself in sentiment and disposition, and, in growing degree, in man's institutions. Thus, the advance of civilization occurs in accordance with God's law. [49]

Hedge defined the end of civilization in terms largely similar to those of his Broad Church. It will be a complete social union in which

> nationality shall no longer divide mankind, when the human family shall consciously unite in one organic whole,--a state combining the greatest freedom of the individual with the greatest compactness of social union, and securing to all members of the common-weal the greatest possible advantage in their connection with each other. [50]

But Hedge warned that such a state as that described above will not arrive without resistance or antagonism, and the opposition of contrary elements, both of man and his institutions. Society will progress, but it will continue to appear in a state of flux as steps forward are met by the forces of resistance. Revolutionary leaps may seemingly appear, but they will be met by the dialectic of opposition and historical continuity. In the end the course of civilization will rely on man, his institutions, and the degree to which God's natural order can be effected in each. This serves as the point from which Hedge's social gospel begins. [51]

NOTES

1. Frederic Henry Hedge, "Dualism and Optimism," in his **Ways of the Spirit and Other Essays** (Boston: Roberts Brothers, 1877), 224; Frederic Henry Hedge, "Arthur Schopenhauer," in his **Atheism in Philosophy and Other Essasy** (Boston: Roberts Brothers, 1884), 80.

2. Hedge, "Schopenhauer," 80; Frederic Henry Hedge, "Our Life is in God," in his **Sermons** (Boston: Roberts Brothers, 1891), 276; Frederic Henry Hedge, "The Theism of Reason and the Theism of Faith," in his **Martin Luther and Other Essays** (Boston: Roberts Brothers, 1888), 316-317; Frederic Henry Hedge, "The Natural History of Theism," in his **Ways of the Spirit**, 120-143. See also Alexander Kearn, "The Rise of Transcendentalism, 1816-1860," in **Transitions in American Literary History**, ed. Harry H. Clark (New York: Octagon Books, Inc., 1967), 284.

3. Frederic Henry Hedge, **Reason in Religion** (Boston: Walker, Fuller, and Company, 1865), 23.

4. Frederic Henry Hedge, **The Regent God** (Boston: American Unitarian Association, 1894), 2.

5. Ibid.

6. Ibid., 3.

7. Ibid.

8. Ibid., 4.

9. Ibid., 2.

10. Ibid., 7-9.

11. Hedge, **Reason in Reliigion**, 41; Frederic Henry Hedge, "Nature: A Problem," Unitarian Review and Religious Magazine, March 1888, 193, 196. See also Henry A. Pochmann, **German Culture in America: Philosophical and Literary Influences: 1600-1900** (Madison, The University of Wisconsin Press, 1957), 157.

12. Harold Clarke Goddard, **Studies in New England Transcendentalism** (1908; rpt. New York: Hillary House Publishers, Ltd., 1960), 114; Ralph Waldo Emerson, "The Divinity School Address: An Address Before the Senior Class in Divinity College, Cambridge, Sunday Evening, July 15, 1838," in **An Anthology of American Literature: Colonial Through Romantic**, ed. George McMichael (New York: Macmillan Publishing Co., Inc., 1980), 1032-1047; Paul Boller, Jr. **American Transcendentalism, 1830-1860: An Intellectual Inquiry** (New York: G. P. Putnam's Sons, 1974), 140-142, 154; "Of Cousin and the Germans, Princeton Review," Christian Examiner, 28 (1840), 382.

13. Hedge, **Reason in Religion**, 113, 119; Hedge, "Nature," 197; Donald N. Koster, **Transcendentalism in America** (Boston: Twayne Publishers, 1975), 41.

14. Frederic Henry Hedge, "The God of Religion, or the Human God," in his **Ways of the Spirit**, 210-213; Frederic Henry Hedge, Letter to Convers Francis, 14 February 1843, Washburn Collection, Massachusetts Historical Society, Boston, Massachusetts; Ralph Waldo Emerson, **The Journals of Ralph Waldo Emerson**, eds.

Edward W. Emerson and W. E. Forbes (Cambridge, Ma.: The Riverside Press, 1909-14), IV, 248-250, 278-279; V, 206; Pochmann, 202, 235.

15. Hedge, "Dualism and Optimism," 238.

16. Ibid., 239.

17. Hedge, "Dualism and Optimism," 241; Hedge, "Nature," 195-197; Frederic Henry Hedge, "Critique of Pessimism," in his **Atheism**, 140; Hedge, "Theism of Reason," 325; Octavius Brooks Frothingham, **Transcendentalism in New England** (1876; rpt. Gloucester, Ma.: Peter Smith, 1965), 292; F. O. Matthiessen, **American Renaissance: Art and Expression in the Age of Emerson and Whitman** (New York: Oxford University Press, 1941), 180.

18. Hedge, "Dualism and Optimism," 243.

19. Ibid.

20. Hedge, "Dualism and Optimism," 245. The topic of inferring good or evil by reasoning from the cause or effect was often discussed by Hedge and Emerson. See Sherman Paul, **Emerson's Angle of Vision: Man and Nature in American Experience** (Cambridge, Ma.: Harvard University Press, 1952), 36. Unlike Emerson, Hedge spent little time considering the nature of humanly perceived reality in the idealistic sense. Occasionally, he questioned if nature has an essence of its own, or whether it is merely the product of human consciousness. But he failed to reach any definite conclusions. The world exists, he concluded, whether it be of the mind or matter, and we must deal with it accordingly. See Frederic Henry Hedge, "Ghost Seeing," in his **Martin Luther**, 250-277; Frederic Henry Hedge, "Questionings," [later "The Idealists"] The Dial, 1 (1841), 290-291. See also Ralph Waldo Emerson, "The Transcendentalists," in **The Transcendentalist Revolt**, ed. George F. Whicher, rev. Gail Kennedy (1949; rpt. Lexington, Ma.: D. C. Heath and Company, 1968), 28-30.

21. Hedge, "Dualism and Optimism," 245; Arthur Christy, **The Orient in American Transcendentalism: A Study of Emerson, Thoreau, and Alcott** (New York: Columbia University Press, 1932), 115.

22. Hedge, "Dualism and Optimism," 245, 251. See Howard D. Brown, **Frederic Henry Hedge, A Memorial Discourse** (Boston: George H. Ellis, 1891), 81.

23. Hedge, "Dualism and Optimism," 249, 251; Frederic Henry Hedge, "Epicurus," in his **Atheism**, 36; Hedge, **Reason in Religion**, 138.

24. Hedge, **Reason in Religion**, 120, 121, 133; Frederic Henry Hedge, "The Lesson of Flowers," in his **Sermons**, 41.

25. Hedge, **Reason in Religion**, 21; Frederic Henry Hedge, "Man in Paradise," in his **Primeval World of Hebrew Tradition** (Boston: Roberts Brothers, 1870), 55.

26. Frederic Henry Hedge, "Paradise Lost," in his **Primeval World,** 103-105.

27. Hedge, "Paradise Lost," 106, 108; Hedge, **Reason in Religion,** 31. See also Ronald Vale Wells, **Three Christian Transcendentalists: James Marsh, Caleb Sprague Henry, Frederic Henry Hedge** (1943; rpt. New York: Octagon Books, 1972), 107-108, 148.

28. Hedge, "Paradise Lost," 105.

29. Ibid.

30. Ibid.

31. Ibid., 119.

32. Ibid., 113.

33. Ibid.

34. Ibid., 114-115.

35. Hedge, **Reason in Religion,** 129-133.

36. Hedge, **Reason in Religion,** 141. See also William R. Hutchison, **The Transcendentalist Ministers: Church Reform in the New England Renaissance** (New Haven: Yale University Press, 1959), 5.

37. Hedge, "Schopenhauer," 92; Hedge, **Reason in Religion,** 9; Wells, 119.

38. Frederic Henry Hedge, "The Failure of Primeval Society," in his **Primeval World,** 184-186; Frederic Henry Hedge, "Progress of Society," Christian Examiner, 16 (1834), 1-21; Boller, 101, 144. As will be seen, Hedge differed from Bancroft on the latter's belief in the superiority of the collective mind over the individual. See George Bancroft, "On the Progress of Civilization," in **The Transcendentalists: An Anthology,** ed. Perry Miller (Cambridge, Ma.: Harvard University Press, 1960), 424; George Bancroft, "The Office of the People in Art, Government, and Religion," in **American Philosophic Addresses: 1700-1900,** ed. Joseph L. Blau (New York: Columbia University Press, 1947), 98, 108; Louis M. Hacker, **The Shaping of the American Tradition** (New York: Columbia University Press, 1947), 365.

39. See Charles Mayo Ellis, **An Essay on Transcendentalism** (1842; rpt. Westport, Ct.: Greenwood Press, Publishers, 1954), 304.

40. Frederic Henry Hedge, "The Way of History," in his **Ways of the Spirit,** 5; Frederic Henry Hedge, "The Method of History," North American Review, III (1870), 313.

41. Hedge, "Way of History," 5-6; Hedge, "Method of History," 314.

42. Hedge, "Way of History," 5-6; Hedge, "Method of History," 314-316; Koster, 4; Boller, 157; Frederic Henry Hedge, "Martin Luther," in his **Martin Luther,** 2.

43. Hedge, "Way of History," 11, Hedge, "Method of History," 320.

44. Hedge, "Method of History," 316; Hedge, "The Failure of Primeval Society," 169; Boller, 172. Hedge saw biblical representation of this in the story of the flood, which he read as an allegory on the dissolution of society by the action of internal moral causes. The flood hastened the extinction of that society, and, therefore, was more remedial than retributory. A whole generation was eliminated, but moral worth (e.g. Noah and his family) survived and flourished. See Frederic Henry Hedge, "The Deluge," in his **Primeval World,** 208-214.

45. Hedge, "The Failure of Primeval Society," 169, 180.

46. Hedge, "Way of History," 12.

47. Ibid., 17.

48. Ibid., 19.

49. Hedge, "Way of History," 19-21; Ellis, 27-42; Frederic Henry Hedge, "Christianity in Conflict with Hellenism," in his **Martin Luther**, 64-98; Frederic Henry Hedge, "Feudal Society," in his **Martin Luther**, 97-128.

50. Hedge, "Way of History," 23.

51. Hedge, "Way of History," 28; Hedge, **Reason in Religion**, 294; Hedge, "Epicurus," 38; Frederic Henry Hedge, **Conservatism and Reform** (Boston: Charles C. Little and James Brown, 1843), 38-39.

Chapter Ten

AN EXERCISE IN PRACTICAL CHRISTIANITY

Frederic Henry Hedge, as we have seen, believed in the evolutionary, progressive orientation of history, based on divine immanence, man's divine nature, his knowledge of God's law, the example of Christ's atonement, and the liberty of man to act within God's natural order. History's end is the Christ-like perfection of man and the establishment of God's heavenly kingdom. The subject to be considered here is the area of worldly societal concern in which man is to participate to prepare the way. Hedge called such participation "practical Christianity." Others have referred to it as his social gospel, for in many ways it anticipated the movement of the same name which followed later in the nineteenth century under figures such as Walter Rauschenbusch, Josiah Strong, and Washington Gladden. Like later practitioners, Hedge felt that practical Christianity was the peculiarly American contribution to Christianity and its goal of the realization of God's will on earth. Further, he, as they, held practical Christianity to be the practical basis of religion without which the spiritual cannot exist and its end never be realized. [1]

Hedge was widely recognized for his devotion to practical Christianity and for his influence on other followers of the social gospel. He was seen as one of the two major practitioners in nineteenth century Unitarianism, itself generally esteemed for its humanitarian causes. As he put it, a minister must "care more for humanity than he does for theology." [2] Before this is construed as implying numerous direct involvements in social issues, as with Gladden and Rauschenbuch, however, it is necessary to make two basic points concerning Hedge's approach. The first point is that he believed progressive reform is best effected through the unfolding of God's spirit in man, who in turn infuses institutions. [3] Any changes in external "trappings," even revolutionary ones, are doomed to failure without this prerequisite. Secondly, the church, as the manifestation of God's word, Hedge believed, is the divinely appointed institution, set apart to do

God's work. He maintained that reformers would do well to work within its ranks, rather than through the more secular approach of the Enlightenment. The pulpit, as Rauschenbush later agreed, is the moral sense of society. [4]

Hedge sought reform, then, from within Unitarianism. He interpreted history, elaborated schemes for the future, and involved himself in areas of reform, but he did so as a denominational leader. He preached the gospel of love, based on the drawing together of religious ideals and secular institutions, with an emphasis on the modern world. He wished to translate the eternal vision into an earthly one. [5] As Hedge put it, "The past was infinitely momentous while we were in it, and the future will be when we are in it, but we are in the present, and it is momentous." [6] This was not a denial of salvation through faith, not an embracing of the gospel of good works. It was the recognition of what he saw as the "genuine fruits" of the truly faithful. [7]

Hedge was confident that the divine in man, or his moral sense, provided his basic impulse to seek an end to disorder, discord, and excess, prevalent in his natural state. For this man seeks to substitute organization, peace, and measure. Further, personal morality is not an end in itself, but a call to action for "the will of God." [8] As with the earlier Puritan moral idealism and the later social gospel, Hedge believed that all men are committed not only to their own personal unfolding, but to the welfare of society at large, the projection of that individual spirit into the collective sense. No man or class is exempt from this commitment, for if he is good, he must will good. If he wills good, he must will the institution which provides the means of securing the highest good. [9]

Hedge believed that the man who wills good has reached the highest stage of life. He referred to that stage as the "heroic" stage or the point at which man considers it "more blessed to give than to receive." To do this man must first accept the obligations of life, mainly responsibility for his fellow man, as well as its tasks and duties. When achieved, this acceptance leads man upward from his childish stage of indulgence and indolence. [10]

Such a view of participatory reform placed Hedge within the mainstream of liberal and Transcendental Unitarianism as espoused by figures such as William E. Channing and Theodore Parker. [11] He was to the "right" of other Transcendentalists, who were generally viewed as more individualistic--and at the same time more notorious--such as Emerson and Thoreau. Emerson was noted for making the point that he did not consider himself "a good man of society" and that he could not take "seriously" those areas of reform proposed for his consideration, such as "the cause of the debtor, of the slave, or the pauper." [12] Thoreau added that he was "too Transcendental" to consider the same, and that he felt it better to go to Mt. Katahdin than to involve himself. Unlike Hedge, Thoreau concluded:

> It is not a man's duty, as a matter of course, to obligate himself to the eradication of any, even the most enormous wrong; he may still properly have other concerns to engage him. [13]

Whether or not these statements accurately reflect the attitudes of the speakers, a point of some controversy, they were popularly attached to them, and to the Transcendental movement. One critic, for example, accused American Transcendentalists of being "out of touch with the concrete things of the practical world." He wrote that they were "lost in the clouds . . . [and] idle dreamers . . . unfitted for any practical contact with the world or any useful service to mankind." [14] Hedge distanced himself from this accusation.

Hedge shared in the dominant Transcendental belief that individual efforts at reform are more beneficial than "the operation of a body," whether public or private. He too feared the possible loss of individual character and independence of thought, for the sake of group effectiveness through solidarity, leading to the retarded progress of truth. Truth is found only in the private communion of self and God, and true reform is based on the "perfect freedom and originality" of the mind, unbiased by party association and public opinion. [15]

Hedge developed his scheme of reform and individual character in an article on "self-culture," a phrase and concept he introduced to American Transcendentalists, but that Emerson later popularized. [16] In that article, he explained that the "true reformer must be by taste averse, by calling exempt, from the practical movement around him." He must be committed to the movement of thought, as well as a "radical in speculation, an ascetic in devotion, a cynic in independence, an anchorite in his habits, and a perfectionist in discipline." He must seek the highest aims of his inner vision and rebuke the superficial attainments, the hollow pretensions, the feeble efforts, and trivial productions of his contemporaries. [17]

Lasting reforms will result from the compromising search for the perfection of man's individual nature. Such efforts are self-sacrificial, in that they are not recognized by a society whose concern for advancement is not of the mind, nor of secular reformers, who offer "a more refined species of sensual enjoyment." The only efficient power in the world, Hedge asserted, is attraction, and that is what the individual of "self-culture" offers to the world. It attracts others to like improvements in themselves. Most secular reforms fail, he believed, because they have not reached such an exemplary state. [18]

Hedge, like later social gospelers, believed that genuinely conceived acts of reform, whether or not they lead to visable consequences, always hold greater good for the doer. It is not merely the deed done, then, that expresses the value of practical Christianity, but the consequential blessing of him who conceives of and wills its exertion. It is the secret of a blessed life, in that man loses himself in some worthy cause or work, sought for its own sake. Hedge added: "The greater the object, the greater and more enduring the satisfaction." This is denied those whose principles and methods, regardless of their merit, are derived from others. [19]

Hedge did not condemn all "combinations for philanthropic purpose," but he readily pointed to their limits. He occasionally met with various groups, such as the Radical Club including reformers such as William Lloyd Garrison and Wendell Phillips, and he joined the Cambridge Anti-Slavery Society. [20] Yet, because these groups lacked the element of personal character development basic to his practical Christianity, as well as a commitment to work at reform from within the ranks of the church, Hedge believed them to be "misguided," and "not the light to come." The fact that these movements were "everywhere springing up," however, "bore witness to the light" to those still "wrapt in sleep." They both reflected the improvement in personal character in the general population and gave visible signs to others of the need for social reform. Even if they accomplished no more, he felt they would lead people to his social gospel. [21]

The stimulus for Hedge's practical Christianity, as for Rauschenbusch and later church reformers, can be found in his conviction of the injustices of the "existing social order." Such injustices, he believed were largely the product of previous, comparatively unenlightened ages, and they had resulted in "the bondage, ignorance, and privation of the many, contrasted with the lot of the privileged few." The result was an unnatural relation, "which suffered one man to riot in abundance wrung from the sweat of his brother, and condemned that brother to life-long hardship." No man, therefore, could conclude that "the final and true destination of man" had been realized, nor that his responsibility to effect that end had yet been relieved. [22]

Hedge urged man to take the role of the "Ideal Christian" in society. He must pursue "self-culture," but he must remain of the world. He must seek the spiritual perfection of inner life, but with the vision he thus gains, he must pursue the correction of worldly error. In Hedge's words, man must "partake of the world's innocent uses while contending against the bad," promoting the welfare of society. Finally, as if in response to Emerson or Thoreau, he concluded that isolation may free an individual from temptation, but it will not accomplish God's will, the creation of His heavenly Kingdom on earth. [23]

Among the numerous related areas with which Hedge concerned himself beyond passing reference were penal reform, education, the Christian Amendment, woman's suffrage, the labor movement, the distribution of wealth, conscience and the state, revolution, the peace movement, and antislavery. As preacher, educator, and public speaker, he sought to instill the highest moral values, which he considered the "indispensable condition" of the highest goal to which man could aspire, namely the reform of his society. These were religious values as well, and as Hedge saw them, the origin of man's purest motives, the source of stability as well as change, and the purifier of his heart as well as eliciter of self-sacrifice and reform. [24]

Some of the areas of reform with which Hedge concerned himself can be briefly summarized. Others are more complicated, including qualifications and elaborations. Further, with the exception of the antislavery issue, there is little evidence of his direct involvement in secular organizations or their activities. As a rule he remained aloof from them, convinced that what he termed the "scholar's calling," as a servant of the people, would be more effective. Thus his writings, preaching, and speeches establish his position. [25]

Penal reform was a major area of concern for Hedge. His proposal was simply put and continuously repeated. Basically, he supported a shift in the perception of prisons as sources of punishment and retribution to institutions of security for society and reformation of the individual. He cited the results of a recent British Parliamentary investigation showing the importance of preparing inmates for gainful employment upon release. Such preparation and employment would assure the minimum of prosperity necessary to moral culture. As Hedge concluded, "It is vain to expect that the hungry and naked will appreciate the highest while the lowest is unprovided for." [26]

A related issue was education. Hedge considered the development of the intellect closely tied to the realization of the individual and to the progress of history and, consequently, to social reform. Education could lead the individual to a highly developed sense of the understanding, for example in the areas of science and history, as well as to a greater appreciation of spiritual truths. The best media of the time for expressions of such truths were literature and the other arts, and the major source for their cultivation were the universities. Thus, Hedge concentrated on university reform. [27]

Hedge presented a major address on university reform to the Harvard alumni on July 18, 1866. One modern scholar has hailed the address as "one of the most significant discussions of higher education, not only in the history of Harvard University but also in American education." [28] In that report, and consistent with his attitude toward his own education, Hedge criticized the current university method, emulated in public schools as well, of textbook recitation and compulsory written exercises. He believed these exercises were aimed at "a somewhat protracted exhibition of themselves [students] at the close of their college course, which, according to a pleasant academic fiction, is termed their 'commencement'." In such a system, he noted, "you hold your subject fast with one hand, and pour knowledge into him with the other. The professors are task masters and police officers, the president the chief of the college police." [29]

Hedge suggested that after a probationary freshman year, followed by a matriculation exam, the system of marks, college rank, and compulsory tasks be abolished. This would give students the freedom of a "true university," namely to select their own studies and teachers. The "rudiments of knowledge," he concluded, could be instilled by compulsory tasks, but "for the formation of the true scholar a season of comparative leisure should be allowed." By comparative leisure he did not mean "cessation of activity, but self-determined activity," the self-command of an individual's time for "voluntary study." Hedge insisted that liberty is an indispensable condition for intellectual growth, and it is the task of the university to provide that liberty. [30]

The Christian Amendment movement of the nineteenth century is not widely known due to its comparatively insignificant impact, but Hedge's reaction to it provides important insights into his attitude toward the role of the church in America. A high point in that movement, that which brought him forward in response, was the meeting of the National Convention to Secure the Religious Amendment to the United States Constitution, held in February 1872, in Cincinnati, Ohio. This assemblage followed two hundred local meetings on the subject and led to a proposal for an amendment for the protection of Bible reading in the public schools, keeping the sabbath, and state recognition of Christian marriage. The convention adopted the following resolution:

> Resolved, that it is the right and duty of the United States, as a nation settled by Christians, a nation of Christian laws and usages, and with Christianity as its greatest social force to acknowledge itself in its written Constitution to be a Christian nation. [31]

Hedge did not attend the National Convention. He publicly spoke out against the amendment and the resolution. He insisted that the convention's "premise" was false and the "enterprise a vain undertaking," not likely to succeed, or, if successful, to result in good to church or state. [32] Hedge agreed that his age had seen the relaxation of sabbatarian discipline, proposals for the discontinuation of Bible use in schools, as well as signs of the general weakening of religious and moral values and of evidence that the United States was basically a Christian, if not a Protestant, nation. To seek the stricter exercise of Christian values through legal recognition of the letter of the law, however, he believed would be ineffective save to recall acts of bigotry and intolerance reminiscent of similar attempts in history. As he asserted, "A simple declaration does not make a nation Christian, if it isn't in spirit." If it were such a nation, it would show in its policy, with or without legal recognition. A social order would result in which God, as revealed in moral law, would be practically recognized as inspiring and shaping the policy of the nation." [33]

Elsewhere, Hedge took another tack. He acknowledged his fear of Roman Catholic ascendancy in the United States due to the increasing rate of immigration, "its compactness," and its "invincible solidarity." Further, he asserted that the founding fathers did not realize the threat posed by Roman Catholicism, with its belief in papal allegience above individual conscience and all other worldly powers. Roman Catholicism posed not only a threat to national allegiance but also to "the best interests of humanity, light, liberty, and progress." He asserted that Roman Catholicism ruled by "seducing the will, by capturing the conscience of its subjects, and through the bondage of the soul." [34] Yet, Hedge maintained that passage of the Christian Amendment, as it was then called, would run the risk of giving Roman Catholicism the opportunity to gain "political overweight" and to influence the course of American history. [35]

Hedge approved of the separation of church and state in America. He saw it as the culmination of reform based on abuses of the past thousand years and, more recently, on the growing number and mutual jealousy of denominations in America. An experiment resulted, placing religion "on the basis of its own sufficient worth, leaving it to its own unaided strength, withdrawing the state from all supervision and dictation of the church, and freeing the church from civil authority." If the church lacked sufficient vitality to survive, to grow, and to become the conscience of the nation under such conditions, Hedge believed it would fail regardless of the legal or nominal recognition of its existence. [36]

Hedge was convinced that women should have the right

to vote, although he failed to get directly involved in any movement toward that end. [37] He insisted that as citizens they had a stake in the country. They were subject to its laws, paid taxes, and were as capable as men in exercising their judgment on public matters. The denial of the right to vote in his day, he believed, was not an intentional act of oppression by writers of the constitution, but a decision based on the general perception of women's self-preferred role in our society. If, at a future date, women demanded the franchise, he believed they would receive it. [38] He warned, however, that he did not believe, as many did, that women would bring any greater reason or conscience to that exercise. There would be no great impact. [39]

Hedge recognized two dominant yet conflicting attitudes toward women in the nineteenth century. The first he saw reflected in Galatians 3:28 "There is neither male nor female." The second he saw in I Corinthians 11:8, 9 "The man is not of the woman, but the woman of the man; neither was the man created for the woman, but the woman for the man." Hedge preferred the first, and he saw it as the likely future outcome of efforts to end sexual discrimination, but he also realized that all people remained subject to the conditions of the moment. It, therefore, became women's duty to work in that direction with "feminine tact" and "practical wisdom," while it was incumbent upon men to meet their efforts with "manly toleration." [40]

Hedge offered further insights into the issue of feminine equality by noting the difference in what he labeled civil and industrial rights versus social and aesthetic ones. In the first case, he saw a natural division, as men had been excluded from the kitchen, laundry, and nursery, and women from the army, bar, and pulpit. As he put it, men had naturally tended toward outdoor life and adventure, while their presence and masculine mind had made their role in business and labor more convenient and "easier to deal with." Thus these assignments were "as natural as the difference in the costume which has always divided male and female," and had "a sense of fitness, propriety of natural affinity, and a felt necessity" precluding cries of "forced compulsion." [41]

Hedge noted that women could make immediate employment gains in the medical profession (provided they treated only those of the same sex), the arts, science, literature, teaching, lecturing, preaching, missionary endeavors, and even the ministry. He insisted, however, that women first had to reconsider the meaning and value of their role in family life and not abandon it. This, Hedge believed, was the first and primary calling of women, "by law of nature," and that it would remain so as long as the home remained "a cherished institution in civil society." What had changed historically, in his mind, and had allowed for greater feminine involvement in the work force, was that the number of families had not kept pace with the growth in population. This had brought about an excess of women without family roles, who were seeking employment in professions outside the home. [42]

Thus, Hedge asserted that the tendency of history would lead to a change in perception and attitude toward women, precluding extensive legal revisions. But, first, he warned, women had to deliver themselves from their low self-perceptions of their "proper calling and destination." He noted that women continued to perceive themselves as "ornaments" rather than as having a "self-subsisting individuality, a self-regulating intelligence." As custom would have it they continued to prefer a "fortunate union" to an "absolute standard of right and good," to aim at "pleasing" rather than knowing, and "to seek their best triumph in external glitter" rather than in the full realization of themselves and their ideals. [43]

Hedge's attitude toward labor was quite simple, as well. Like Orestes Brownson's, his theory was concerned with the distribution of wealth and property. To begin with, he believed that "the great disparities of human life" in his day had been caused largely by the facility with which one class of men had availed themselves with the labor of another without adequate compensation. [44] This had both created an untenable socio-economic position for laborers and demeaned their calling. At one point, Hedge concluded:

> Society as we know it, is upborne by a host of proletaries, who toil in deeps beneath our feet, and sow in discomfort and privation what we reap in comfort and ease. [45]

He saw the organization of labor as a positive step in reconciling both problems and possibly avoiding the armed class struggle predicted by Brownson. [46] It would demand a higher state of economic well being in which "the class of labor shall divide more equally with the capitalist the product of their united action, as well as the reestablishment of the notion of labor as being "in harmony with the highest culture" and exemplifying those values of discipline and growth seen in Christ's own example. Thus, the true basis of mutual dependence of employer and employed would be reestablished. [47]

Hedge believed that one source of social prejudice against labor had been the schools. He felt that the educational system of his day was "one-sided" in educating the brain rather than the hand. It falsely separated the intellectual from the laborer. He suggested that the system be replaced with one that embraced the whole man in all his scope. Improvement might begin by allowing the university student to study mechanics and the workingman to study at the university. In the end, the first would be skilled in some mechanical art to complement his intellectual attainments, while the second would be spared a life of labor with a barren mind. [48]

Of related interest to Hedge was the disparity he observed in America's distribution of property, which he believed was related to the disparity in labor compensation. He asserted that the origin of land ownership was in forceful possession, whether by government, company, or individual, and that control by might had been the rule ever since. [49] Though this argument called into question the equity of the basis of land ownership, he waived the argument, assumed the existence of land ownership, and considered its current operation. Given its existence, Hedge insisted that property should be distributed according to the needs and labors of the individual. There was enough earth to do this and to insure that no one would want or suffer. This, Hedge held to be the essential function of society and one of the reasons for its formation. [50]

Although asserting that this equitable system would someday be brought about, Hedge allowed that this change would not occur in his lifetime. Since some owned disproportionately more, at the expense of those who had little, he stressed a sense of obligation. Because the rich own their property by the consent and aid of society, which allows them to accumulate it, they are bound to give a proportionate part not only in taxes but also in voluntary contributions to social needs, to the aid and relief of the poor and distressed. Inordinate wealth does not justify inordinate self-gratification. Instead it "reckons a debt of honor," which if not paid leads to social disgrace and moral depredation. [51]

It is important to add that Hedge did not see the realization of his economic commonwealth in socialism. He felt socialism, in general, took "no account of the moral destination of man, as an individual." Further, he found it "essentially Epicurean, irreligious, and grovelling, making pleasure the only good," or deficient in all the best elements of human nature. As to its application in Fourierist schemes such as that of George Ripley at Brook Farm, which he had refused to join, Hedge saw only "ominous import, suggesting ideas of disorganization, contempt of authority, corruption of morals, licentiousness, and infidelity." Fourierism was "too gay and festal, for human nature's daily food," with "no recognition of the holy ministry of sorrow." In a word, it was "too French." [52]

One area of concern to Hedge, as well as to other Transcendentalists, was the place of the individual conscience within society. With the emphasis he and the others placed on the inviolability of human, divine intuition, consideration had to be given to instances where conclusions drawn from that source clashed with the dictates of society, no matter how restricted that government might be in its scope. This tied into Hedge's theory on revolution.

Although Hedge opposed revolution as a means of effecting change, he insisted that government be limited in its subjugatory powers, and that only in instances where those limits were exceeded might revolution be warranted. This began from his basic premise that government has no right to exact obedience when the moral sense of the subject forbids it. This destroys conscience, which, as we have seen earlier, is the product of man's divinely intuitive insight into the will of God, and which serves as the only true basis for obedience to law. Hedge's theory on the limits of government, which in its ideal resembles Thoreau's maxim of minimal government, is intended to preclude such difficulty, but he realized that situations of excessive government would occur nonetheless. [53]

Hedge did not follow the dictates of Friedrich Jacobi that "government was a compact with the Devil." [54] Instead, in the tradition of seventeenth century Puritanism, William Ellery Channing, and George Bancroft, he believed that the role of government is to provide the environment in which man could be true to his divine nature and spiritually unfold. It should provide protection for man's exercise of his natural right and promote social organization for the purpose of practical Christianity, not available in a savage or natural state. Further government should embody the wisdom of the ages as received by man and unfolded from age to age. [55]

Yet, as with Thoreau, he insisted that government should pass no laws requiring the individual to violate his will. If it did, Hedge noted that the first problem of the individual would not be to obey for the sake of society, but to be true to himself. [56] Government should not absolve the individual from his obligation to moral law, and that obligation necessitates the free interpretation by the individual of that law:

> For if I have a conscience--if I really believe in a law of God, in my accountableness to that law, and in all which that fact implies, then my obedience to that law, involving as it does my moral well-being, is more to me than society or anything that society can give. [57]

It should be noted that Hedge applied this line of reasoning even to that legislation conscientiously passed by legislators with reference to their own moral values but contested by a small number of constituents claiming the same allegiance. Even in this case, which he believed seldom occurred, the individual conscience must be respected and guaranteed. Clearly Hedge did not hold Bancroft's faith in the supremacy of the group to the individual mind, a basic tenet of Jacksonian America. [58] He qualified himself only in the sense that those in opposition should be

> sober and intelligent citizens, whose social position, education, moral and religious standing afford a reasonable guarantee of their competency to judge, and their sincerity in deciding such questions, and make it highly improbable that they are governed by caprice or impelled by fanaticism, or possessed with a lawless and destructive spirit. [59]

In this case, government should carefully reconsider its action and refrain from forced conformity. With such opposition individuals are forced to choose opposition to God or government. The first alternative is the usual route, whereby government crushes resistance to its authority, but at the same time destroys its purpose and the well-being of its constituency. The second could lead to revolution; people will not obey what they do not respect. [60]

Even if those who control government feel they are right, they have an obligation to respect the scruples of minorities, if perceived as sincere, by repealing laws that violate conscience, or by modifying their application and obligation. Society cannot absolve men from their allegiance to conscience. Government, therefore, cannot cancel allegiance to conscience. Society exists only by a compromise with individual freedom, to secure a greater good, the realization of man's divinity. But "some limit it must have, or society would be unqualified oppression and endless evil." The balance should be struck between securing the general good without violating the individual, and the limit is reached when the individual is asked to concede morally more than he gets in return. Society does not have to violate this limit, but if it does, it has no right to exist. [61]

Upon these grounds revolution may take place. Whereas, as shown earlier, Hedge believed revolutions could not effect lasting change without changes within the spirit of society, revolutions are justified, or even necessary when external institutions prevent the cultivation of that same spirit, as in the case of violations of conscience. Once again, however, he noted that this seldom is the case because despotism breeds passive obedience and violations of conscience, leading to acceptance of subjugation in most cases. This passive spirit is a more effective subjugator than armed force. This passive spirit must change before revolutions can happen and be successful. If not, revolutions will not occur or equally despotic governments will replace older ones. With the necessary, prior change having occurred, the revolution will have already been won before the first shot is fired. [62]

Examples used by Hedge of instances in which external revolutions had failed for the above reasons include the French Revolution of 1789 and those which followed in Brazil, Mexico, Colombia, and Europe of 1848. The "character" of those nations was not ready. [63] No lasting change had been attempted. Social and moral evils, the true sources of inequities, were ignored for political change. One dynasty was replaced with another. "The purse and bayonet" remained hand in hand and continued to plague each of these nations. [64]

Hedge felt the American Revolution was successful because the ideas of liberty had been established among the American people prior to the revolution and, thereafter, incorporated into their constitution. British aggression, he believed, merely precipitated that impulse, but the revolution had already begun in the minds of the people and would have led to self-government with or without the war. In this case, although the method of revolution, or violence, remained invalid, the principle of the American Revolution justified it. Further, the American Revolution was not an attempt at revolutionary change, something Hedge believed could not supersede evolutionary progress, because America had already evolved to its liberated state. Finally the American Revolution was allowable because it removed an impediment to America's moral growth and reasserted its freedom to observe the laws of nature. [65]

Hedge felt the American government should continue to grow with the wisdom of each age, or it too would be subject to revolution. [66] He suggested that democracy is the best form of government, but that to see it as without fault is a political fallacy. Democracy is the most firmly based of all governments on equality. It establishes a political equality, from which Hedge believed social equality naturally follows. American democracy allows government by representation and participation, based on intellectual and moral fitness, while it promises a society in which economic opportunity will be available for all. Hedge concluded that the United States was the best example of its time of "civil independence, spiritual emancipation, individual scope . . . unbound thought, and the free pen." [67]

Hedge suggested that American democracy, however, is not without a tendency to subvert personal liberties. Tyranny of the monarchy can be replaced by sovereignty of the people, but the latter, in turn, can become a tyranny of the majority, not an uncommon criticism, as seen, for example, in Alexis de Tocqueville's **Democracy in America.** [**68**] This, Hedge believed, would be most likely to occur if politics were allowed to become "a trade for self-profit," pitting majorities against minorities for their own power and office, instead of a means to effect the best for the people. [**69**] Thus, we return to his concern for the individual conscience, even in a democratic nation.

Hedge's argument against war was essentially the same as that against revolution, except that war is even less likely to have those extenuating circumstances that justify revolution. War is unchristian. It betrays sacred trusts and violates moral obligations, but it also needlessly squanders spiritual and material resources. [**70**] War is the epitome of man's inhumanity toward man, and its abolition is man's most "sublime" and difficult task. At times removal of war appears almost impossible due to its myriad causes and manifestations. But war is caused by people who are too little influenced by moral considerations to care about the evils they create, so the solution lies with them. [**71**]

Hedge believed that to bring peace people must be reformed. Those who make war are in a brutal, unregenerate, and spiritless stage, originating in and enkindling malevolent passions. Man is capable of moral and spiritual progress, however, but to achieve this progress he must be infused with moral law. People acting in concert with God's will do not make war. A government composed of such people will not make war. [**72**]

Hedge's concept of a peace movement, then, was not a secular movement dealing with institutions, international agreements, societies, and individual understandings, all of which can leave personal advantages in war. It was a movement for the realization of religious truths in man and their diffusion as principles throughout society. [**73**] If, as Hedge believed, peace conferences of the day, such as that at Brussels and Paris, had their "farcical side," they did appear to indicate a growing sense of that spirit necessary to bring peace. [**74**]

As with revolutions, however, Hedge was prepared to justify some instances of war as they related to conscience and moral law. As he put it, "War is bad, but war is not the worst that can be." The betrayal of sacred trusts is worse, as is shrinking from natural responsibilities. In these cases war may be justified or even a duty. [**75**] These "righteous" wars, to Hedge were those against the oppression of civil or religious liberties, private judgment, self-government, and moral values, all necessary for furthering civilization. Among examples he cited of justified wars were those waged by the Greeks in the Persian War of ancient times, the German Protestant princes in the Thirty Years War of the seventeenth century, and the North in the American Civil War. [**76**]

Hedge opposed slavery in the same vein as he opposed the oppression of all men. First, he opposed the ownership of any man by another. Further, he saw the same humanity in the slave that he saw in the master, except that the slave's humanity was not allowed to develop according to the eternal plan that lay at the foundation of his being. Slavery defied moral law. Its manifestation in the South gave slavery a visible and physical order, which to Hedge, was serpent-like and which threatened the existence of the nation itself. He saw no alternative to killing the serpent, save "defanging" or "disabling" it for the future. [**77**]

Hedge was more involved in the anti-slavery movement than in any other area of reform. This was true of most American Transcendentalists and Unitarians. In 1834 he joined the Cambridge Anti-Slavery Society. In 1835 he gave a public address in Bangor titled "British Emancipation of West Indies Slaves." In 1845, he and other Unitarian ministers gathered in a special meeting to "discuss their duties in relation to American slavery." They issued a finding that slavery was "utterly opposed to the principle of Christianity" and declared that they would do all they could to "create a public opinion to secure the overthrow of the institution." [**78**]

In a June 1854 letter, Hedge commented on the public's reaction to the recapture of a fugitive slave in Boston. First, in response to the subdued public response, he said he did not see how people could have done otherwise, "with a thousand armed men to keep them in check." He went on to add, however, that he would have found it more satisfactory if some demonstration, however ineffectual, had been made, even if some lives had been sacrificed "in the cause of freedom." He added, "until that is the case I am convinced there will be no end to the surrender of fugitives." [**79**]

In the same letter Hedge called for an antislavery organization, armed "for such exigencies," notably the rescue of fugitive slaves from recapture. He wrote of his disdain for the "alacrity" with which the Boston and Massachusetts governments had been enforcing the Fugitive Slave Act. He concluded, "the universal sense of justice" should outweigh the fact that "the law must be obeyed," a point made by Thoreau and Senator William Seward. [**80**]

In 1856, Hedge spoke in Providence, Rhode Island, against Representative Preston Brooks' attack on Senator Charles Sumner on the floor of the Senate. Sumner had delivered his discourse, "The Crime against Kansas," in which he cast aspersions on Southern slavery in general and Stephen Douglas and the absent Senator from South Carolina, Andrew Butler, in particular. Brooks, Butler's nephew, sought revenge for his uncle. Hedge, like most Northerners, recoiled in horror. [**81**]

During the Civil War, Hedge lent his efforts to the "Sanitary Commission" [82] and took the time to comment on the war and the state of the nation. In 1861, for example, he spoke of how the first year of the war had elicited "a thrill of patriotic joy" out of the end of passive submission to an evil institution and the expectation of a speedy resolution. Yet the war had dragged on with no end in sight, despite the North's "vast resources and superabundant strength." Hedge attributed this failure of the North to gain a quick victory not to a problem of leadership or organization, or even of a unity of purpose, but to "infirmities and faults" which lay at the heart of the nation. Among these were self-conceit and intellectual and moral looseness. [83]

The union's self-conceit grew out of its "vainglorious persuasion" that the American people were "the greatest people on earth, and the wisest that ever occupied the earth." Hedge found such a view not only boastful, but the result of confusing America's destiny with its current situation. The American character would someday mature to be the finest fruit yet produced on earth, he believed, but for the moment American could claim no such "pre-eminent rank." He felt what had been seen as signs of America's greatness was only material progress. Material progress had resulted from the bounty of the continent and the rare opportunity Americans had to use it. Beyond that Americans' weaknesses were quite evident, namely their "intellectual and moral looseness." [84]

America's intellectual looseness, Hedge believed, was in part due to "the very condition of our republican society." American society had afforded success in the form of a prosperous career without demanding a high degree of culture or education. He saw this situation as especially true of public men, whom he considered the "worst educated, worst trained, and worst mannered" of any comparable nation. The result for most Americans had been a certain "superficiality," "crudeness," and "want of discipline and of thorough and effective training." Such laxity had led to moral looseness. [85]

Hedge wrote that moral looseness was manifest in the American people's want of reverence and subordination, which formed "so conspicuous a trait of our nationality." This he believed, had been causing a problem for military supervision at that point in the war. America's emphasis on the superiority of each individual had led to an inordinate disdain for subordination, "the first and fundamental principle . . . of social order," and to moral indifference. Moral indifference had led to a decline in American character. In this sense Hedge believed the war had anticipated even greater evils threatening the nation than slavery itself.

The war, therefore, could be seen as a blessing, rectifying America's moral transgressions and righting their noble experiment. [86]

Hedge urged his fellow Americans to reassert their moral character by fighting on in the war with "unabated zeal and indominitable hearts." To seek a compromise peace was "the voice of reason, frightful and hateful." Slavery was "the great weakness of the land," and it threatened American liberty, union, and national character. [87]

In 1863 Hedge was drawn once again to comment on the course of the war. This time he translated essentially the same errors listed above into an allegory of bodily illness. Secession and the Civil War were visible manifestations of a raging fever caused by a "falsification" of the nature of the Constitution and the moral law therein included. An errant national will, tolerant of moral evil--especially slavery--had subverted its conscience and a new and false union had been established which could not last. Instead, through its infected system, the "fever" had broken out cathartically into a civil war. What was needed was a return to a new national consensus based on a "higher law," identified with organic principles and ideas lying at the base of society, such as the rights of man and Christian law. "The patient is young, and life is strong," Hedge reminded his readers, and "God is gracious." Therefore, He will save the nation if "we repent of former sins . . . and make proof of . . . [our] restitution." [88]

In 1865, Hedge spoke out against those who "through excessive caution" were "conceding" to the South. In response to the growing controversy between radical and moderate Republicans, he accused the cautious of "conceding" because of their false assumption that the Union could be saved by conciliation. [89] Six years later, however, he criticized the radicals for their excesses of "demonstrations and cheap enthusiasms," as well as their continued "mouthing and railing of the antislavery platform." [90]

The object of Hedge's practical Christianity was the realization of a "heavenly kingdom" on earth, where individual, spiritual and social perfection and equality would exist for all men:

> Every truth and right which Christianity achieves over the selfish passions of man, like the abolition of slavery and the emancipation of women; every principle of justice which gains ascendancy in human legislation, which incorporates itself within civil government and becomes an organic element of society, such as political equality; every institution which labors

> in the name of Christ for the relief of human misery and the furtherance of human well-being, such as hospitals for the sick and insane and ministries to the poor,--is a step in that progressive incarnation of divine attributes in humankind, which illustrates and fulfills the prophetic prayer of Christ, "that they all may be one in us." [91]

Hedge believed the solution of practical problems comes through the cultivation and extension of man's divine nature and of religion of love. The object of this cultivation is to give the soul "the scope and reverence which God intended." It is to insure that future generations will see "a nation such as the world has never yet known. Millions upon millions of free, enlightened, and virtuous citizens will enjoy equal rights and equal blessings, filling every valley and nook of the vast territory with the proofs of their wisdom, and the fruits of their genius." [92]

Yet Hedge continually warned that tendencies among the American people were retarding or even threatening to destroy progress toward that end. In addition to those noted above, he cited political ambitions, love of money and office, overdependence on the growing luxury of the cities, and readiness with which Americans aped the follies and vices of elder nations, extravagance of fashion, and disproportionate wealth. In the end, the threat to America and to its role in human progress lay not abroad but within. Hedge found America to be a viable experiment in liberty, but he insisted that men qualify for liberty only in proportion to "the moral chains" they are able to place on their baser appetites, rapacity, and vanity. He concluded: "It is ordained in the eternal constitution of things, that men of intemperate minds cannot be free; their fashions forge their fetters." [93]

To fail at his practical Christianity, Hedge believed, would be not only to tolerate the iniquities of the world, but to fail to assert the very purpose of religion or God's will. In the end, the spirit of Christ demands:

> Have you ministered to the wants and infirmities of your brotherman? Have you fed the hungry and relieved them that were distressed? Have you given so much as a cup of cold water in the name of humanity, in the name of Christ? [94]

This, Hedge believed, is the standard by which we will be judged. Therefore, "let this be the standard by which we judge." [95]

NOTES

1. Frederic Henry Hedge, **Practical Goodness, The True Religion** (Boston: American Unitarian Association, 1840), 11, 13; Frederic Henry Hedge, "The Way of Historic Atonement," in his **Ways of the Spirit and Other Essays** (Boston: Roberts Brothers, 1877), 101; Frederic Henry Hedge, "Personality," in his **Martin Luther and Other Essays** (Boston: Roberts Brothers, 1888), 300-301; Frederic Henry Hedge, **An Oration, Pronounced Before the Citizens of Bangor, on the Fourth of July, 1838, The Sixty-Second Anniversary of American Independence** (Bangor, Me.: Samuel S. Smith, 1838), 29-30; Frederic Henry Hedge, **On the Use of the Word Evangelical** (Providence: Knowles, Anthony, and Co., 1854), 6. See also George H. Williams, **Rethinking the Unitarian Relationship with Protestantism: An Examination of the Thought of Frederic Henry Hedge** (Boston: The Beacon Press, 1949), 24-25, 98; Walter Rauschenbusch, "Christianity and the Social Crisis," in **Theology in America: The Major Protestant Voices from Puritanism to Neo-Orthodoxy** (New York: The Bobbs-Merrill Company, Inc., 1967), 536.

2. The other major nineteenth century, Unitarian practitioner of practical Christianity was James Freeman Clarke. William R. Hutchison, **The Transcendentalist Ministers: Church Reform in the New England Renaissance** (New Haven: Yale University Press, 1959), 138; Joseph Haroutunian, **Piety Versus Moralism: The Passing of the New England Theology** (Hamden, Ct.: Archon Books, 1964), 179; Henry A. Pochmann, **German Culture in America: Philosophical and Literary Influences: 1600-1900** (Madison: The University of Wisconsin Press, 1957), 147; Frederic Henry Hedge, **Christianity Confined to No Sect** (Bangor, Me.: Samuel S. Smith, 1844), 12.

3. Frederic Henry Hedge, "The Way of Historic Christianity," in his **Ways of the Spirit**, 91; Frederic Henry Hedge, "Nothing to Draw With," in his **Sermons** (Boston: Roberts Brothers, 1891), 67; Frederic Henry Hedge, "Strength in Weakness," in his **Sermons**, 219; Paul F. Boller, Jr., **Freedom and Fate in American Thought From Edwards to Dewey** (Dallas: Southern Methodist University Press, 1978), 67.

4. Frederic Henry Hedge, **Reason in Religion** (Boston: Walker, Fuller, and Company, 1865), 135; Hedge, **Practical Goodness**, 3; Frederic Henry Hedge, **The Leaven of the Word** (Boston: Dutton and Wentworth, 1849), 13; Frederic Henry Hedge, **An Address Delivered Before the Graduating Class of the Divinity School in Cambridge, July 15, 1849** (Cambridge, Ma.: John Bartlett, 1849), 29; Frederic Henry Hedge, "Man in Paradise," in his **The Primeval World of Hebrew Tradition** (Boston: Roberts Brothers, 1870), 64-65; Frederic Henry Hedge, "The Baptist and the Christ; or Reformers and Humanity," in his **Sermons**, 141-142; Frederic Henry Hedge, "Love is of God," in his **Sermons**, 270; Rauschenbusch, "Christianity and the Social Crisis," 534-535; Elizabeth Flowers and Murray G.

Murphy, **A History of Philosophy in America** (New York: Capricorn Books, 1977), I, xvi, xviii.

5. Hedge, **Leaven of the Word,** 13-15; Hedge, "Love is of God," 261-275; Frederic Henry Hedge, "Love Cancels Obligations," in his **Sermons,** 180; Frederic Henry Hedge, "The Doctrine of Endless Punishment," Christian Examiner, 67 (1859), 128.

6. Hedge, **Leaven of the Word,** 11; Frederic Henry Hedge, "The Religion of the Present," Christian Examiner, 67 (1859), 54.

7. Hedge explained that while the truly faithful cannot be detected by their actions, their total absence or evil nature infers moral deficiency or corruption. Hedge, **Reason in Religion,** 322-323.

8. Hedge, **Practical Goodness,** 5; Frederic Henry Hedge, "Ethical Systems," in his **Martin Luther,** 232.

9. Hedge, **Practical Goodness,** 5, 16; Hedge, "Man in Paradise," 59; Hedge, "Love Cancels Obligations," 182; Paul F. Boller, Jr., **American Transcendentalism, 1830-1860: An Intellectual Inquiry** (New York: G. P. Putnam's Sons, 1974), 172; Rauschenbusch, "Christianity and the Social Crisis," 535, 542; Winthrop Hudson, **American Protestantism** (Chicago: University of Chicago Press, 1969), 142-144; Edwin Scott Gaustad, **A Religious History of America** (New York: Harper and Row, Publishers, 1966), 242.

10. Frederic Henry Hedge, "Three Views of Life," in his **Sermons,** 2, 6, 12, 19; Hedge, "Historic Atonement," 99-100.

11. See for example William Ellery Channing, "Importance of Religion to Society," in his **The Works of William Ellery Channing** (New York: Burt Franklin, 1970), 187-188; William Ellery Channing, "The Great Purposes of Christianity," in **Works,** 246-255; Herbert W. Schneider, **A History of American Philosophy** (New York: Columbia University Press, 1963), 107, 110.

12. Boller, **American Transcendentalism,** 94, 102; Ralph Waldo Emerson, "The Transcendentalist," in **The Transcendentalist Revolt,** ed. George F. Whicher, rev. Gail Kennedy (1949; rpt. Lexington, Ma.: D. C. Heath and Company, 1968), 35.

13. Boller, **American Transcendentalism,** 107, 110.

14. Harold Clarke Goddard, **Studies in New England Transcendentalism** (1908; rpt. New York: Hillary House Publishers, Ltd., 1960), 113. See also Donald N. Koster, **Transcendentalism in America** (Boston: Twayne Publishers, 1975), 41-48; Octavius Brooks Frothingham, **Transcendentalism in New England** (1876; rpt. Gloucester, Ma.: Peter Smith, 1965), 138-139; Charles Crowe, **George Ripley: Transcendentalist and Utopian Socialist** (Athens: University of Georgia Press, 1967), 126.

15. Frederic Henry Hedge, **A Sermon Preached Before the Ancient and Honorable Artillery Company, on Their CXCVIth Anniversary, June 2, 1834** (Boston: J. H. Eastburn, 1834), 13-14; Williams, 24-25; Hedge, "The Baptist and the Christ," 146-147; Ralph Waldo Emerson, "New England Reformers," in his **Essays** (New York: E. P. Dutton and Co., Inc., 1947), 340.

16. Frederic Henry Hedge, "The Art of Life, the Scholar's Calling," The Dial, 1 (1840), 174-182; Frothingham, 150; Ralph Waldo Emerson, "Self-Reliance," in his **Essays,** 51; W. H. Werkmeister, **A History of Philosophical Ideas in America** (New York: The Ronald Press Company, 1949), 42.

17. Hedge, "Art of Life," 175-182.

18. Hedge, "Art of Life," 176-181. See also Lawrence Buell, **Literary Transcendentalism: Style and Vision in the American Renaissance** (Ithaca, N.Y.: Cornell University Press, 1973), 92.

19. Hedge, **Artillery Company Sermon,** 12-14; Hedge, "The Baptist and the Christ," 145-146; Hedge, "Love Cancels Obligations," 182; Hedge, "Art of Life," 181; Hedge, "Personality," 304; Hedge, "Nothing to Draw With," 66; Sydney E. Ahlstrom, "Walter Rauschenbusch: Champion of the Social Gospel," in **Theology in America**, 532.

20. Van Wyck Brooks, **New England: Indian Summer** (New York: E. P. Dutton and Company, Inc., 1950), 123-127; George Willis Cooke, **Unitarianism in America: A History of Its Origin and Development** (Boston: American Unitarian Association, 1902), 360; Julia Ward Howe, **Reminiscences: 1819-1899** (1899, rpt. New York: Negro University Press, 1969), 285.

21. Hedge, "Art of Life," 182.

22. Frederic Henry Hedge, **Seventeen Hundred Fifty-Eight and Eighteen Hundred Fifty-Eight, a New Year's Discourse** (Boston: Phillips, Sampson and Company, 1858), 18; Frederic Henry Hedge, **The National Entail** (Boston: Wright and Potter, 1864), 9-13; Hedge, **Fourth of July Oration**, 35-36; Sydney Ahlstrom, "Theology in America: A Historical Survey," in **Religion and American Life,** eds. A. Leland Jamison and James Ward Smith (Princeton: Princeton University Press, 1969), 296; Rauschenbusch, "Christianity and Social Crisis," 534; Walter Rauschenbusch, "A Theology for the Social Gospel," in **Theology in America**, 583.

23. Hedge, "The Baptist and the Christ," 142-145.

24. Frederic Henry Hedge, "The Way of Religion," in his **Ways of the Spirit**, 36; Hedge, **Practical Goodness,** 3; Frederic Henry Hedge, **Conservatism and Reform** (Boston: Charles C. Little and James Brown, 1843), 4; Frederic Henry Hedge, "Progress of Society," Christian Examiner, 16 (1834), 112.

25. Hedge, "Art of Life," 175-182.

26. Frederic Henry Hedge, "The Nineteenth Century," Christian Examiner, 48 (1850), 382-384.

27. Boller, **American Transcendentalism**, 116-120; Frederic Henry Hedge, **An Introductory Lecture Delivered at the Opening of the Bangor Lyceum, November 15, 1836** (Bangor, Me.: Nourse, Smith, Duran and Thatcher, 1836), 3, 23-27.

28. Orie W. Long, **Frederic Henry Hedge: A Cosmopolitan Scholar** (Portland, Me.: The Southworth-Anthoensen Press, 1940), 41.

29. Frederic Henry Hedge, "University Reform, An Address to the Alumni of Harvard, at Their Triennial Festival, July 19, 1866," Atlantic Monthly, Sept. 1866, 301.

30. Hedge, "University Reform," 301-302; Hedge, **Lyceum Introductory Lecture**, 23-27.

31. Frederic Henry Hedge, **Shall the Nation, by a Change in Its Constitution, Proclaim Itself Christian?** (Cambridge, Ma.: John Wilson and Son, 1872), 5.

32. Ibid.

33. Frederic Henry Hedge, "Ecclesiastical Christendom," Christian Examiner, 51 (1851), 122; Frederic Henry Hedge, "Martin Luther," in his **Martin Luther**, 35; Hedge, **Christianity Confined to No Sect**, 5.

34. Hedge, "Martin Luther," 35.

35. Hedge, **Shall the Nation Proclaim Itself Christian**, 7-10; Frederic Henry Hedge, "The Churches and the Church," Christian Examiner, 41 (1846), 210.

36. Hedge, **Shall the Nation Proclaim Itself Christian**, 18; Hedge, **Christianity Confined to No Sect**, 5; Frederic Henry Hedge, **Conscience and the State** (Providence: Joseph Knowles, 1851), 14.

37. Frederic Henry Hedge, Letter to Caroline H. Dall, 28 October 1861, Dall Collection, Massachusetts Historical Society, Boston, Massachusetts.

38. Ibid.

39. Hedge, Letter to Dall, 28 October 1861; Frederic Henry Hedge, "Male and Female," The Monthly Religious Magazine, Oct. 1867, 246-247; Frederic Henry Hedge, "The Best Government," Christian Examiner, 72 (1862), 336.

40. Hedge, "Male and Female," 424; Hedge, Letter to Dall, 28 October 1861.

41. Hedge, "Male and Female," 242, 243, 245.

42. Hedge, "Male and Female," 244-248; Hedge, Letter to Dall, 28 October 1861.

43. Hedge, "Male and Female," 250-251.

44. Hedge, "Man in Paradise," 61; Orestes A. Brownson, "The Laboring Classes," in **The Transcendentalists: An Anthology**, ed. Perry Miller, (Cambridge, Ma.: Harvard University Press, 1960), 437.

45. Frederic Henry Hedge, "European Travel," Christian Examiner, 53 (1852), 246.

46. Brownson, "Laboring Classes," 437; Alexander Kearn, "The Rise of Transcendentalism, 1815-1860," in **Transitions in American Literary History**, ed. Harry H. Clark (New York: Octagon Books, Inc., 1967) 301; Joseph L. Blau, **American Philosophic Addresses: 1700-1900** (New York: Columbia University Press, 1947), 173.

47. Frederic Henry Hedge, "The Gospel of Manual Labor," in his **Sermons**, 112, 118; Hedge, "Love Cancels Obligations," 172-173; Hedge, "The Nineteenth Century," 376; Hedge, "European Travels," 247.

48. Hedge, "Manual Labor," 114, 117; Hedge, **Lyceum Introductory Lecture**, 17.

49. Hedge, "Man in Paradise," 60-61.

50. Hedge, "Man in Paradise," 60-61; Hedge, **Bangor Fourth of July Oration**, 35-36.

51. Hedge, "Man in Paradise," 138.

52. Hedge, "The Nineteenth Century," 376. Hedge did not feel the same disdain for "all things French." One acquaintance recorded, for example, that he found the French theater quite "to his liking." Howe, 300.

53. Hedge, **Conscience and the State**, 14; Henry David Thoreau, "Civil Disobedience," in **Walden and Other Writings of Henry David Thoreau**, ed. Brooks Atkinson (New York: The Modern Library, 1950), 635; Werkmeister, 74.

54. Hedge, "The Best Government," 314; Thoreau, "Civil Disobedience," 635.

55. Hedge, "The Best Government," 317-318; William Ellery Channing, "Spiritual Freedom," in his **Works**, 173; Blau, 97; Hedge, "Progress of Society," 20.

56. Hedge, **Conscience and the State**, 14.

57. Ibid., 9.

58. George F. Whicher, "Introduction," in **The Transcendentalist Revolt**, vii; Arthur M. Schlesinger, Jr., "Jacksonian Democracy and Literature," in **The Transcendentalist Revolt**, 10.

59. Hedge, **Conscience and the State**, 7.

60. Ibid., 5-7.

61. Hedge, **Conscience and the State**, 9, 14-15; Hedge, "Ethical Systems," 245.

62. Hedge, **Bangor Fourth of July Oration**, 5-6.

63. Hedge, **Bangor Fourth of July Oration**, 20, 22, 23; Arthur Alphonse Ekirch, Jr., **The Idea of Progress in America, 1815-1860** (New York: Columbia University Press, 1944), 55; Joseph Henry Allen, **Sequel to "Our Liberal Movement"** (Boston: Roberts Brothers, 1897), 50.

64. Hedge, "The Nineteenth Century," 375; Hedge, **Leaven of the Word**, 15-16.

65. Hedge, **Bangor Fourth of July Oration**, 4-15; Hedge, "The Nineteenth Century," 375; Hedge also cited the nineteenth century struggle of "Christian Crete" against their "Mahometan oppressors" as a justifiable revolution. Frederic Henry Hedge, **Live Soberly** (Boston: F. A. Searle, 1867), 4-21.

66. Hedge, "Progress of Society," 20.

67. Hedge, "Martin Luther," 2; Hedge, "The Best Government," 324-330.

68. Alexis de Tocqueville, **Democracy in America**, Transl. Henry Reeve (1835; rpt. New York: Vintage Books, 1945), 269.

69. Hedge, "The Nineteenth Century," 373-374; Hedge, "The Best Government," 322-323.

70. Hedge, "The Nineteenth Century," 378-380.

71. Hedge, **Artillery Company Sermon**, 15.

72. Hedge, **Artillery Company Sermon**, 22-23; Frederic Henry Hedge, "The Way of History," in his **Ways of the Spirit**, 33.

73. Hedge, **Artillery Company Sermon**, 16-19, 23-27; Hedge, "European Travel," 245.

74. Hedge, "The Nineteenth Century," 377.

75. Ibid., 381.

76. Hedge, "The Way of History," 33; Frederic Henry Hedge, "Cain, or Property and Strife as Agents in Civilization," in his **Primeval World**, 139-141. See also Frederic Henry Hedge, "Address to the Germans of Boston, Faneuil Hall, July, 1870," The Index, 27 August 1870, 2-3.

77. Hedge, **The National Entail**, 16; Cooke, 359.

78. Cooke, 360.

79. Frederic Henry Hedge, Letter to Convers Francis, 5 June 1854, Washburn Collection, Massachusetts Historical Society, Boston, Massachusetts.

80. Hedge, Letter to Francis, 5 June 1854; Henry David Thoreau, "Slavery in Massachusetts," in Atkinson, 666; Louis Filler, **The Crusade Against Slavery: 1830-1860** (New York: Harper and Row, Publishers, 1960), 200.

81. William H. Lyon, **Frederic Henry Hedge: Seventh Minister of the First Parish in Brookline, 1856-1872** (Brookline, Ma.: First Parish in Brookline, 1906), 12.

82. Hedge, Letter to Francis, 5 June 1854.

83. Frederic Henry Hedge, **The National Weakness** (Boston: Walker, Wise, and Company, 1861), 3.

84. Ibid., 7-8.

85. Ibid., 7-9.

86. Ibid., 10-13.

87. Ibid., 15-19.

88. Frederic Henry Hedge, **The Sick Woman: A Sermon for the Time** (Boston: Prentiss and Deland, 1963), 9-15.

89. Frederic Henry Hedge, **Discourse on Edward Everett** (Boston: George C. Rand and Avery, 1965), 16.

90. Frederic Henry Hedge, "The Faithful Servant," in **Services in Memory of Ezra Stiles Gannett** (Boston: American Unitarian Association, 1871), 36.

91. Frederic Henry Hedge, "The Way of Historic Christianity," in his **Ways of the Spirit**, 91-92.

92. Hedge, **Bangor Fourth of July Oration**, 35-38; Hedge, "The Way of History," 27; Hedge, "The Way of Religion," 39; Williams, 25; Ronald Vale Wells, **Three Christian Transcendentalists: James Marsh, Caleb Sprague Henry, Frederic Henry Hedge** (New York: Octagon Books, 1972), 130-131.

93. Hedge, **Bangor Fourth of July Oration**, 25-27.

94. Hedge, **Christianity Confined to No Sect**, 12.

95. Ibid.

Chapter Eleven

PORTRAIT OF AN ENLIGHTENED CONSERVATIVE

Frederic Hedge was a Transcendentalist. He fully accepted its most basic tenet, which held that man had the innate capacity to arrive intuitively at truths not open to the understanding. He based his affirmation of intuitive knowledge on his belief in man's divine nature, through which man received supernatural insights into God's law. These insights could then be unfolded naturally by a process of spiritual growth, as man's nature more closely approximated that of God. From this foundation Hedge developed his concepts of Christology, will, conscience, perfection, immortality, heaven, revelation, ecumenicity, historicism, and social gospel. He incorporated nearly the full range of nineteenth century American intellectual issues.

The original motive of Transcendentalism, and the motive from which he did not stray, was the need to answer Lockean sensualism. The Lockean school dominated philosophy and theology of the day and exercised what Hedge and other Transcendentalists believed was a deadening influence on religion, especially Unitarianism. Most American Transcendentalists, including Hedge, were or had been Unitarians, and they believed their creed to be both the culmination of centuries of religious development and the hope for man's future. Thus, the concern for an infusion of new life blood. [1]

Beyond this point, no one party within Unitarianism or one school of philosophy could claim Frederic Hedge. He was both one of the most intellectually radical and ecclesiastically conservative thinkers of his day. He belonged both to the "party of hope" and to the "party of memory." His lectures and writings continually revealed a vision of man's future, based on his faith in the inevitability of man's continued realization of what God originally intended him to be. This realization would occur first in the individual and then in the collective sense. At the same time, Hedge's words portray a man unshakingly aware of the past and present and of man's capacity to harm as well as to aid God's will. From this realistic view of man's history and nature arose his conservative insistence upon the restraints of ecclesiastical tradition. [2]

Hedge incorporated these two inclinations consistently and convincingly into his theological and philosophical formulations. This dichotomy can be better understood when viewed on the broader scale included in this discussion than in previously completed, narrower analyses limited alone to his two decades of direct involvement with American Transcendentalism. By their very limits earlier studies have missed the greater part of Hedge's intellectual development, and, as a result, a fuller understanding of the continuity of its integral parts.

A popular thesis labels Hedge as the most "disappointing" and "disappointed" of America's first Transcendentalists. [3] The case for this thesis relies on the comments of contemporaries such as Emerson, Fuller, and Ripley, and a misreading of Hedge's enthusiasm and concerns for the movement. It ignores many of his earliest writings and points to the exclusion of Hedge from Octavius B. Frothingham's study of American Transcendentalism as proof of its contention. [4] Finally, this explanation has gained credence because it is consistent with a broader view of American Transcendentalism as rising and falling in the three decades leading to the Civil War. [5] Some of the more substantive points are considered below.

The case for Frederic Hedge's "fall from grace" with American Transcendentalism generally recalls the importance of his article "Coleridge's **Literary Character**" and the acclaim it received among the "like-minded." It establishes his "pivotal" role in the American Transcendentalist movement by citing his nearly sole responsibility for bringing German Transcendental philosophy to America, establishing the Transcendental Club, and leading the movement toward the creation of The Dial. It notes comments such as that of Mary Moody Emerson (Ralph Waldo Emerson's aunt) in 1838 referring to Hedge as the "Moses" of American Transcendentalism, and then refers to his reluctance to contribute to The Dial, once established, and his critical comments on the movement and its leaders dating from the 1840s. [6]

One example often cited is an exchange between Fuller, Hedge, and Emerson in 1840 and 1841. Fuller and Emerson were seeking Hedge's greater involvement in The Dial, if no longer as editor, which he had declined, then at least as contributor. On January 1, 1840, Fuller wrote to him seeking "solid bullion," or "melodies" (contributions) that she believed he could compose so "that all the stones will advance to form a city of refuge for the just." [7] He declined the invitation, citing temporary poor health and financial embarrassment as making him "less enterprising and more diffident." He did, however, suggest topics for future articles. [8]

On March 30, 1840, Emerson wrote to Fuller voicing disappointment over Hedge's response. He obviously discounted Hedge's excuse and called it a "sad letter," one over which, he felt, Hedge would later "grieve." He added that he and Hedge were not quite "meeting" on matters of the mind, lately, and that a "fence" had developed between them. [9]

In the spring of 1842, Emerson wrote to Hedge reminding him that he was one of the original "friends and favorers" of The Dial and asked for contributions. [10] This time Hedge sent a copy of his **Conservatism and Reform** and offered future translations and articles on "relations" or the church. [11] Although Emerson accepted his offer of a translation of "Shelling's Introductory Lecture in Berlin," he returned **Conservatism and Reform** and suggested a separate publication. Emerson praised many of the points in **Conservatism and Reform** and used them in an article of his own on the topic, but he wrote that he had "several moral reservations" about Hedge's article. Basically, its recognition of the fruits of conservatism used in tandem with reform, and Hedge's appeal for the reconciliation of radicals and conservatives in a rational manner, offended Emerson's Transcendental sensibilities. [12] Emerson commented:

> The sentence which began with an attack on the conservatives ended with a blow at the reformers; the first clause was applauded by one party and the other party had their revenge and gave their applause before the period was closed. [13]

Ultimately, Hedge contributed four articles to The Dial and praised its content, but his hesitancy to do more bothered him as well. [14] He noted that he "prized" the four volumes of the journal among the "choicest of treasures" of his library, and that he felt it contained some of Emerson's, Parker's, Fuller's and Thoreau's best work, "not to speak of writers less absolute and less famous." [15]

In two other private letters, Hedge explained his position more fully. In the first, written to Margaret Fuller in 1840, he said he feared that by identifying himself publicly with Transcendentalists such as Emerson and Alcott, he would "stand forth as an atheist in disguise," as they were so perceived. [16] Three years later he sounded the same note in a letter to Convers Francis, adding Theodore Parker to his list of dissenters. He noted that he wished to avoid the "wild mania of Transcendentalism" and its "heretical tendencies." [17]

The division between Emerson and Hedge soon came to involve the preaching of Christianity itself. By 1845, he had publicly stated that due to Emerson's quarrels with particular issues, he could not consider Emerson a Christian any longer "in the usual and distinctive sense of the term." [18] In 1864, Hedge wrote to Caroline Dall explaining that although he considered Emerson one of his "oldest and best friends," he would not let him "stand" in his pulpit. Hedge noted that he had denied Emerson this privilege during an earlier visit to Bangor even though people in his congregation had expected him to allow Emerson to speak. He explained that he had formulated his stand as a member of the Christian church. Emerson "wanted more liberty than Christianity allowed," and although Hedge "honored" Emerson's "honesty" and "consistency," he insisted that Emerson had willingly left the pulpit. He did not respect "the fundamental position or claims" of Christianity, which Hedge listed as the Lordship of Christ and the superhuman authority of Christianity. Hedge therefore believed that his responsibility, despite his personal relationship with Emerson, was not to allow Emerson to preach. [19] He took a similar stand on Parker in 1859. [20]

The point is readily apparent that Hedge had developed an uncomfortable intellectual relationship with Emerson, Fuller, Ripley, and others of like persuasion. Emerson's disappointment has been noted. Fuller criticized Hedge for sacrificing the "high ground for middle ground." [21] Theodore Parker referred to him as "a man of unstable water. You put your finger on him, and he ain't there." [22] All three would have agreed with Henry James, Sr., who called Hedge "indecisive little Dr. Hedge." [23]

It should be stressed that this divisiveness was an intellectual one and not unique among Transcendentalists, who seldom agreed on anything beyond the most basic points. [24] At the same time, Hedge remained close friends with, and was highly respected by, Emerson, Fuller, and Ripley. In 1845, for example, in the midst of Hedge's quarrel with Emerson over The Dial, Emerson wrote to William Furness comparing Hedge to "one of those slow growing pear trees whose fruit is finer every year and at last becomes a beurre incomparable." [25] In 1846 Emerson created a list of "kindred spirits," that he envisioned as "an unrivaled company," if they were to move to Concord. Although his list of good companions never proceeded beyond the visionary stage, Hedge was on that list. [26] In 1847, Emerson wrote two letters in which he first noted that he "esteemed" and "respected" Hedge "always more and more," and then referred to him as the "chief supporter of the cause of good letters in this country." [27]

In 1845, Hedge published an article in which he acknowledged Emerson's "heresies and sins," but he went on to call him "a most loving and sincere spirit." He praised Emerson for his bold and original thinking, his stand on individual genius, and his assertion of Christian moral truths and principles, which Hedge held to be the spirit if not the substance of Christianity. He insisted that Emerson possessed "all the intellectual qualifications of a great poet" and "the vision and the faculty divine." [28]

When Emerson died in 1882, Ellen Emerson, his widow, asked Hedge, as one of Emerson's "proper friends," to speak at his funeral. [29] Although an accident prevented his doing so, Hedge did pay tribute to Emerson in an address to the annual meeting of the American Unitarian Association later that year. In that address, he recalled Emerson's leadership as a "philosophical essayist" and "lyric poet." He praised his interest in "creative and constructive reform" and called Emerson "an emancipator . . . by the positive, affirmative method," and "a prophet,--the greatest . . . this country or this age has known." [30]

The increasing intellectual divisiveness between Hedge and Emerson, Fuller, and Ripley was not based on the defection of Hedge from previously stated, fundamental Transcendental beliefs. Instead, the split developed because Hedge grew clearer and more insistent in rejecting principles and ideas that he had rejected from the very beginning and to which the others had evolved. These principles and ideas included the more radical opposition to existing institutions, distrust of the past, sole reliance on individual intuition, dismissal of New Testament miracles, and degrading of social reform movements. [31]

Those points upon which Hedge differed with Emerson, Fuller, Ripley, and other radical Transcendentalists have been discussed in this study. They are explained on the scale of his larger intellectual scheme, beyond Transcendentalism, and are seen in both his radical and conservative perspectives. Moreover, by reviewing the relevant chapters of this work, including the dates of those references cited, it can be seen that Hedge's position on these issues had been formulated and stated even before his split with Emerson and the others became apparent. [32]

Clearly, Hedge's views did not change. They were from the beginning balanced by radical impulses and conservative restraints, the first serving as cases in point for the others. In the beginning, his emphasis on the positive aspects of Transcendentalism was more popularly received, because American Transcendentalists were looking for intellectually recognized champions, a role Hedge certainly fit. His constraints became more evident in the years to follow, because he refused to follow the others in their radical, secular move away from the majority of the Transcendental Club. The majority remained within the Unitarian Church and represented the mainstream of American Transcendentalism. [33] Octavius B. Frothingham labeled this group the "eminent orthodox divines who accepted it [Transcendentalism] in accordance with the Christian scheme, and used it in fact as an efficient support for the doctrine of the church." [34]

Hedge remained constant, when he felt the others had "slipped their moorings" or "gone up as dust." [35] In 1867, he commented on the formative years of the Transcendental Club:

> Some thirty years ago, a club was formed of young men, mostly preachers of the Unitarian connection, with a sprinkling of elect ladies,--all fired with the hope of a new era in philosophy and religion, which seemed to them about to dawn upon the world. There was something in the air,--a boding of some great revolution,--some new avatar of the spirit, at whose birth their expectations were called to assist. . . .
> For myself, though I hugely enjoyed the sessions, and shared many of the ideas which ruled the enclave, and the fermentation they engendered, I had no belief in ecclesiastical revolutions to be accomplished with set purpose; I seemed to discern a power and meaning in the old, which the more impassioned would not allow. I had even then made up my mind, that the method of revolution is not discession [sic] but development. My historic conscience, then as since, balanced my neology, and kept me ecclesiastically conservative, though intellectually radical. [36]

Hedge noted that the Transcendental movement was "neither so glorious nor so vile an apparition as one side and the other would make it." It was not the "pure spirit of health," nor the "goblin damned." It was not "destined to supersede other systems," but it was "destined to take an equal rank by their side." What it did do, in Hedge's mind, was to "furnish a new impulse to thought" and "enlarge, somewhat, the horizon of life." It restored man's confidence in his "native instincts" and, thus, would prove to be "an advance over ages past," once accepted. This, he felt confident, would occur in time, as every new philosophy went through a period of rejection upon its introduction and prior to its acceptance, including the currently reigning sensualism. [37]

The consistency established here for Hedge's approach to Transcendentalism has been shown to be the case throughout the entire realm of his consideration. He always considered himself, and was perceived by others, to be among the intellectual vanguard. One contemporary referred to him as "one of the principal actors in a great drama of progressive thought," while another commented that his progressive intellect led him to "an atmosphere in which most men--even intellectual men--find it difficult to breathe today." [38] He resented compromise on the introduction of new ideas, and he sought not popularity if it involved accommodation purchased at too dear a price. He did not shrink from considering the most delicate or momentous questions of his day, and he was never appalled by any results to which his thoughts led. [39] He believed that new ideas, regardless of how unpopular or distasteful, comprised an essential element of man's progressive future.

Hedge was unboundedly optimistic because he believed man's divine nature would continuously seek to rejoin itself with God. He saw it as an inevitable course toward perfectibility, based upon the freedom of man to act in concert with God's will. This would lead to an unfolding of God's spirit within man, possible only through the free and open reception of His word, through man's divine intuition. [40]

At the same time, Hedge was always aware of the limits within which intellectual radicalism should operate. "Next to originality," he stated, "the most distinctive characteristic of genius is a right proportion between the productive and regulative forces of the mind." [41] His faith was in evolution, not revolution, and in the fact that the future would be tied to historical and ecclesiastical continuity, not rupture or institutional destruction. In sum, Hedge always defended intellectual conservatism, when it protected the wisdom of the past and offered stability. He supported radicalism, provided it was "of disciplined thought, not of impatience, pugnacity, and self-conceit." Without radicalism growth could not occur. But, in the end, Hedge favored that "historic sense" which acknowledged the good in both these tendencies. His "historic sense" insisted that both conservative and radical tendencies were "polarizations of a truth that neither quite comprehended." [42] One contemporary observed, for example, that despite Hedge's liberal stance, there was "scarcely a doctrine that separated the orthodox from the liberal world, under which he did not find a greater truth." [43]

Hedge felt that the working of the human mind,

> like all the processes of planetary life, has its appointed methods, and is, from the beginning to end, a series of evolutions, in which every phase is connected, by necessary sequence, with every other phase, and the first movement contains the last.

Thus no philosophy is absolutely true or false, but instead "one of many factors in that process by which truth is continually approximated and never reached." [44]

The process that Hedge had in mind is reflected in the historical process within Christianity at large, and within Anglo-American Christianity in particular, resulting from the continued tension between legalism and antinomianism. [45] The process is dialectial and the direction that results for knowledge is necessarily diagonal, or the progressive product of antithetical radicalism and conservatism. Hedge saw this development represented both in his own intellectual processes, and, on a larger scale, in that including the interaction of figures such as himself, Emerson, Fuller, and Ripley with those such as Andrews Norton and Francis Bowen. [46] Within himself he was the antithesis of what he called his "intellectual radicalism" and "ecclesiastical conservatism." The diagonal which resulted, and which best describes what Hedge stood for, was in his own words, "enlightened conservatism." [47]

Perry Miller once questioned why Frederic Hedge, with all his advantages of intellect and position, failed to make "more of a mark than he did." [48] Miller was, of course, viewing Hedge as falling away from Emerson, Alcott, Ripley, Fuller, and others who rose to popularity on the crest of their radical Transcendentalism. Some critics have answered by pointing to Hedge's years in Bangor, away from the hub of Transcendental development. [49] Others have reflected on his "unassuming nature." [50]

Possibly the answer to Miller lies hidden in a comment by one of Hedge's contemporaries and fellow Transcendental Club members, Elizabeth Peabody. Twenty years after what is generally agreed to be the demise of American Transcendentalism, she observed that if Frederic Hedge had assumed the leadership of American Transcendentalism, "he might have introduced Transcendentalism in such a way that it would not have become identified with the extreme individualism which is now perhaps indelibly associated with it in America." [51]

Clearly unrestrained individualism has been "indelibly" associated with American Transcendentalism, and those, such as Hedge, who led its more moderate mainstream have largely been forgotten. Those central figures remain to be considered more carefully, if we are to understand the larger focus and effectiveness of American Transcendentalism on nineteenth century American intellectual life. The study of Frederic Henry Hedge offers a point from which to begin.

NOTES

1. See Chapter Three and Frederic Henry Hedge, Letter to James Elliot Cabot, 3 December 1836, Emerson Collection, Harvard University Archives, Cambridge, Massachusetts.

2. Terms used by R. W. B. Lewis in his **The American Adam: Innocence, Tragedy, and Tradition in the Nineteenth Century** (Chicago: University of Chicago Press, 1968), 7; Frederic Henry Hedge, "The Destinies of Ecclesiastical Religion," Christian Examiner, 82 (1867), 12; Raymond William Adams, "Frederic Henry Hedge," **Dictionary of American Biography** (1932), IV, 498.

3. Joel Myerson, **The New England Transcendentalists and The Dial: A History of the Magazine and Its Contributors** (Rutherford, N.J.: Farleigh Dickinson University Press, 1980), 156. See also Herbert W. Schneider, **A History of American Philosophy** (New York: Columbia University Press, 1963), 240.

4. Hedge's absence from Frothingham's books may be explained by the author's personal estimate of Hedge following Hedge's opposition to Frothingham in the Unitarian--Free Religion controversy (see Chapter Nine). It is further seen in Frothingham's generally acknowledged insistence upon including only the radical "like-minded" in his book, those whom he saw as most representative of the movement. This latter point will be considered. Octavius Brooks Frothingham, **Transcendentalism in New England** (1876; rpt. Gloucester, Ma.: Peter Smith, 1965), 103; Joseph Henry Allen, **Sequel to "Our Liberal Movement"** (Boston: Roberts Brothers, 1897), 147; Stanley M. Vogel, **German Literary Influences on the American Transcendentalists** (New York: Archon Books, 1970), 114.

5. Vernon L. Parrington, **The Romantic Revolution in America: 1800-1860** (New York: Harcourt, Brace and World, Inc., 1954), 464-465; Van Wyck Brooks, **The Flowering of New England** (New York: E. P. Dutton and Company, Inc., 1952), 539; Henry A. Pochmann, **German Culture in America: Philosophical and Literary Influences: 1600-1900** (Madison, The University of Wisconsin Press, 1957), 243.

6. Ralph Barton Perry, **The Thought and Character of William James** (Boston: Little, Brown, and Company, 1935), I, 88; Frederic Henry Hedge, Letter to Caroline Dall, 1 February 1877, as quoted in Caroline H. Dall, **Transcendentalism in New England: A Lecture Delivered Before the Society for Philosophical Enquiry, Washington, D.C., May 7, 1895** (Boston: Roberts Brothers, 1897), 15; Mary Moody Emerson, Letter to Frederic Henry Hedge, 20 December 1838, as quoted in Martha Ilona Tuomi, "Dr. Frederic Henry Hedge: His Life and Works to the End of His Bangor Pastorate, 1805-1850," M.A. Thesis, University of Maine 1934, 63; Bronson Alcott, **The Journals of Bronson Alcott**, ed. Odell Shepard (Boston: Little Brown

and Company, 1938), 70; Frederic Henry Hedge, "Characteristics of Genius," Atlantic Monthly, February 1868, 256; William T. Harris and F. B. Sanborn, **A. Bronson Alcott, His Life and Philosophy** (Boston: Roberts Brothers, 1893), 1, 269; Clarence L. F. Gohdes, **The Periodicals of American Transcendentalism** (Durham, N.C.: Duke University Press, 1931), 9.

7. Margaret Fuller, Letter to Frederic Henry Hedge, 1 January 1840, Fuller Family Papers, Harvard University Archives, Cambridge, Massachusetts.

8. Frederic Henry Hedge, Letter to Margaret Fuller, 20 January 1840, Fuller Family Papers, Harvard University Archives, Cambridge, Massachusetts.

9. "To Margaret Fuller," 30 March 1840, **The Letters of Ralph Waldo Emerson**, ed. Ralph D. Rusk (New York: Columbia University Press, 1939), II, 270-271.

10. "To Frederic Henry Hedge," 23 March 1842, in **Letters of Emerson,** III, 37.

11. Frederic Henry Hedge, Letter to Ralph Waldo Emerson, 4 April 1842, Poor-Hedge Letters, Schlesinger Library, Radcliffe College, Cambridge, Massachusetts.

12. "To Frederic Henry Hedge," 1 September 1842, in **Letters of Emerson, III**, 84; Ralph Waldo Emerson, **The Journals of Ralph Waldo Emerson,** eds. Edward W. Emerson and W. E. Forbes (Cambridge, Ma.: The Riverside Press, 1909-1914), VIII, 31.

13. As quoted in William R. Hutchison, **The Transcendentalist Ministers: Church Reform in the New England Renaissance** (New Haven: Yale University Press, 1969), 139.

14. Frederic Henry Hedge, Letter to Caroline H. Dall, 1 February 1877, in Dall, 17; Tuomi, 73.

15. Hedge, "Destinies of Ecclesiastical Religion," 13.

16. Frederic Henry Hedge, Letter to Margaret Fuller, 24 March 1840, Fuller Family Papers, Harvard University Archives, Cambridge, Massachusetts.

17. Frederic Henry Hedge, Letter to Convers Francis, 14 February 1843, Washburn Collection, Massachusetts Historical Society, Boston, Massachusetts.

18. Frederic Henry Hedge, "Emerson's Writings," Christian Examiner, 38 (1845) 94-95.

19. Frederic Henry Hedge, Letter to Caroline H. Dall, 28 September 1864, Dall Collection, Massachusetts Historical Society, Boston, Massachusetts.

20. Frederic Henry Hedge, "Dr. Furness's Word to Unitarians," Christian Examiner, 68 (1859), 435.

21. As quoted in Joel Myerson, "Frederic Henry Hedge and the Failure of Transcendentalism," Harvard Library Bulletin, 23 (1975), 408. See also Julia Ward Howe, **Reminiscences: 1819-1899** (1899; rpt. New York: Negro University Press, 1969), 296.

22. Theodore Parker, Letter to Convers Francis, March 1848, Parker Collection, Boston Public Library, Boston, Massachusetts.

23. Perry, 88.

24. At various times, Emerson, Fuller, and Ripley criticized one another as well. Fuller once noted that Emerson "always seems to be on stilts." Emerson found Fuller "a little too impetuous for his nature," and Ripley faulted Emerson for emphasizing esthetics at the expense of religion. Paul F. Boller, Jr., **American Transcendentalism, 1830-1860: An Intellectual Inquiry** (New York: G. P. Putnam's Sons, 1974), xvii, xviii; Charles Crowe, **George Ripley: Transcendentalist and Utopian Socialist** (Athens: University of Georgia Press, 1967), 84; Doreen Hunter, "Frederic Henry Hedge, What Say You?" American Quarterly, 32 (1980), 187.

25. As quoted in Ronald Vale Wells, **Three Christian Transcendentalists: James Marsh, Caleb Sprague Henry, Frederic Henry Hedge** (New York: Octagon Books, 1972), 101.

26. Emerson, **Journals,** VIII, 172.

27. "To William Furness," 6 April 1847, as quoted in Horace Howard Furness, **Records of a Lifelong Friendship, 1807-1882** (Boston: Houghton Mifflin, 1910), 61; "To Thomas Carlyle," 2 June 1847, **The Correspondence of Emerson and Carlyle** (New York: Columbia University Press, 1964), 424; "To Thomas Carlyle," 4 June 1847, **Correspondence of Emerson and Carlyle,** 425.

28. Hedge, "Emerson's Writings," 90-114.

29. Wells, 101-102; Frederic Henry Hedge, "Memorial Address," in Joseph Henry Allen, **Our Liberal Movement in Theology: Chiefly as Shown in Recollections of the History of Unitarianism in New England** (Boston: Roberts Brothers, 1892), 212; Frederic Henry Hedge, "Emerson the Philosopher and the Poet," The Literary World, 25 May 1882, 176-177.

30. Hedge, "Memorial Address," 212.

31. A point raised but not developed by Myerson, "Frederic Henry Hedge," 409; Hunter, 196.

32. See, for example, references to "Emmanuel Swedenborg" (1833), "Progress and Society" (1834), **Conservatism and Reform** (1843), **Christianity Confined to No Sect** (1844), and "The Churches and the Church" (1846). Note also the qualifications Hedge placed on Transcendentalism in general, and on the German Transcendentalists in particular, in "Coleridge's **Literary Character**" (1833), as discussed in Chapter Three and as touted by Emerson and other Transcendentalists as one of the earliest and most seminal works of American Transcendentalists.

33. Schneider, 246; Donald N. Koster, **Transcendentalism in America** (Boston: Twayne Publishers, 1975), 69; Pochmann, 219-220; Boller, xiv; Hutchison, 3; Octavius Brooks Frothingham, **Recollections and Impressions: 1822-1890** (New York: G. P. Putnam's Sons, 1891), 136; Stow Persons, **Free Religion: An American Faith** (Boston: Beacon Press, 1963), 19; Henry David Gray, **Emerson: A Statement of New England Transcendentalism as Expressed in the Philosophy of Its Chief Exponent** (New York: Frederick Ungar Publishing Co., 1958), 16; Thomas Wentworth Higginson, **Margaret Fuller Ossoli** (1884; rpt. New York: Haskell House Publishers, 1968), 144; Walter Harding, **The Days of Henry Thoreau** (New York: Alfred A. Knopf, 1966), 12; Myerson, "Frederic Henry Hedge," 404-405.

34. Frothingham, **Transcendentalism**, 353. See also Howe, 282-285.

35. Hedge, "Destinies of Ecclesiastical Religion," 14.

36. Ibid. 12-13.

37. Frederic Henry Hedge, **Conservatism and Reform** (Boston: Charles C. Little and James Brown, 1843), 32-34.

38. John W. Chadwick, **Frederic Henry Hedge: A Sermon** (Boston: George H. Ellis, Publisher, 1890-1891), 14; William H. Lyon, **Frederic Henry Hedge: Seventh Minister of the First Parish in Brookline, 1856-1872** (Brookline, Ma.: First Parish in Brookline, 1906), 15.

39. C. Everett, "Frederic Henry Hedge," The Christian Register, 28 August 1890, 551; Howard N. Brown, **Frederic Henry Hedge, A Memorial Discourse** (Boston: George H. Ellis, 1891), 3; Frederic Henry Hedge, "The Two Religions," in his **Ways of the Spirit and Other Essasys** (Boston: Roberts Brothers, 1877), 292; Frederic Henry Hedge, "The Art of Life, The Scholar's Calling," The Dial, 1 (1840), 182.

40. Hedge, **Conservatism and Reform**, 38; Frederic Henry Hedge, Letter to Caroline H. Dall, 11 January 1864, Dall Collection, Massachusetts Historical Society, Boston, Massachusetts; Frederic Henry Hedge, Letter to Caroline H. Dall, 22 February 1865, Dall Collection, Massachusetts Historical Society, Boston, Massachusetts; Frederic Henry Hedge, Letter to Henry Bellows, 17 October 1877, Bellows Collection, Massachusetts Historical Society, Boston, Massachusetts; Frederic Henry Hedge, Letter to Henry Bellows, 7 April 1878, Bellows Collection, Massachusetts Historical Society, Boston, Massachusetts. See also Wells, 98-100; Hedge, "Genius," 150; Chadwick, 29; Frederic Henry Hedge, "And Wished for the Day," in his **Sermons** (Boston: Roberts Brothers, 1891), 197.

41. Hedge, "Genius," 153.

42. Hedge, "Destinies of Ecclesiastical Religion," 15. See also Frederic Henry Hedge, **The Faithful Servant** (Boston: American Unitarian Association, 1871), 29; Frederic Henry Hedge, "Antisupernaturalism in the Pulpit," Christian Examiner, 77 (1864), 145-159.

43. Lyon, 16. See also Frederic Henry Hedge, **Reason in Religion,** (Boston: Walker, Fuller, and Company, 1865), 307-310; Frederic Henry Hedge, "Romanism and Its Worship," Christian Examiner, 56 (1854), 223-224; Frederic Henry Hedge, "Ecclesiastical Christendom," Christian Examiner, 51 (1851), 113-116, 126; Frederic Henry Hedge, "Dr. Huntington on the Trinity," Christian Examiner, 68 (1860), 236-267.

44. Hedge, **Conservatism and Reform,** 30; Allen, **Sequel to "Our Liberal Movement,"** 20-21.

45. Wesley T. Mott, "Emerson and Antinomianism: The Legacy of the Sermons," American Literature, 50 (1978), 370.

46. Hedge, **Conservatism and Reform,** 38; Frederic Henry Hedge, "All Things to All Men," in his **Sermons,** 200. See also Hunter, 198; Wells, 115, 146; Frederic Henry Hedge, **Recent Inquiries in Theology, By Eminent English Churchmen; Being Essays and Reviews** (Boston: Walker, Wise, and Company, 1861), xiii; and for comparison Frederic Henry Hedge, "Science and Faith," in his **Martin Luther and Other Essays** (Boston: Roberts Brothers, 1888), 173-183; Frederic Henry Hedge, "Classic and Romantic," in his **Martin Luther**, 184-205; Frederic Henry Hedge, "Ethical Systems," in his **Martin Luther**, 225-249.

47. Hedge, **Conservatism and Reform,** 11-13.

48. Perry Miller, **The Transcendentalists: An Anthology** (Cambridge, Ma.: The Harvard University Press), 67.

49. Vogel, 118; Hutchison, 47.

50. Orie W. Long, **Frederic Henry Hedge: A Cosmopolitan Scholar** (Portland, Me.: The Southworth-Anthoensen Press, 1940), 53; Howe, 300.

51. Elizabeth Peabody, **Reminiscences of Reverend William Ellery Channing** (Boston: Roberts Brothers, 1880), 371.

SELECT BIBLIOGRAPHY

I. Works by Frederic Henry Hedge

Hedge, Frederic Henry. **An Address Delivered at the Funeral of Mrs. Hannah C. Stearns of Brookline on Sunday, November 8, 1857.** Boston: David Clapp, 1857.

--------. **An Address Delivered Before the Graduating Class of the Divinity School in Cambridge, July 15, 1849.** Cambridge, Ma.: John Bartlett, 1849.

--------. **Address in Memory of Reverend William Ellery Channing, D.D., at the Arlington Street Church, Boston, on Sunday Evening, October 6, 1867.** Boston: John Wilson, 1867.

--------. "Address to the Germans of Boston, Faneuil Hall, July 27, 1870." The Index, 27 August 1869, 2-3.

--------. "Antisupernaturalism in the Pulpit, An Address Delivered to the Graduating Class of the Divinity School, Cambridge, July 17, 1864." Christian Examiner, 77 (1864), 145-159.

--------. "Arthur Schopenhauer." Christian Examiner, 76 (1864), 46-60.

--------. "The Art of Life, the Scholar's Calling." The Dial, 1 (1840), 175-182.

--------. **Atheism in Philosophy, and Other Essays.** Boston: Roberts Brothers, 1884.

--------. **Atonement in Connection With the Death of Christ.** Boston: American Unitarian Association, 1866.

--------. "Bartol's **Pictures of Europe.**" Christian Examiner, 59 (1855), 427-437.

--------. "Bellow's **Suspense of Faith.**" Christian Examiner, 67 (1859), 286-288.

--------. "The Best Government." Christian Examiner, 72 (1862), 313-336.

--------. "The Broad Church." Christian Examiner, 69 (1860), 54-66.

--------. "Brook's **Faust.**" Christian Examiner, 63 (1857), 1-18.

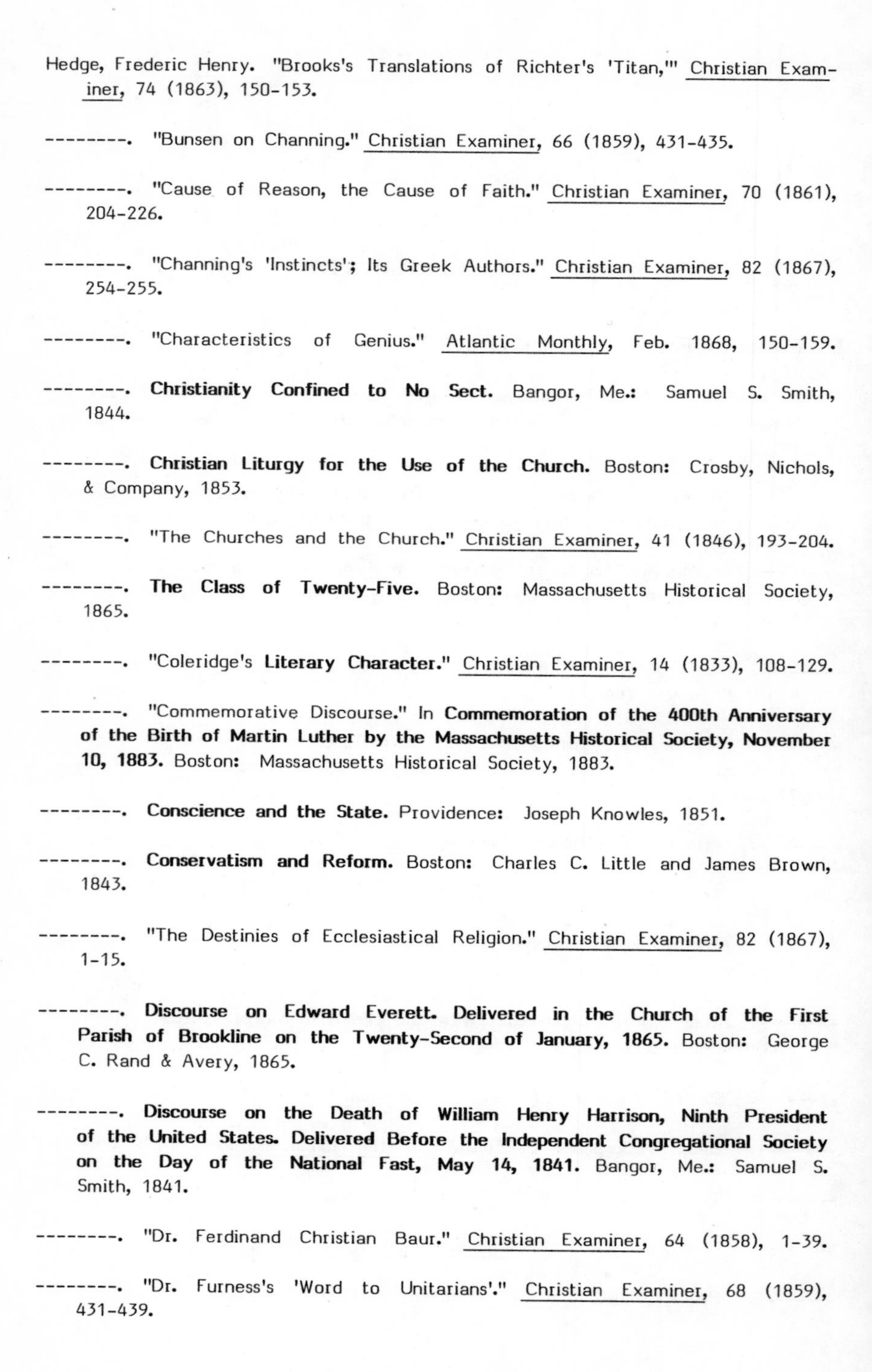

Hedge, Frederic Henry. "Brooks's Translations of Richter's 'Titan,'" Christian Examiner, 74 (1863), 150-153.

--------. "Bunsen on Channing." Christian Examiner, 66 (1859), 431-435.

--------. "Cause of Reason, the Cause of Faith." Christian Examiner, 70 (1861), 204-226.

--------. "Channing's 'Instincts'; Its Greek Authors." Christian Examiner, 82 (1867), 254-255.

--------. "Characteristics of Genius." Atlantic Monthly, Feb. 1868, 150-159.

--------. **Christianity Confined to No Sect.** Bangor, Me.: Samuel S. Smith, 1844.

--------. **Christian Liturgy for the Use of the Church.** Boston: Crosby, Nichols, & Company, 1853.

--------. "The Churches and the Church." Christian Examiner, 41 (1846), 193-204.

--------. **The Class of Twenty-Five.** Boston: Massachusetts Historical Society, 1865.

--------. "Coleridge's **Literary Character.**" Christian Examiner, 14 (1833), 108-129.

--------. "Commemorative Discourse." In **Commemoration of the 400th Anniversary of the Birth of Martin Luther by the Massachusetts Historical Society, November 10, 1883.** Boston: Massachusetts Historical Society, 1883.

--------. **Conscience and the State.** Providence: Joseph Knowles, 1851.

--------. **Conservatism and Reform.** Boston: Charles C. Little and James Brown, 1843.

--------. "The Destinies of Ecclesiastical Religion." Christian Examiner, 82 (1867), 1-15.

--------. **Discourse on Edward Everett. Delivered in the Church of the First Parish of Brookline on the Twenty-Second of January, 1865.** Boston: George C. Rand & Avery, 1865.

--------. **Discourse on the Death of William Henry Harrison, Ninth President of the United States. Delivered Before the Independent Congregational Society on the Day of the National Fast, May 14, 1841.** Bangor, Me.: Samuel S. Smith, 1841.

--------. "Dr. Ferdinand Christian Baur." Christian Examiner, 64 (1858), 1-39.

--------. "Dr. Furness's 'Word to Unitarians'." Christian Examiner, 68 (1859), 431-439.

Hedge, Frederic Henry. "Dr. Huntington on the Trinity." Christian Examiner, 68 (1860), 236-267.

--------. "The Doctrine of Endless Punishment." Christian Examiner, 62 (1859), 98-128.

--------. "Ecclesiastical Christendom." Christian Examiner, 51 (1851), 112-134.

--------. "Emerson's Writings." Christian Examiner, 38 (1845), 87-106.

--------. "Emerson the Philosopher and the Poet." The Literary World, 25 May 1882, 176-177.

--------. "Emmanuel Swedenborg." Christian Examiner, 15 (1833), 193-218.

--------. "European Travel." Christian Examiner, 53 (1852), 239-258.

--------. **The Faithful Servant.** Boston: American Unitarian Association, 1871.

--------. "Furness's Schiller's 'Song of the Bell'." Christian Examiner, 48 (1850), 507-508.

--------. "G. H. Lewes, **The Life and Works of Goethe.**" North American Review, 82 (1856), 564-568.

--------. "Goethe's 'Marchen'." In **The Life and Genius of Goethe: Lectures at the Concord School of Philosophy.** Ed. Franklin B. Sanborn. Boston: Ticknor & Company, 1886.

--------. "The Gospel According to Paul." Christian Examiner, 63 (1857), 391-403.

--------. **Gospel Invitations.** Boston: American Unitarian Association, 1846.

--------. "Holmes's 'Elsie Venner'." Christian Examiner, 70 (1861), 459-462.

--------. "Hosmer's **Short History of German Literature.**" Unitarian Review and Religious Magazine, March 1879, 248-253.

--------. **Hours With the German Classics; Masterpieces of German Literature Translated Into English.** New York: The German Publication Society, 1913.

--------, and Frederic D. Huntington, eds. **Hymns for the Church of Christ.** Boston: Crosby, Nichols, & Company, 1853.

--------. **An Introductory Lecture Delivered at the Opening of the Bangor Lyceum, November 5, 1836.** Bangor, Me.: Nourse, Smith, Duren & Thatcher, 1836.

--------. "Irony." Atlantic Monthly, Oct. 1870, 414-425.

--------. **The Leaven of the Word.** Boston: Dutton & Wentworth, 1849.

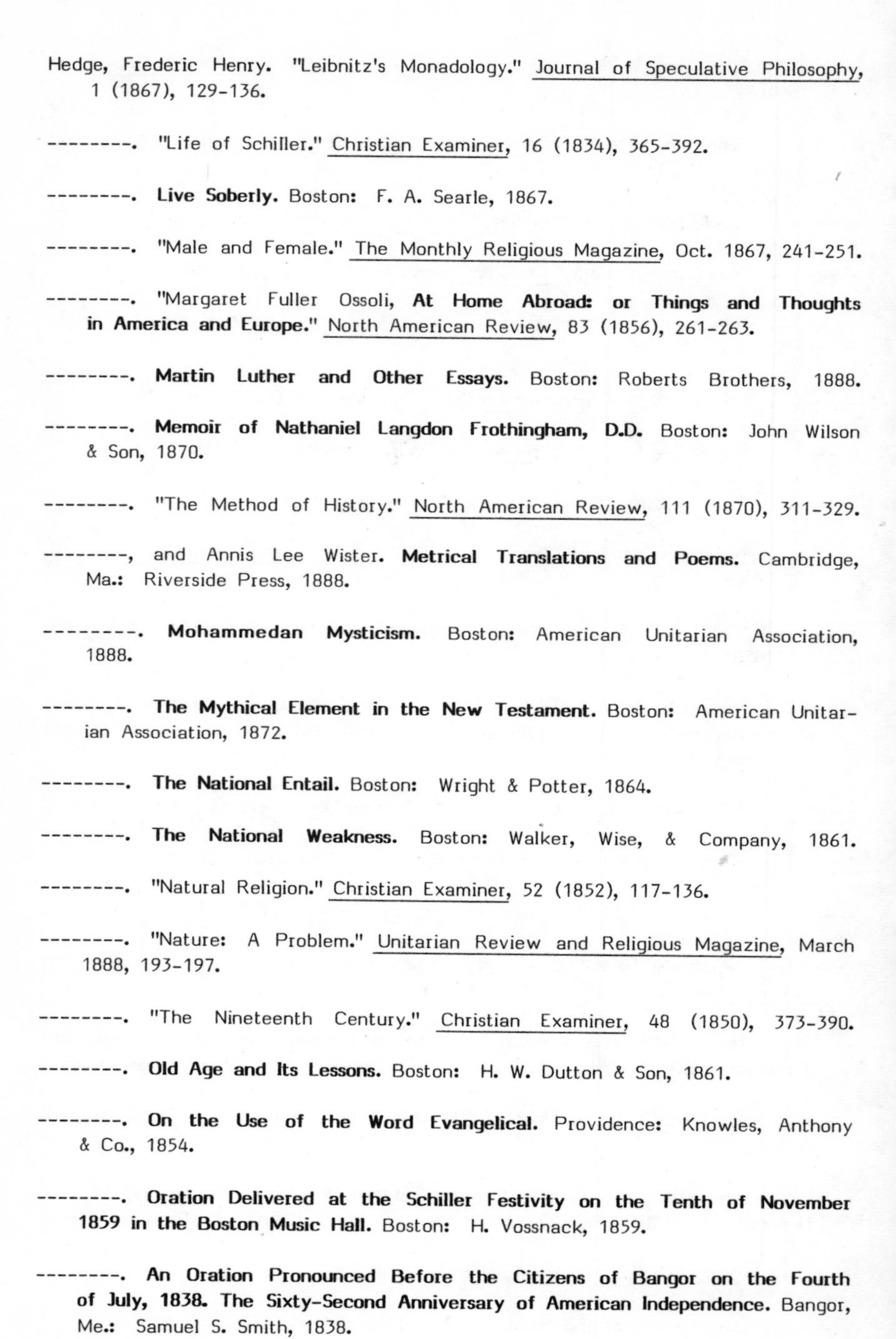

Hedge, Frederic Henry. "Leibnitz's Monadology." Journal of Speculative Philosophy, 1 (1867), 129-136.

--------. "Life of Schiller." Christian Examiner, 16 (1834), 365-392.

--------. **Live Soberly.** Boston: F. A. Searle, 1867.

--------. "Male and Female." The Monthly Religious Magazine, Oct. 1867, 241-251.

--------. "Margaret Fuller Ossoli, **At Home Abroad: or Things and Thoughts in America and Europe.**" North American Review, 83 (1856), 261-263.

--------. **Martin Luther and Other Essays.** Boston: Roberts Brothers, 1888.

--------. **Memoir of Nathaniel Langdon Frothingham, D.D.** Boston: John Wilson & Son, 1870.

--------. "The Method of History." North American Review, 111 (1870), 311-329.

--------, and Annis Lee Wister. **Metrical Translations and Poems.** Cambridge, Ma.: Riverside Press, 1888.

--------. **Mohammedan Mysticism.** Boston: American Unitarian Association, 1888.

--------. **The Mythical Element in the New Testament.** Boston: American Unitarian Association, 1872.

--------. **The National Entail.** Boston: Wright & Potter, 1864.

--------. **The National Weakness.** Boston: Walker, Wise, & Company, 1861.

--------. "Natural Religion." Christian Examiner, 52 (1852), 117-136.

--------. "Nature: A Problem." Unitarian Review and Religious Magazine, March 1888, 193-197.

--------. "The Nineteenth Century." Christian Examiner, 48 (1850), 373-390.

--------. **Old Age and Its Lessons.** Boston: H. W. Dutton & Son, 1861.

--------. **On the Use of the Word Evangelical.** Providence: Knowles, Anthony & Co., 1854.

--------. **Oration Delivered at the Schiller Festivity on the Tenth of November 1859 in the Boston Music Hall.** Boston: H. Vossnack, 1859.

--------. **An Oration Pronounced Before the Citizens of Bangor on the Fourth of July, 1838. The Sixty-Second Anniversary of American Independence.** Bangor, Me.: Samuel S. Smith, 1838.

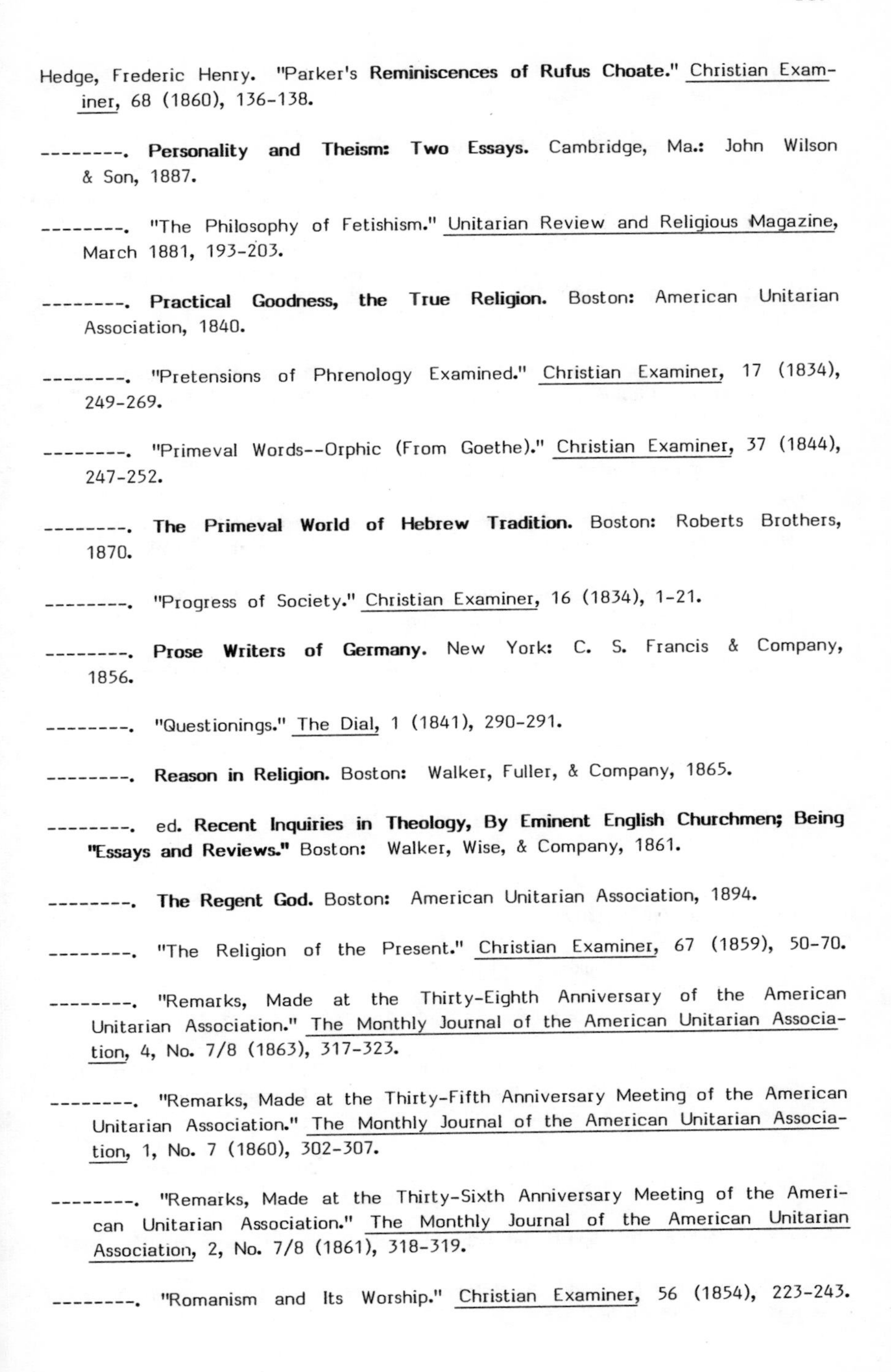

Hedge, Frederic Henry. "Parker's **Reminiscences of Rufus Choate.**" Christian Examiner, 68 (1860), 136-138.

--------. **Personality and Theism: Two Essays.** Cambridge, Ma.: John Wilson & Son, 1887.

--------. "The Philosophy of Fetishism." Unitarian Review and Religious Magazine, March 1881, 193-203.

--------. **Practical Goodness, the True Religion.** Boston: American Unitarian Association, 1840.

--------. "Pretensions of Phrenology Examined." Christian Examiner, 17 (1834), 249-269.

--------. "Primeval Words--Orphic (From Goethe)." Christian Examiner, 37 (1844), 247-252.

--------. **The Primeval World of Hebrew Tradition.** Boston: Roberts Brothers, 1870.

--------. "Progress of Society." Christian Examiner, 16 (1834), 1-21.

--------. **Prose Writers of Germany.** New York: C. S. Francis & Company, 1856.

--------. "Questionings." The Dial, 1 (1841), 290-291.

--------. **Reason in Religion.** Boston: Walker, Fuller, & Company, 1865.

--------. ed. **Recent Inquiries in Theology, By Eminent English Churchmen; Being "Essays and Reviews."** Boston: Walker, Wise, & Company, 1861.

--------. **The Regent God.** Boston: American Unitarian Association, 1894.

--------. "The Religion of the Present." Christian Examiner, 67 (1859), 50-70.

--------. "Remarks, Made at the Thirty-Eighth Anniversary of the American Unitarian Association." The Monthly Journal of the American Unitarian Association, 4, No. 7/8 (1863), 317-323.

--------. "Remarks, Made at the Thirty-Fifth Anniversary Meeting of the American Unitarian Association." The Monthly Journal of the American Unitarian Association, 1, No. 7 (1860), 302-307.

--------. "Remarks, Made at the Thirty-Sixth Anniversary Meeting of the American Unitarian Association." The Monthly Journal of the American Unitarian Association, 2, No. 7/8 (1861), 318-319.

--------. "Romanism and Its Worship." Christian Examiner, 56 (1854), 223-243.

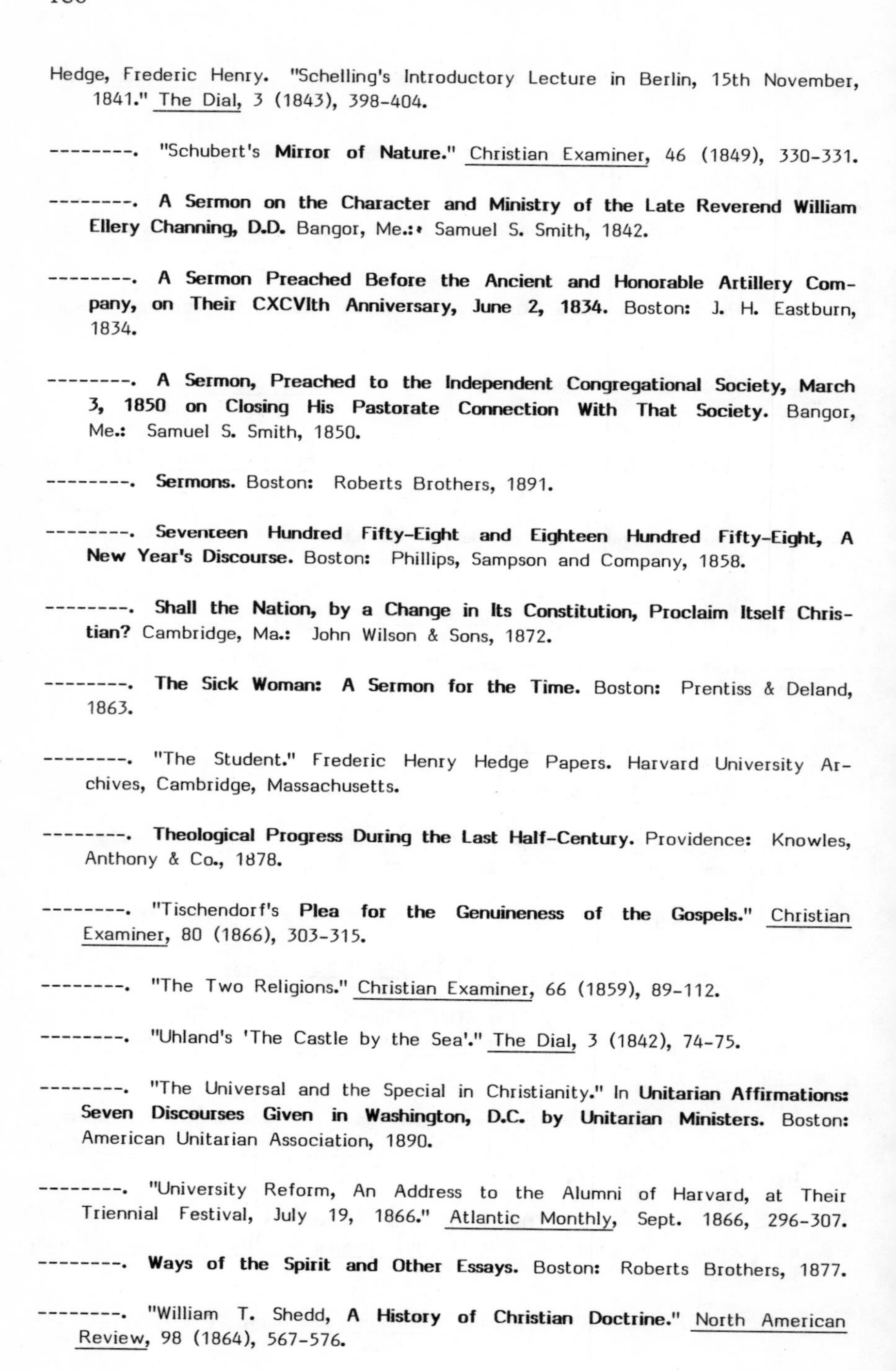

Hedge, Frederic Henry. "Schelling's Introductory Lecture in Berlin, 15th November, 1841." The Dial, 3 (1843), 398-404.

--------. "Schubert's **Mirror of Nature.**" Christian Examiner, 46 (1849), 330-331.

--------. **A Sermon on the Character and Ministry of the Late Reverend William Ellery Channing, D.D.** Bangor, Me.: Samuel S. Smith, 1842.

--------. **A Sermon Preached Before the Ancient and Honorable Artillery Company, on Their CXCVIth Anniversary, June 2, 1834.** Boston: J. H. Eastburn, 1834.

--------. **A Sermon, Preached to the Independent Congregational Society, March 3, 1850 on Closing His Pastorate Connection With That Society.** Bangor, Me.: Samuel S. Smith, 1850.

--------. **Sermons.** Boston: Roberts Brothers, 1891.

--------. **Seventeen Hundred Fifty-Eight and Eighteen Hundred Fifty-Eight, A New Year's Discourse.** Boston: Phillips, Sampson and Company, 1858.

--------. **Shall the Nation, by a Change in Its Constitution, Proclaim Itself Christian?** Cambridge, Ma.: John Wilson & Sons, 1872.

--------. **The Sick Woman: A Sermon for the Time.** Boston: Prentiss & Deland, 1863.

--------. "The Student." Frederic Henry Hedge Papers. Harvard University Archives, Cambridge, Massachusetts.

--------. **Theological Progress During the Last Half-Century.** Providence: Knowles, Anthony & Co., 1878.

--------. "Tischendorf's **Plea for the Genuineness of the Gospels.**" Christian Examiner, 80 (1866), 303-315.

--------. "The Two Religions." Christian Examiner, 66 (1859), 89-112.

--------. "Uhland's 'The Castle by the Sea'." The Dial, 3 (1842), 74-75.

--------. "The Universal and the Special in Christianity." In **Unitarian Affirmations: Seven Discourses Given in Washington, D.C. by Unitarian Ministers.** Boston: American Unitarian Association, 1890.

--------. "University Reform, An Address to the Alumni of Harvard, at Their Triennial Festival, July 19, 1866." Atlantic Monthly, Sept. 1866, 296-307.

--------. **Ways of the Spirit and Other Essays.** Boston: Roberts Brothers, 1877.

--------. "William T. Shedd, **A History of Christian Doctrine.**" North American Review, 98 (1864), 567-576.

Hedge, Frederic Henry. "Woodbury's Burnside." Christian Examiner, 82 (1867), 252, 253.

II. Letters Written by, to, or about Hedge (Not in collections listed in IV)

Bancroft, George. Letter to Edward Everett. 14 November 1818. Bancroft Collection. Massachusetts Historical Society, Boston, Massachusetts.

--------. Letter to Edward Everett. 20 February 1819. Bancroft Collection, Massachusetts Historical Society, Boston, Massachusetts.

--------. Letter to Edward Everett. 1 August 1819. Bancroft Collection. Massachusetts Historical Society, Boston, Massachusetts.

--------. Letter to Edward Everett. 25 September 1819. Bancroft Collection. Massachusetts Historical Society, Boston, Massachusetts.

--------. Letter to Edward Everett. 4 November 1819. Bancroft Collection. Massachusetts Historical Society, Boston, Massachusetts.

--------. Letter to Edward Everett. 28 December 1820. Bancroft Collection. Massachusetts Historical Society, Boston, Massachusetts.

--------. Letter to Edward Everett. 2 April 1821. Bancroft Collection. Massachusetts Historical Society, Boston, Massachusetts.

--------. Letter to Edward Everett Hale. 31 December 1864. Bancroft Collection. Massachusetts Historical Society, Boston, Massachusetts.

--------. Letter to Levi Hedge. 23 January 1821. Bancroft Collection. Massachusetts Historical Society, Boston, Massachusetts.

--------. Letter to Levi Hedge. 6 March 1821. Bancroft Collection. Massachusetts Historical Society, Boston, Massachusetts.

Emerson, Ralph Waldo. Letter to Frederic Henry Hedge. 12 July 1834. Hedge Papers. Bangor Historical Society, Bangor, Maine.

Fuller, Margaret. Letter to Frederic Hedge. 1 February 1835. Frederic Henry Hedge Papers. Harvard University Archives, Cambridge, Massachusetts.

Hedge, Frederic Henry. Letter to Nathan Appleton. 23 September 1859. Appleton Collection. Massachusetts Historical Society, Boston, Massachusetts.

--------. Letter to Henry Bellows. 22 April 1856. Bellows Collection. Massachusetts Historical Society, Boston, Massachusetts.

--------. Letter to Henry Bellows. 2 May 1856. Bellows Collection. Massachusetts Historical Society, Boston, Massachusetts.

Hedge, Frederic Henry. Letter to Henry Bellows. 16 May 1858. Bellows Collection. Massachusetts Historical Society, Boston, Massachusetts.

--------. Letter to Henry Bellows. 24 March 1865. Bellows Collection. Massachusetts Historical Society, Boston, Massachusetts.

--------. Letter to Henry Bellows. 13 January 1872. Bellows Collection. Massachusetts Historical Society, Boston, Massachusetts.

--------. Letter to Henry Bellows. 17 October 1877. Bellows Collection. Massachusetts Historical Society, Boston, Massachusetts.

--------. Letter to Henry Bellows. 24 January 1878. Bellows Collection. Massachusetts Historical Society, Boston, Massachusetts.

--------. Letter to Henry Bellows. 7 April 1878. Bellows Collection. Massachusetts Historical Society, Boston, Massachusetts.

--------. Letter to Henry Bellows. 23 June 1878. Bellows Collection. Massachusetts Historical Society, Boston, Massachusetts.

--------. Letter to James Elliot Cabot. 3 December 1836. Emerson Collection. Harvard University Archives, Cambridge, Massachusetts.

--------. Letter to Caroline H. Dall. 28 September 1864. Dall Collection. Massachusetts Historical Society, Boston, Massachusetts.

--------. Letter to Caroline H. Dall. 11 January 1865. Dall Collection. Massachusetts Historical Society, Boston, Massachusetts.

--------. Letter to Caroline H. Dall. 22 February 1865. Dall Collection. Massachusetts Historical Society, Boston, Massachusetts.

--------. Letter to Ralph Waldo Emerson. 14 June 1836. Poor-Hedge Letters. Schlesinger Library, Radcliffe College, Cambridge, Massachusetts.

--------. Letter to Ralph Waldo Emerson. 4 April 1842. Poor-Hedge Letters. Schlesinger Library, Radcliffe College, Cambridge, Massachusetts.

--------. Letter to Convers Francis. 14 February 1843. Washburn Collection. Massachusetts Historical Society, Boston, Massachusetts.

--------. Letter to Lucy Hedge. 1 April 1836. Poor-Hedge Letters. Schlesinger Library, Radcliffe College, Cambridge, Massachusetts.

--------. Letter to Charles Lowe. 24 March 1865. Frederic Henry Hedge Papers. Andover-Harvard Theological Library, Cambridge, Massachusetts.

--------. Letter to Charles Lowe. 19 September 1865. Frederic Henry Hedge Papers. Andover-Harvard Theological Library, Cambridge, Massachusetts.

Hedge, Frederic Henry. Letter to Charles Lowe. 26 January 1866. Frederic Henry Hedge Papers. Andover-Harvard Theological Library, Cambridge, Massachusetts.

--------. Letter to Charles Lowe. 29 January 1866. Frederic Henry Hedge Papers. Andover-Harvard Theological Library, Cambridge, Massachusetts.

--------. Letter to Charles Lowe. 26 February 1866. Frederic Henry Hedge Papers. Andover-Harvard Theological Library, Cambridge, Massachusetts.

--------. Letter to Charles Lowe. 7 June 1866. Frederic Henry Hedge Papers. Andover-Harvard Theological Library, Cambridge, Massachusetts.

--------. Letter to Charles Lowe. 21 November 1866. Frederic Henry Hedge Papers. Andover-Harvard Theological Library, Cambridge, Massachusetts.

--------. Letter to James de Normandie. 9 January 1877. Bellows Collection. Massachusetts Historical Society. Boston, Massachusetts.

--------. Letter to John Graham Palfrey. 16 June 1833. Frederic Henry Hedge Papers. Harvard University Archives, Cambridge, Massachusetts.

--------. Letter to G. C. Smith. 5 September 1867. Frederic Henry Hedge Papers. Andover-Harvard Theological Library, Cambridge, Massachusetts.

--------. Letter to George Ware. 23 May 1864. Frederic Henry Hedge Papers. Andover-Harvard Theological Library, Cambridge, Massachusetts.

Hedge, Lucy. Letter to Frederic Henry Hedge. 17 December 1835. Poor-Hedge Letters. Schlesinger Library, Radcliffe College, Cambridge, Massachusetts.

Kirkland, John Thornston. Letter to Frederic Henry Hedge. 16 September 1872. Frederic Henry Hedge Papers. Harvard University Archives, Cambridge, Massachusetts.

Parker, Theodore. Letter to Convers Francis. March 1848. Parker Collection. Boston Public Library, Boston, Massachusetts.

III. Directly Related Works by Hedge's Contemporaries

Abbot, Francis Ellington, and James Freeman Clarke. **The Battle of Syracuse, Two Essays.** Boston: The Index Association, 1875.

Abbot, Francis Ellington. "Positivism in Theology." Christian Examiner, 80 (1866), 234-267.

Allen, Joseph Henry, and Richard Eddy. **A History of the Unitarians and the Universalists in the United States.** New York: The Christian Literature Co., 1894.

Allen, Joseph Henry. **Our Liberal Movement in Theology: Chiefly as Shown in Recollections of the History of Unitarianism in New England.** Boston: Roberts Brothers, 1892.

Allen, Joseph Henry. **Sequel to "Our Liberal Movement."** Boston: Roberts Brothers, 1897.

Atkinson, Brooks, ed. **Walden and Other Writings of Henry David Thoreau.** New York: Modern Library, 1950.

Bode, Carl, ed. **The Best of Thoreau's Journals.** Carbondale: Southern Illinois University Press, 1967.

Bowen, Daniel. **Assumed Authority: A Review of Reverend Dr. Hedge's Address Entitled "Antisupernaturalism in the Pulpit."** Boston: Walker, Wise, & Company, 1864.

Bowen, Francis, "Berkeley and His Philosophy." Christian Examiner, 24 (1838), 310-345.

--------. **Critical Essays.** Boston: Roberts Brothers, 1842.

--------. "Locke and the Transcendentalists." Christian Examiner, 23 (1837), 170-194.

--------. **Modern Philosophy, From Descartes to Schopenhauer and Hartman.** New York: Charles Scribner's Sons, 1887.

--------. "Transcendentalism." Christian Examiner, 23 (1837), 371-385.

--------. "Transcendental Theology." Christian Examiner, 30 (1841), 189-223.

Burnap, George W. "The Importance of Systematic Theology, and the Duty of the Unitarian Clergy in Relation to It." Christian Examiner, 49 (1850), 165-184.

Cabot, James Elliot. **A Memoir of Ralph Waldo Emerson.** 2 vols. Boston: Houghton Mifflin & Company, 1895.

Chadwick, John White. **Old and New Unitarian Belief.** Boston: George H. Ellis, 1901.

--------. **Theodore Parker: Preacher and Reformer.** Boston: Houghton Mifflin and Company, 1900.

Channing, William Ellery. **The Works of William Ellery Channing.** 2 vols. 1846; rpt. New York: Burt Franklin, 1970.

Channing, William H., and James F. Clarke, and Ralph Waldo Emerson, eds. **Memoirs of Margaret Fuller Ossoli.** 3 vols. London: Richard Bentley, 1852.

Clarke, James Freeman. **Memorial and Biographical Sketches.** Boston: Houghton, Osgood & Company, 1878.

Commager, Henry Steele, ed. **Theodore Parker, An Anthology.** Boston: Beacon Press, 1960.

Conway, Moncure Daniel. **Autobiography, Memories and Experiences of Moncure Daniel Conway.** 2 vols. 1904; rpt. New York: Negro University Press, 1969.

Cook, Joseph. **Transcendentalism, With Preludes on Current Events.** Boston: James R. Osgood & Company, 1878.

Cranch, Leonora Scott, ed. **The Life and Letters of Christopher Pearse Cranch.** 1917; rpt. New York: AMS Press, 1969.

Dall, Caroline H. **Transcendentalism in New England: A Lecture Delivered Before the Society for Philosophical Enquiry, Washington D.C., May 7, 1895.** Boston: Roberts Brothers, 1897.

Eliot, Samuel Atkins, ed. **Heralds of a Liberal Faith.** 4 vols. 1900; rpt. Boston: Beacon Press, 1952.

Ellis, Charles Mayo. **An Essay on Transcendentalism.** 1842; rpt. Westport, Ct.: Greenwood Press, 1954.

Ellis, George E. **A Half-Century of the Unitarian Controversy.** Boston: Crosby, Nichols, & Company, 1857.

Emerson, Edward W., and W. E. Forbes, eds. **The Journals of Ralph Waldo Emerson.** 10 vols. Cambridge, Ma.: Riverside Press, 1909-1914.

Emerson, Ralph Waldo. **Essays.** New York: E. P. Dutton & Co., Inc., 1947.

--------. "American Scholar: An Oration Delivered Before the Phi Beta Kappa Society at Cambridge, August 31, 1837." In **Anthology of American Literature.** New York: Macmillan Publishing Co., Inc., 1980. Vol. I, 1024-1036.

--------. "The Divinity School Address: An Address Delivered Before the Senior class in Divinity College, Cambridge, Sunday Evening, July 15, 1838." In **Anthology of American Literature.** New York: Macmillan Publishing Co., 1980. Vol. I, 1032-1047.

--------. "Nature." in **Anthology of American Literature.** New York: Macmillan Publishing Co., Inc., 1980. Vol. I, 997-1024.

First Annual Report of the Executive Committee of the Free Religious Association. Boston: W. F. Brown and Co., 1868.

Free Religion. Report of Addresses at a Meeting Held in Boston, May 30, 1867 to Consider the Conditions, Wants, and Prospects of Free Religion in America, Together With the Constitution of the Free Religious Association There Organized. Boston: Adams & Co., 1867.

Frothingham, Octavius Brooks. **Boston Unitarianism: 1820-1850, A Study of the Life and Work of Nathaniel Langdon Frothingham.** New York: G. P. Putnam's Sons, 1890.

--------. **George Ripley.** 1883; rpt. New York: AMS Press, 1970.

--------. **A Memoir of William Henry Channing.** Boston: Houghton Mifflin, 1886.

--------. **Recollections and Impressions: 1822-1890.** New York: G. P. Putnam's Sons, 1891.

--------. **Transcendentalism in New England, A History.** 1876; rpt. Gloucester, Ma.: Peter Smith, 1965.

Furness, Horace Howard. **Records of a Lifelong Friendship, 1807-1882.** Boston: Houghton Mifflin, 1910.

Gillett, E. H. "History and Literature of the Unitarian Controversy." Historical Magazine, April 1871, 316-324.

Hale, Edward Everett, ed. **James Freeman Clarke: Autobiography, Diary, and Correspondence.** Boston: Houghton Mifflin & Company, 1892.

--------. "The National Conference of Unitarian Churches." Christian Examiner, 16 (1865), 409-430.

Harris, William T., and F. B. Sanborn. **A. Bronson Alcott, His Life and Philosophy.** 2 vols. Boston: Roberts Brothers, 1893.

Hedge, Levi. **Elements of Logick; or a Summary of the General Principles and Different Modes of Reasoning.** Cooperstown, N.Y.: H. & E. Phinney, 1849.

Herrnstadt, Richard L. **The Letters of A. Bronson Alcott.** Ames: The Iowa State University Press, 1969.

Higginson, Thomas Wentworth. **Margaret Fuller Ossoli.** 1884; rpt. New York: Haskel House Publishers, Ltd., 1968.

Howe, Julia Ward. **Reminiscences: 1819-1899.** 1899; rpt. New York: Negro University Press, 1969.

Howe, M. A. De Wolfe, ed. **The Life and Letters of George Bancroft.** 2 vols. New York: Charles Scribner's Sons, 1908.

Le Breton, Anna Letitia, ed. **Correspondence of William Ellery Channing and Lucy Aiken From 1826 to 1842.** Boston: Roberts Brothers, 1874.

Memoir of William Ellery Channing With Extracts From His Correspondence and Manuscripts. 3 vols. Boston: William Crosby & H. P. Nichols, 1848-1860.

"National Unitarian Convention." The Monthly Journal of the American Unitarian Association, 6, No. 5 (1865), 209-215.

Norton, C. E. ed. **Correspondence of Thomas Carlyle and Ralph Waldo Emerson, 1834-1872.** 2 vols. Boston: Houghton Mifflin Company, 1883.

"Of Cousin and the Germans, Princeton Review." Christian Examiner, 28 (1840), 378-389.

"Our Denominational Position." The Monthly Journal of the American Unitarian Association, 7, No. 7/8 (1866), 333-335.

Parsons, T. "Transcendentalism, Part I." New Jerusalem Magazine, Dec. 1840, 137-140.

--------. "Transcendentalism, Part II." New Jerusalem Magazine, June 1841, 380-388.

Peabody, Elizabeth. **Reminiscences of Reverend William Ellery Channing.** Boston: Roberts Brothers, 1880.

Potter, William J. **The Free Religious Association: Its Twenty-Five Years and Their Meaning--An Address for the Twenty-Fifth Anniversary of the Association, at Tremont Temple, Boston, May 27, 1892, Preceded by a Brief Sketch of the Annual Convention.** Boston: Free Religious Association of America, 1892.

Rusk, Ralph D., ed. **The Letters of Ralph Waldo Emerson.** 6 vols. New York: Columbia University Press, 1939.

Sanborn, F. B. **Recollections of Seventy Years.** 2 vols. Boston: Richard G. Badger, 1909.

"Second Meeting of the National Conference of Unitarian and Other Christian Churches." The Monthly Journal of the American Unitarian Association, Nov. 1866, 481-500.

Shepard, Odell, ed. **The Journals of Bronson Alcott.** Boston: Little, Brown & Company, 1938.

Slater, Joseph, ed. **The Correspondence of Emerson and Carlyle.** New York: Columbia University Press, 1964.

Sprague, William B. **Annals of the American Pulpit; or Commemorative Notices of Distinguished American Clergymen of the Various Denominations, From the Early Settlement of the Country to the Close of the Year 1855, With Historical Introductions.** 9 vols. New York: Robert Carter & Brothers, 1857-1869.

Wade, Mason, ed. **The Writings of Margaret Fuller**, New York: Viking Press, 1941.

Walker, J. "Schaf on Protestantism." Christian Examiner, 39 (1845), 220-225.

Ware, William ed. **American Unitarian Biography: Memoir of Individuals Who Have Been Distinguished by Their Writings, Character, and Efforts in the Cause of Liberal Christianity.** 2 vols. Cambridge, Ma.: James Munroe & Company, 1850.

Weiss, John ed. **Life and Correspondence of Theodore Parker, Minister of the Twenty-Eighth Congregational Society, Boston.** 2 vols. New York: D. Appleton & Company, 1864.

IV. Sources on Hedge and His Work

A. Hedge's Contemporaries

Abbott, F. H. "Theism and Christianity." Christian Examiner, 79 (1865), 157-174.

Alger, R. "Frederic Henry Hedge and F. D. Huntington. **Hymns for the Church of Christ.**" Christian Examiner, 55 (1853), 468-472.

Allen, Joseph Henry. "A Memory of Dr. Hedge." The Unitarian Review and Religious Magazine, Sept. 1890, 266-270.

--------. "Frederic Henry Hedge." The Unitarian Review and Religious Magazine, Oct. 1890, 281-301.

Bartol, Cyrus A., and S. K. Lothrop. "Four Score Years: Personal Tribute to Dr. Hedge." The Christian Register, December (?) 1885, 1.

Bartol, Cyrus A. "Hedge's **Reason in Religion.**" Christian Examiner, 79 (1865), 84.

"Biographical Sketch of Frederic Henry Hedge." The Christian Register, 28 August 1890, 551.

Brown, Howard N. "Frederic Henry Hedge." In **Heralds of a Liberal Faith.** ed. Samuel A. Eliot. Boston: American Unitarian Association, 1910. Vol. IV, 158-167.

--------. **Frederic Henry Hedge, A Memorial Discourse.** Boston: George H. Ellis, 1891.

Chadwick, John W. **Frederic Henry Hedge: A Sermon.** Boston: George H. Ellis, 1890-1891.

Ellis, George E. "Old Faith and New Knowledge." Christian Examiner, 69 (1860), 351-401.

Everett, Charles C. "Dr. Hedge." The Christian Register, 28 August 1890, 549-551.

"Frederic Henry Hedge," The Nation, 28 August 1890, 165.

"Frederic Henry Hedge." New York Times, 23 August 1890, Sec. 1, p. 4, col. 6.

Furness, H. H. "Prose Writers of Germany." Christian Examiner, 44 (1848), 263-273.

Harris, William T. "Frederic Henry Hedge, D.D." Journal of Speculative Philosophy, 11 (1877), 107-108.

Hillard, G. S. "Sermon, June 2, 1834." Christian Examiner, 17 (1834), 169-177.

Kneeland, Stillman Foster. **Seven Centuries in the Kneeland Family.** New York: Stillman Foster Kneeland, 1897.

Lyon, William H. **Frederic Henry Hedge: Seventh Minister of the First Parish in Brookline, 1856-1872.** Brookline, Ma.: First Parish in Brookline, 1906.

Perry, Bliss. "Frederic Henry Hedge." In **The Early Years of the Saturday Club, 1855-1870.** ed. Edward Waldo Emerson. Boston: Houghton Mifflin Company, 1918.

"Reason in Religion." The New Jerusalem Magazine, Nov. 1865, 290-293.

Ward, Richard. "Editorial." The New Jerusalem Magazine, Nov. 1871, 387-388.

B. Later Studies

Adams, Raymond William. "Frederic Henry Hedge." **Dictionary of American Biography** (1932).

Carley, Peter King. "The Early Life and Thought of Frederic Henry Hedge: 1805-1850." Ph.D. Dissertation, Syracuse University 1973.

Hunter, Doreen. "Frederic Henry Hedge, What Say You?" American Quarterly, 32 (1980), 186-201.

Long, Orie W. **Frederic Henry Hedge: A Cosmopolitan Scholar.** Portland, Me.: The Southworth-Anthoensen Press, 1940.

Myerson, Joel. "Frederic Henry Hedge and the Failure of Transcendentalism." Harvard Library Bulletin, 23 (1975), 396-410.

Tuomi, Martha Ilona. "Dr. Frederic Henry Hedge: His Life and Works to the End of His Bangor Pastorate, 1805-1850." M.A. Thesis, University of Maine 1934.

Wells, Ronald Vale. **Three Christian Transcendentalists: James Marsh, Caleb Sprague Henry, Frederic Henry Hedge.** 1943; rpt. New York: Octagon Books, 1972.

Williams, George H. **Rethinking the Unitarian Relationship With Protestantism: An Examination of the Thought of Frederic Henry Hedge.** Boston: Beacon Press, 1949.

V. Other Sources, Collections, and Cited Materials

Ahlstrom, Sydney E. **A Religious History of the American People.** New Haven: Yale University Press, 1973.

--------. ed. **Theology in America: The Major Protestant Voices From Puritanism to Neo-Orthodoxy.** New York: Bobbs-Merrill Company, Inc., 1967.

Allen, Gay Wilson. **Waldo Emerson: A Biography.** New York: Viking Press, 1981.

Anderson, Paul Russell, and Max Harold Fisch. **Philosophy in America, From the Puritans to James.** New York: D. Appleton-Century Company, Inc., 1939.

Bartlett, William Irving. **Jones Very, Emerson's "Brave Saint."** New York: Greenwood Press, 1968.

Bates, Ernest Sutherland. "Levi Hedge." **Dictionary of American Biography** (1932).

Bishop, Jonathan. **Emerson on the Soul.** Cambridge, Ma.: Harvard University Press, 1964.

Blau, Joseph L. ed. **American Philosophic Addresses: 1700-1900.** New York: Columbia University Press, 1947.

--------. **Men and Movements in American Philosophy.** New York: Prentice-Hall, Inc., 1952.

--------. ed. **Social Theories of Jacksonian Democracy: Representative Writings of the Period 1825-1850.** New York: Bobbs-Merrill Company, Inc., 1954.

Boas, George, ed. **Romanticism in America: Papers Contributed to a Symposium Held at the Baltimore Museum of Art, May 13, 14, and 15, 1940.** Baltimore: Johns Hopkins Press, 1940.

Boller, Paul F., Jr. **American Transcendentalism, 1830-1860: An Intellectual Inquiry.** New York: G. P. Putnam's Sons, 1974.

--------. **Freedom and Fate in American Thought From Edwards to Dewey.** Dallas: Southern Methodist University Press, 1978.

Branch, E. Douglas. **The Sentimental Years: 1836-1860.** New York: D. Appleton-Century Company, 1934.

Bratton, Fred Gladstone. **The Legacy of the Liberal Spirit: Men and Movements in the Making of Modern Thought.** New York: Charles Scribner's Sons. 1943.

Braun, Frederick Augustus. **Margaret Fuller and Geothe. The Development of a Remarkable Personality, Her Religion and Philosophy, and Her Relation to Emerson, James Freeman Clarke and Transcendentalism.** 1910; rpt. New York: Henry Holt and Company, 1971.

Brooks, Van Wyck. **The Flowering of New England.** New York: E. P. Dutton & Company, Inc., 1952.

--------. **New England: Indian Summer.** New York: E. P. Dutton & Company, Inc., 1950.

Brown, Arthur W. **A Biography of William Ellery Channing: Always Young for Liberty.** Syracuse: Syracuse University Press, 1956.

--------. **Margaret Fuller.** New York: Twayne Publishers, Inc., 1964.

Buell, Lawrence. **Literary Transcendentalism: Style and Vision in the American Renaissance.** Ithaca, N.Y.: Cornell University Press, 1973.

Burr, Nelson R. **A Critical Biography of Religion in America.** Princeton: Princeton University Press, 1961.

Bush, Clive. **The Dream of Reason: American Consciousness From Independence to the Civil War.** London: Edward Arnold, 1977.

Cameron, Kenneth Walter. **Emerson Among His Contemporaries: A Harvest of Estimates, Insights, and Anecdotes From the Victorian Literary World and an Index.** Hartford: Transcendental Books, 1967.

--------. **Young Emerson's Transcendental Vision: An Exposition of His World View With an Analysis of the Structure, Background, and Meaning of Nature.** Hartford: Transcendental Books, 1971.

Canby, Henry Seidel. **Thoreau.** Boston: Houghton Mifflin Company, 1939.

Carofiol, Peter C. "James Marsh to John Dewey: The Fate of Transcendental Philosophy in American Education." The Journal of the American Renaissance, 24 (1978), 1-11.

Carpenter, Frederic Ives. **Emerson Handbook.** New York: Hendricks House, Inc., 1953.

Christy, Arthur. **The Orient in American Transcendentalism: A Study of Emerson, Thoreau, and Alcott.** New York: Columbia University Press, 1932.

Cohen, Morris R. **American Thought: A Critical Sketch.** Glencoe, Il.: The Free Press, 1954.

Commager, Henry Steele. **Theodore Parker.** Boston: Little, Brown, & Company, 1936.

Conner, Frederic William. **A Study of the Interpretation of Evolution by American Poets From Emerson to Robinson.** Gainesville: University of Florida Press, 1949.

Cooke, George Willis. **Historical and Biographical Introduction to the Dial.** 1902; rpt. New York: Russell & Russell, 1961.

Cooke, George Willis. **Unitarianism in America: A History of Its Origin and Development.** Boston: American Unitarian Association, 1902.

Crowe, Charles. **George Ripley: Transcendentalist and Utopian Socialist.** Athens: University of Georgia Press, 1967.

Curti, Merle. **The Growth of American Thought.** New York: Harper & Brothers, 1943.

Diehl, Carl. **Americans and German Scholarship, 1770-1870.** New Haven: Yale University Press, 1978.

Dirks, John Edward. **The Critical Theology of Theodore Parker.** New York: Columbia University Press, 1948.

Ekirch, Arthur Alphonse, Jr. **The Idea of Progress in America, 1815-1860.** New York: Columbia University Press, 1944.

Firkins, O. W. **Ralph Waldo Emerson.** New York: Houghton Mifflin Company, 1915.

Fisch, Max H., ed. **Classic American Philosophers.** New York: D. Appleton-Century Crofts, Inc., 1951.

Flower, Elizabeth and Murray G. Murphy. **A History of Philosophy in America.** 2 vols. New York: Capricorn Books, 1977.

Friedrich, Carl J., ed. **The Philosophy of Kant: Immanuel Kant's Moral and Political Writings.** New York: Modern Library, 1949.

Gabriel, Ralph Henry. **The Course of American Democratic Thought: An Intellectual History Since 1815.** New York: Ronald Press, 1940.

Gaustad, Edwin Scott. **A Religious History of America.** New York: Harper & Row Publishers, 1966.

Ginger, Ray, ed. **American Social Thought.** New York: Hill & Wang, 1961.

Gittleman, Edwin. **Jones Very: The Effective Years: 1833-1840.** New York: Columbia University Press, 1967.

--------. ed. **The Minor and Later Transcendentalists, A Symposium.** Hartford: Transcendental Books, 1969.

Goddard, Harold Clarke. **Studies in New England Transcendentalism.** 1908; rpt. New York: Hillary House Publishers, Ltd. 1960.

Gohdes, Clarence L. F. **The Periodicals of American Transcendentalism.** Durham, N.C.: Duke University Press, 1931.

Goldfarb, Clare R. and Russell M. Goldfarb. **Spiritualism and Nineteenth Century Letters.** Teaneck, N.J.: Farleigh Dickinson University Press, 1978.

Gray, Henry David. **Emerson: A Statement of New England Transcendentalism as Expressed in the Philosophy of Its Chief Exponent.** 1917; rpt. New York: Frederic Ungar Publishing Co., 1958.

Griggs, Earl Leslie. **Coleridge Fille: A Biography of Sara Coleridge.** New York: Oxford University Press, 1940.

Hacker, Louis M. **The Shaping of the American Tradition.** New York: Columbia University Press, 1947.

Harding, Walter. **The Days of Henry Thoreau.** New York: Alfred A. Knopf, 1966.

--------. ed. **Thoreau: A Century of Criticism.** Dallas: Southern Methodist University Press, 1965.

Harmon, Frances B. **The Social Philosophy of the St. Louis Hegelians.** New York: Frances B. Harmon, 1943.

Haroutunian, Joseph. **Piety Versus Moralism: The Passing of the New England Theology.** Hamden, Ct.: Archon Books, 1964.

Harrison, John S. **The Teachers of Emerson.** New York: Haskell House, 1966.

Hicks, John H., ed. **Thoreau in Our Season.** Amherst: University of Massachusetts Press, 1966.

Hofstadter, Richard. **Social Darwinism in American Thought.** New York: George Braziller, Inc., 1965.

Hopkins, Vivian C. **Spires of Form: A Study of Emerson's Aesthetic Theory.** New York: Russell & Russell, 1965.

Howard, Claud. **Coleridge's Idealism: A Study of Its Relationship to Kant and to the Cambridge Platonists.** Boston: Gorham Press, 1979.

Howe, M. A. De Wolfe, ed. **Later Years of the Saturday Club, 1870-1920.** 1927; rpt. Freeport, N.Y.: Books for Libraries Press, 1968.

Hovenkamp, Herbert. **Science and Religion in America: 1800-1860.** Philadelphia: University of Pennsylvania Press, 1978.

Hudson, Winthrop. **American Protestantism.** Chicago: University of Chicago Press, 1969.

Hutchison, William R. **The Transcendentalist Ministers: Church Reform in the New England Renaissance.** New Haven: Yale University Press, 1959.

Jamison, A. Leland, and James Ward Smith, eds. **The Shaping of American Religion.** Princeton: Princeton University Press, 1969.

Jones, Rufus M. **Studies in Mystical Religion.** London: Macmillan & Co., Limited, 1923.

Kant, Immanuel. **Critique of Practical Reason.** Trans. Lewis White Beck. New York: Bobbs-Merrill Company, Inc., 1956.

--------. **Critique of Pure Reason.** Trans. F. Max Müller. Garden City, N.Y.: Anchor Books, 1966.

--------. **Religion Within the Limits of Reason Alone.** Trans. Theodore M. Greene and Hoyt H. Hudson. New York: Harper & Row, Publishers, 1960.

Kearn, Alexander. "The Rise of Transcendentalism, 1815-1860." In **Transitions in American Literary History.** ed. Harry H. Clark. New York: Octagon Books, Inc., 1967.

Koster, Donald N. **Transcendentalism in America.** Boston: Twayne Publishers, 1975.

Kring, Walter Donald. **Liberals Among the Orthodox: Unitarian Beginnings in New York City: 1819-1839.** Boston: Beacon Press, 1974.

Ladu, Arthur. "Channing and Transcendentalism." American Literature, 11 (1939), 129-137.

Leighton, Walter L. **French Philosophers and New England.** New York: Greenwood Press, 1968.

Lewis, R. W. B. **The American Adam: Innocence, Tragedy, and Tradition in the Nineteenth Century.** Chicago: University of Chicago Press, 1968.

Locke, John. **An Essay Concerning Human Understanding.** 2 vols. 1690; rpt. New York: Dover Publications, Inc., 1959.

Loewenberg, James. "Darwin Comes to America, 1859-1900." Mississippi Valley Historical Review, 28 (1941), 339-368.

Long, Orie William. **Literary Pioneers: Early American Explorers of European Culture.** 1935; rpt. New York: Russell & Russell, Inc., 1963.

Mathiessen, F. L. **American Renaissance: Art and Expression in the Age of Emerson and Whitman.** New York: Oxford University Press, 1941.

Maynard, Theodore. **Orestes Brownson: Yankee, Radical, Catholic.** New York: Macmillan Company, 1943.

Mc Loughlin, William G. **Revivals, Awakening, and Reform: An Essay on Religion and Social Change in America, 1607-1977.** Chicago: University of Chicago Press, 1978.

Miller, F. De Wolfe. **Christopher Pearse Cranch and His Caricatures of New England Transcendentalism.** Cambridge, Ma.: Harvard University Press, 1951.

Miller, Perry, ed. **The Transcendentalists: An Anthology.** Cambridge, Ma.: Harvard University Press, 1960.

Mott, Wesley T. "Emerson and Antinomianism: The Legacy of the Sermons." American Literature, 50 (1978), 369-397.

Muelder, Walter G., Anne V. Schlabach, and Lawrence Sears, eds. **The Development of American Philosophy: A Book of Readings.** Boston: Houghton Mifflin Company, 1960.

Muirhead, John H. **The Platonic Tradition in Anglo-Saxon Philosophy: Studies in the History of Idealism in England and America.** New York: Macmillan Company, 1931.

Mumford, Lewis. **The Golden Day: A Study in American Literature and Culture.** New York: Boni & Liveright, 1926.

Myers, Henry Alonzo. **Are Men Equal? An Inquiry Into the Meaning of American Democracy.** Ithaca, N.Y.: Cornell University Press, 1955.

Myerson, Joel. **The New England Transcendentalists and the Dial: A History of the Magazine and Its Contributors.** Rutherford, N.J.: Farleigh Dickinson University Press, 1980.

Parrington, Vernon L. **The Romantic Revolution in America: 1800-1860.** Vol. II of **Main Currents in American Thought.** New York: Harcourt, Brace & World, Inc., 1954.

Parsons, Thornton H., and Myron Simon, eds. **Transcendentalism and Its Legacy.** Ann Arbor: University of Michigan Press, 1966.

Paul, Sherman. **Emerson's Angle of Vision, Man and Nature in American Experience.** Cambridge, Ma.: Harvard University Press, 1952.

--------. **The Shores of America: Thoreau's Inward Exploration.** Urbana: University of Illinois Press, 1958.

Perry, Ralph Barton. **The Thought and Character of William James.** 2 vols. Boston: Little, Brown, & Company, 1935.

Persons, Stow. **Free Religion: An American Faith.** Boston: Beacon Press, 1963.

Pochmann, Henry A. **German Culture in America: Philosophical and Literary Influences: 1600-1900.** Madison: University of Wisconsin Press, 1957.

--------. **New England Transcendentalism and St. Louis Hegelianism: Phases in the History of American Idealism.** Philadelphia: Carl Schurz Memorial Foundation, Inc., 1948.

Porte, Joel. **Representative Man: Ralph Waldo Emerson in His Time.** New York: Oxford University Press, 1979.

Provost, Gary. **A Brief History of Unitarian Universalism.** Boston: Unitarian Universalists Association, 1980.

Schneider, Herbert W. **A History of American Philosophy.** 2nd ed. New York: Columbia University Press, 1963.

Smith, Timothy L. **Revivalism and Social Reform in Mid-Nineteenth Century America.** New York: Abingdon Press, 1957.

Sweet, William Warren. **Religion in the Development of American Culture: 1765-1840.** New York: Charles Scribner's Sons, 1952.

Tanner, Tony. **The Reign of Wonder: Naivety and Reality in American Literature.** Cambridge, England: Cambridge University Press, 1965.

Tocqueville, Alexis de. **Democracy in America.** 2 vols. Trans. Henry Reeve. New York: Vintage Books, 1945.

Townsend, Harvey Gates. **Philosophical Ideas in the United States.** New York: American Book Company, 1934.

Tyler, Alice Felt. **Freedom's Ferment: Phases of American Social History From the Colonial Period to the Outbreak of the Civil War.** New York: Harper & Row, 1962.

Vogel, Stanley M. **German Literary Influences on the American Transcendentalists.** 1955; rpt. New York: Archon Books, 1970.

Wade, Mason. **Margaret Fuller: Whetstone of Genius.** New York: Viking Press, 1940.

Washburn, Wilcomb. "The Oriental Roots of American Transcendentalism." The Southwestern Journal, 4 (1949), 152-153.

Weiskel, Thomas. **The Romantic Sublime: Studies in the Structure and Psychology of Transcendence.** Baltimore: Johns Hopkins University Press, 1976.

Wellek, René. "The Minor Transcendentalists and German Philosophy." New England Quarterly, 15 (1942), 652-680.

Werkmeister, W. H. **A History of Philosophical Ideas in America.** New York: Ronald Press Company, 1949.

Whicher, George F., ed. **The Transcendentalist Revolt.** rev. Gail Kennedy. Lexington, Ma.: D. C. Heath & Company, 1968.

Whicher, Stephen E. **Freedom and Fate: An Inner Life of Ralph Waldo Emerson.** 1953; rpt. Philadelphia: University of Pennsylvania Press, 1971.

Williams, Daniel Day. **The Andover Liberals: A Study in American Theology.** New York: Octagon Books, 1970.

Wright, Conrad. **The Liberal Christian: Essays on American Unitarian History.** Boston: Beacon Press, 1970.

INDEX